SMALL TOWN
RENAISSANCE

SMALL TOWN RENAISSANCE

A STORY OF THE MONTANA STUDY

by

Richard Waverly Poston

GREENWOOD PRESS, PUBLISHERS
WESTPORT, CONNECTICUT

Library of Congress Catalog Card Number: 76–109300
ISBN: 0–8371–3843–4

Originally published in 1950 by Harper & Brothers, Publishers

Reprinted with the permission of Harper & Row, Publishers, New York

First Greenwood Reprinting: 1971

Greenwood Press, 88 Post Road West, Westport, CT 06881
An imprint of Greenwood Publishing Group, Inc.

Printed in the United States of America

The paper used in this book complies with the
Permanent Paper Standard issued by the National
Information Standards Organization (Z39.48–1984).

10 9 8 7 6 5 4 3 2

TO

MARJORIE

MY WIFE

CONTENTS

PREFACE

This is a story about some men and women in Montana engaged in an experiment designed to strengthen and improve the lot of our small American towns. I am convinced that in this experiment, known as The Montana Study, there is to be found a secret by which people throughout all America, rich or poor, educated or uneducated, can make their lives richer, more enjoyable, and more worth while. And so I should like to narrate the story of this experiment, the trials, the struggles, the mistakes, the conflicts, of the men and women who have helped to achieve its objectives.

The experiment itself has been fraught with rumor and misunderstanding. It has had to operate in the face of almost unbelievable odds—a situation which to many has remained even yet an unsolved mystery. In the pages that follow I have tried to set forth the reasons for such misunderstanding, and to mark the pitfalls that others who embark upon similar programs may wish to avoid. To do this, my task has not been easy. The book deals with real people and real places. Many will disagree with my findings, will become hostile upon reading my conclusions. However, this cannot be avoided, nor should I wish to avoid it at a sacrifice of what to me is a true statement of the events as they actually occurred. In some instances the situations narrated will have changed due to the lapse of time between the dates of my investigation and the date of publication, but the principles involved will last indefinitely.

In the Appendix I have presented a step-by-step outline of the group organization and study guide used in the Montana experiment, which I hope will be of further assistance to others.

As for myself, I had no part in the experiment. I learned of it through reading the newspapers, and did not meet those engaged in the work until after I had begun my investigations. My purpose in writing the narrative is to tell a story that I think should be told for its value to our American democracy. The University at Missoula is my Alma Mater, for eight years Montana was my home; and I shall always have a deep sense of faith in this state and its people. This, together with my years of experience as an investigator for our American Government, comprised the personal equipment with which I began my research. I have listened to the story as it was told to me by those on both sides of the issue. I have examined the record as I found it through long and diligent investigation; I have written my findings and conclusions.

At the end of the book I have acknowledged my appreciation to the hundreds of witnesses who contributed to my research. I should now like to acknowledge the assistance of the Newberry Fellowships in Midwestern Studies, which helped in a larger way than I can express to make the writing of this book possible, but which in no way directed my course, and can in no way be held responsible for the statements herein.

RICHARD WAVERLY POSTON

Seattle, Washington
September 1, 1949

SMALL TOWN
RENAISSANCE

1

A Future in the Making

"Bring up Plummer!"

The sharp voice of a vigilante cut through the night and struck into the heart of a man facing death.

"Can't a man have time to pray?" the bandit pleaded.

"Do your praying up there," said the vigilante, motioning to the crude gallows where the bodies of Plummer's two friends were still twitching from the end of the hangman's ropes.

A waiting noose was quickly adjusted around the man's throat. There was little time for praying. With a rude heave he was hoisted upward, then dropped. A sudden jerk, and it was all over.

Mounting their horses, the band of vigilantes rode off over the crackling snow, leaving the stiffening bodies of Henry Plummer, outlaw sheriff of Bannack, and his two murderous deputies swinging in the freezing wind.

Sunday, the 10th day of January, 1864, was drawing to a close, and law and order were dawning in Montana.

Through the operations of the vigilantes a community had united in group action for the welfare of its people. But it was the last time for years to come that community welfare was to become again a goal of concerted effort in Montana.

Explored by Lewis and Clark in 1805, this new territory had been a wilderness frontier where men sought riches and adventure. They had fought for its furs. They had cheated and lied to the Indians. They had built fortunes for the trading companies, and they had blazed trails that opened a route to civilization. But civilization was not the motive that drove them. It was a period of exploitation sharpened by the intense rivalry of competing fur companies. Permanence, farming, and community life were discouraged as obstructions to the fur trade. Women and families were not wanted. It was a world for men who could survive by individual superiority, and the thinking of generations yet unborn was being conditioned.

Then in July, 1862, John White, trudging through the Rocky Mountain wilderness with a small party of weary travelers, stopped on Grasshopper Creek, and discovered gold—rich yellow gold! News of their discovery spread through the West, and almost overnight Bannack, Montana, a roaring metropolis of 5000 gold-crazed citizens, burst into being.

A year later Bill Fairweather uncovered the riches of nearby Alder Gulch, the diggin's that yielded up a hundred million dollars, and more men poured into Montana. At the foot of sweeping hillsides that rise to the great mountain heights surrounding these distant valleys of gold, tents, shacks, and rough-hewn cabins mushroomed from the sagebrush, and 12,000 men spread over the creek bottoms, probing into rich-laden sands. Fabulous Virginia City, Central, Junction, Summit, Highland, Nevada City sprang out of nowhere.

Following close on the tracks of the prospectors came the gamblers, the dancing girls and women for hire, and on the wave of riches rode the gunmen, plundering and shooting their way to fame in the romantic legends of western history and song.

Saloons and hurdy-gurdy houses lined wagon-choked streets of the new communities, and from swinging doors blared the music, laughter, and swearing of drunken mobs. Valley tan at four bits a shot poured over the bars, roulette wheels clicked at a thousand dollars a spin, dice rolled on the felt-padded tables, and ten thousand dollars in gold dust went down the drain.

Here in this Montana mining hub swarmed one of the largest collections of murderers and swift-riding bandits the West has ever known. Guns blazed through town and canyon. Hardly a stage left Bannack or Virginia City without encountering masked riders with their familiar command to "Throw up your hands!"

During the closing months of 1863 these outlaws murdered over a hundred men for their gold, and hundreds of others were robbed under threats of death if they dared mention the experience. Notorious Henry Plummer, the suave, dashing sheriff of Bannack, was leader of the gang. The federal government had no time to worry about bad men in so remote a western territory, and lawlessness surged unchecked.

Out of this emergency rose the vigilantes; tough, fast-shooting, determined citizens who believed that quick death was the only cure for a road agent. They knew no law save that made and enforced by themselves. It was a country without established courts, prosecutors, or judges. No decent woman was safe on the streets, no semblance of civilized society could grow until this lawless element was erased. And before the citizens' committee had finished, Henry Plummer and thirty-one members of his gang had died at the end of a rope.

This was the state of early life in Montana. It had progressed beyond a fur frontier, but there was still nothing to encourage permanence. Few, if any, of those who came to the newly discovered gold fields had any intention of settling a community or building a state. They came with one idea only—to clean up and get out. Theirs was a motive of exploitation, of individual achievement. And it was only when their lives had been threatened, and their gold had been menaced, that community welfare entered their code of living.

Their industry was temporary by nature. As one placer was exhausted they moved on to another. Mobility was the key to success. While the restless moved on, others moved in, and they were soon gone, too. Virtuous women and families were liabilities. Communities existed by chance. And today there is almost no trace of Central, Junction, Summit, Highland, or Nevada City. In Bannack, where once lived and caroused the 5000, winds sweep through blocks of deserted buildings, and only the ghost of a city that used to be marks her forgotten streets. Virginia City still remains, but with only a fraction of her former population, and within the walls of her ancient houses is locked the story of a glamorous but unstable past.

While men toiled for gold in the rich placers of the mountains, the frontier call was being answered in other parts of the territory, and a new struggle for wealth was unfolding on the dry Montana plains. This was the ancestral home of the Blackfeet, the Assiniboine, the Gros Ventre, and the Crow. Wolves and coyotes lurked in the ravines. Elk, antelope, and deer grazed the highlands, and great herds of buffalo blackened the prairie. For generations Nature had maintained her perfect balance.

Then came the white man.

Enraged by this invasion of their native land, a violation of existing treaties, Indian braves sprang into action. Beating war drums resounded across the plains, and vicious fighting flared wherever the enemies met. Troops of the U. S. Army were rushed into the bedlam. Old forts were enlarged and new ones built. The only good Indian was a dead Indian, and the invaders began working on that thesis.

"The plains must be cleared for civilization!" they cried.

Then in about 1875 a demand for hides from eastern leather interests hit the West, and professional hunters joined the invasion. Whole herds of buffalo were shot down at a time, their carcasses left to rot in the sun. Extermination was hastened by western railroad expansion, and in 1882 the Northern Pacific alone shipped 200,000 hides out of Montana. By 1884 an estimated four million buffalo had been slaughtered on the Montana plains, and as the hunters disappeared, bone men took their places. Bones for fertilizer brought twelve to eighteen dollars a ton, and the years 1884-86 saw mountains of bones piled along railroad sidings. Then the bones were gone. Within fifteen years after the invasion began the Indians had been crushed and the buffalo had passed into history.

But the western beef industry was mounting to a bonanza. Early in the seventies Texas longhorns were driven onto the Northern Plains, and the reckless days of Montana's open range had begun. Here was a land of luxuriant grass that for centuries had supported the buffalo. Its former Indian owners were being swept away, and it belonged to the United States. Unsurveyed, unfenced, it was free for the taking. And so the cattlemen took it. Under federal laws they could not buy it, they could not lease it. But nothing could stop them from using it —except perhaps another cattleman who got there first. It was man against man for land to which none of them had legal right. It was man against nature; against racing prairie fires that blotted out the sun and left blackened carcasses smouldering in acres of ashes; against wind-driven blizzards that cut down frozen cattle; man against drought that left parched earth with no water for cattle to drink and no food for cattle to eat.

Yet here was a new opportunity to get rich and get out. Stories were told of men building fortunes. And as this news spread eastward, big business invaded Montana. On came the speculators, the cattle barons, financed by eastern and European capitalists.

It was hazardous business, but men could afford to risk fortunes in this gamble for gold on the hoof. It was an industry of nomads on horseback. Every man for himself, and if you couldn't take it you could get out.

Over the trails from Texas, from California, Oregon, and Washington, the cattle came; driven by the men on horseback—men with broadbrimmed hats, leather chaps, high-heeled boots with shiny spurs, and six-guns on their belts. The American cowboy had become an institution. And with him came his songs, his spirit of courage, and to-hell-with-the-devil living.

It was a man's world, out there under the sky, with cattle as far as you could see. It was adventurous living and it was fun, but it was lonely. Months passed. And the cowboys hit town. They got rip-roarin' stinkin' drunk. There were wild women, barroom brawls, screaming and cursing, and galloping horsemen shot up the town. A spree of spending, then back to the range. This was the Golden West. An era that America would never forget.

But the range couldn't take it. Weakened by overgrazing, the grasses began to give way. Then came the droughts with their swirling clouds of dust. And then came the winters. Ranch thermometers dropped to sixty below zero as winds came screaming from the north. Deep snow covered the plains. Cattle died by the thousands. Then more winters, more droughts. The big outfits went broke, and the colorful days of the open range had become legend, another episode in western history.

Instability had become a part of things. And the background to life in Montana today was being made.

While the furious drama of the open range moved on toward its inevitable end, the curtain was rising on one of the greatest industrial developments the West has ever seen. Out of a multimillion-dollar industry men were to witness the growth of an economic colossus destined to shape the lives of thousands of people; a private institution that would some day become the most powerful single influence in the political, social, and economic life of Montana. The kings of copper were making their debut.

The development of quartz mining with its costly machinery called for the investment of real capital, and Montana was ushered into another phase of history. Most of the prospectors who struck it rich in the early gold fields soon departed for more comfortable living elsewhere, and many had painlessly unloaded their riches into the hands of eager gamblers, or the silk-skirted laps of hurdy-gurdys. Saving was not a virtue of the frontiersman. So in seeking money to finance the quartz mines men had to look beyond the borders of Montana. Thus, control of Montana's richest industrial resource moved eastward and finally settled at No. 25 Broadway, New York City.

In the mines financed by eastern capitalists, rich veins of silver were uncovered, and with the rise of silver came Butte.

"A mile high and a mile deep!"

Probably more money has been won and lost in Butte, Montana, than in any other city its size in the world. This, in days not long past, was the city of whiskey with beer chasers, of roulette wheels, card sharks, bought-off judges and politicians, rioting mobs, and prostitutes in downtown windows beckoning men from the street. It was not an atmosphere conducive to social or moral restraint. But in fifty years this city produced more than $2,200,000,000 in mineral wealth.

Butte's dominant financial figure during the silver boom was a Scotch-Irishman named William Andrews Clark. Intelligent, and dignified in appearance, Clark was ostensibly a well-bred gentleman. But in his pursuit of wealth and prestige he was not limited by ethical procedure. By 1878, with his mines, banks, and smelter, Clark was well on his way to becoming the King of Butte, when Marcus Daly, an Irishman who was no less gifted at conniving, invaded his territory. Experienced from Nevada's Comstock Lode, and with money to spend, Daly bought a Butte silver mine, the Anaconda, and in it discovered the world's richest vein of copper.

Determined to drive each other from the state, these two men fought violently for political and financial control of Montana. From Butte's mines both contestants built fortunes running into millions. Daly gained control of the richest copper deposits in Butte Hill and Clark was elected to the United States Senate.

These were the days when senators were elected by state legislatures, so Clark practically put Montana's legislature on his personal pay roll. In 1899, he is reported to have bribed forty-seven legislators for a total of more than $400,000. A portion of the bribe was exposed on the floor of the legislature, and through the personal efforts of Daly, was brought to the attention of Congress. Clark resigned his seat and returned to Montana for revenge. With the help of debonair Frederick

Augustus Heinze, who later became one of the most colorful figures in American mining, Clark managed to buy enough votes to elect a legislature in 1900 that sent him back to Washington where he served six years as the Gentleman from Montana.

This was all part of Montana's political and financial development. Then, in 1898, Marcus Daly began the negotiations with Henry H. Rogers of Standard Oil which led to the formation of one of the largest trusts in financial history—the Amalgamated Copper Company. With assets of only $39,000,000, the corporation was capitalized at $75,000,000, its stock divided into 750,000 shares, and sold to the public. Through stock market manipulations the entrepreneurs quickly cleaned up $15,000,000 for themselves and gained control of the combine. A new contestant, Amalgamated Copper, was now ready to operate in Montana.

Yet one obstacle blocked its path—Frederick Augustus Heinze.

Young, handsome, and vivacious, endowed with a love for liquor and women, and an unquenchable zest for battle and achievement, Heinze became the only man in the financial world able to so consistently thwart the interests of Standard Oil. And because this was a land where men had learned to glorify individual conquest, Heinze— a financial Napoleon who thought of no one but himself—became the hero of Butte, champion of the little man. This was indicative of the extent to which life on the frontier had conditioned the people's thinking, and to this day that kind of thinking has not ceased entirely.

Heinze had come to Montana only nine years earlier as a hundred-dollar-a-month mining engineer. After gaining valuable knowledge of the copper veins, he embarked upon a business career of his own and in a few years had established a smelter and acquired a few mining properties, including the Rarus Mine, and a small plot of ground on Butte Hill no larger than a small house lot.

Claiming the ore in Amalgamated's richest mines apexed in his small plot of ground Heinze bored from his own shafts into those of his enemy and began lifting out tons of copper. Meanwhile, he bought off the Butte judges and brought action to prevent the trust from working its own shafts. Flooded by more than a hundred suits the courts began handing down the decisions he asked, while Heinze worked feverishly turning copper from Amalgamated's mines into the money he needed to keep fighting. With his own newspaper, the

Reveille, and in public addresses Heinze attacked the trust politically, calling it every despicable name in the dictionary, plus those of his own.

Heinze was a master psychologist, and in his efforts to marshal the public against Amalgamated he repeatedly demonstrated his skilled understanding of the emotional appeal.

In one of his famous speeches to the people of Butte, he shouted, "My fight against the Standard Oil is your fight. In this glorious battle . . . you and I are partners. We stand or fall together. If they crush me tomorrow they will crush you the day following. They will cut your wages and raise the tariff in the company store on every bite you eat and every rag you wear. They will force you to dwell in Standard Oil houses while you live and you must be buried in Standard Oil coffins when you die. Your enemies are a combination of ruthless pirates who have trampled under foot every law of God and man. . . . Those people are my enemies, fierce, bitter, implacable, but they are your enemies too. Let them win . . . and they will inaugurate conditions in Montana that will blast its fairest prospect and make its very name hateful to those who love liberty. In this fight you and I, my friends, are partners and allies."

But the battle was not limited to words alone. Hand-to-hand encounters were fought in mine corridors underground. Steam blasts, floods, and dynamite explosions were pressed into use as the war mounted in tempo. For eight years the conflict boiled at an intensity hitherto unknown in the history of capitalism. Finally, by his terrific offensive, Heinze had precipitated a drastic reduction in Amalgamated stocks. Through court injunctions he had fought the giant to a standstill, robbed it of millions of dollars worth of copper, brought one of its richest subsidiaries into receivership, and prevented it from paying dividends to the parent company although profits were pyramiding to millions in the corporate treasury.

Meanwhile Amalgamated was extending its ownership into other parts of Montana. Whole forests were stripped from the mountains as the great company tore into the vitals of Montana's natural resources. Then came the counteroffensive against Heinze.

Suddenly and without warning Amalgamated's operations were closed, and thousands of men were without work. The work stoppage spread rapidly through Montana and soon more thousands were without work as dozens of other businesses all dependent on Amalgamated's operations and the salaries of its employees, closed. Winter was looming ahead.

The strategists of Amalgamated, now fighting for survival, were demanding that Heinze sell certain stock which had provided the grounds for many of his lawsuits; and under the threat of starvation held over the people of Montana, were demanding that the Governor call a special session of the legislature to pass a law enabling Amalgamated to transfer Heinze's suits from the Butte courts to other jurisdictions.

Heinze, now at the peak of his career, appealed to the citizens of Butte. On the courthouse steps before a mob of 10,000 he denounced the trust, and temporarily regained public support.

But the odds were too great. Heinze was doomed, and the sovereign state of Montana found itself at the mercy of a private trust.

With his people crying for jobs, the Governor called the legislature into special session and the law Amalgamated demanded was passed. Heinze was forced to sell out to the trust, and a few years later the man who had fought Standard Oil to a standstill, was dead.

Amalgamated emerged as the dominant power in Montana's economy.

In 1911, the Supreme Court of the United States rendered a decision which dissolved the Standard Oil trust. Amalgamated became the Anaconda Copper Mining Company, but in the reorganization lost none of its economic position in Montana.

In 1912, Montana saw the organization of the Montana Power Company, which is today the state's only financial institution in Anaconda's league. And in Montana these two companies, with interdependent interests, important common officials, and mutual political and social policies, are in a class by themselves. Together they are referred to by Montanans simply as "the Company." Their combined ownership extends from one end of the state to the other, including mines, timber, stores, dams, power plants, and about half of the state's daily newspapers.

And whether the Company's present managers like it or not, this economic dominance has had far-reaching social effects on Montana. Both Company and anti-Company propaganda has often veered from the truth. And the end result has been the creation of an unhealthy social condition where officials are often elected because they are either for or against the Company, where one economic group can exercise undue influence in legislative lobbying, where objective reporting on local issues is frequently limited in the press, and where factional prejudice prevents state-wide cooperation for the mutual welfare of both the people and the Company.

Legislators coming to the state capital are often taken captive by Company lobbyists, skilled in the art of human relations, without knowing what has happened. Actually, however, it is doubtful that the Company is today the all-powerful political force people think it is, for in late years some of the Company-backed politicians have suffered terrific beatings at the polls. Yet in every phase of public life, including the university system, there is a state-wide tradition that people must be careful lest they irritate the Company and thereby endanger their jobs or their financial security. And since there are enough instances of Company influence to keep this tradition alive, a fear psychology has so permeated the life of Montana that many are paralyzed by a danger that is often imaginary. In Montana's vast spaces people are isolated from each other. They lack adequate interchange of news and opinions, and the idea that they can be the masters of their own social and cultural destiny is only rising on the horizon.

The builders of Butte made wealth grow out of the wilderness. They became famous in the annals of Montana history. But they intensified the motive of exploitation. The individualistic attitude and disregard for wholesome community life that dominated the frontier were even more firmly entrenched. Mining was an extractive industry to begin with, and as the natural resources were exploited, more and more of Montana's wealth went East. The psychology of "clean up and get out" changed slightly to "clean up and ship out." In proportion to the wealth she produced Montana realized few of the benefits her resources provided. There was little incentive for the development of local processing and manufacturing industries to utilize the raw materials from her mines and forests. Thus, Montana became little more than a source of supply for eastern industrialists; a colony to be tapped for the building of stable communities elsewhere, but with little regard for those who lived in the colony. It was a one-way process with much flowing out and little flowing in.

Underlying this pattern of economic development was a frontier society, heedless of its own welfare and future security. Few of those who helped make this historic background realized or cared what the consequences of their acts would be on today's generations, but in their desire for individual achievement and in the speed of their operations, they were laying a foundation for many of the social problems that now plague the children who followed them.

While the quartz miners moved forward in their desire for riches and the war of the copper kings boiled over Butte, railroads were spanning the continent, and Jim Hill was pushing his Great Northern toward the Pacific Coast. Hill, and others like him, envisioned on the high plains east of the Rockies a vast kingdom of small wheat farms that would make the prairie "blossom like the rose," and make profits for the railroads. In Congress the politicians with their homestead laws were offering 160 or 320 acres of land in the West, free to anybody who could prove up. To the railroad promoters, this was meat and drink. By colorful oratory and national advertising they stirred people to a frenzy of acquisition. Thousands of homesteaders expecting quick riches from the soil streamed into Montana. Drab shack towns sprang up around rail stops. Land offices boomed. Speculators cleaned up. And the greatest wave of incoming population in Montana's history was under way.

But neither Congress nor Jim Hill and his fellow promoters knew the plains. For it took more than 320 acres to wrest a living from this sun-baked country, and much of it was not suitable for wheat farming to begin with. Professor Carl F. Kraenzel of Montana State College has called this the land of variability at the margin, and with annual rainfall at twenty inches or less, it took only a slight variation to drop below that margin which makes the difference between boom and bust.

For permanent prosperity this is a region requiring special agricultural techniques, but the people who promoted and settled it were not aware of those techniques. Nor would they listen to the few who warned them. Land was free, rail fares were cheap, and credit was good. They could clean up in a few years and get out.

For a while the weather was favorable and profits were good. More homesteaders kept coming and more farms were opened to cultivation. Then more good rains and the record wheat prices of World War I. Eastern Montana was "busting its buttons." Then with the invention of tractors even more land could be plowed. And in a few years millions of acres of sod were turned upside down.

Eventually there came a break in the price of wheat. And with that break the weather moved into a drought. High dry winds descended upon the homesteaders and blew their soil away. Banks failed. Life savings disappeared. Homesteads were abandoned and towns were deserted. Ruin had come to the plains.

Yet even while prosperity flourished, homesteading on the plains was no easy life. Towns were far apart. Most of them were little more than rail depots where newcomers unloaded and the disillusioned departed. Barren and monotonous, they were the utilitarian product of railroad promoters, whose minds were no more cluttered by thoughts of cultural stability than were the land speculators who helped lure the homesteaders. Quick profits were their chief attraction. Community life, homes, promoters—all were tailored to this dominant motive. The cultural services provided by stable churches and schools, by established tradition and community planning, were notably lacking. Women were often unhappy and in the battle against hardships thousands of men were discouraged. For those who sought only to get rich and get out there was no incentive to build strong communities, and the odds were against those who sought permanent homes. Security and stability were virtually impossible, for the very basis of society was in conflict with nature. And in the plains communities of today this era of "homestead and busted" has left its indelible mark.

Joseph Kinsey Howard has pointed out that from 1921 to 1925, half the farmers in Montana lost their land through foreclosure, through the twenties nearly two hundred banks closed, and 60,000 people left the state. A difficult period of adjustment followed, and then came the world-wide depression of the thirties. Another prolonged drought teamed up with the depression, and by 1935 a fourth of all the people in Montana were on relief. Stability was still not in sight.

With World War II, high wheat prices came back, the weather returned to a period of abundant moisture, and prosperity was again in the ascendancy. In 1948 one eastern Montana farmer told the author that while his farm yielded only $500 in 1934, his profits from that same farm in 1947 were more than $40,000 net. The plains are still a region of variability at the margin, and the variation has now exceeded that margin.

Today modern farming practices adapted especially to the plains region have placed Montana's agricultural economy on a more permanent footing. Through research by the federal government, by the State College at Bozeman, and from the hard lessons of experience, many of the hazards have been eliminated from farming on the plains, but the job of building stable communities with a rich and satisfying life has only been started.

Montana had its beginnings in bloodshed, vigilante hangings, and corporate intrigue. It was exploited for its furs. Its gold was dissipated in an orgy of spending and riotous living. In less than thirty years its millions of buffalo were slaughtered, and the open-range livestock industry had come and gone. There was a relentless fight for its silver, the war of the copper kings, and the rise of a dominant economic group. There was unrestricted logging in its forests, wasting of its soil, and exploitation of its plains. And on this thesis a Western Empire was built.

Each historical episode brought a new flow of migrants, all seeking riches. From the fur frontier to the present day, mobility has been a major characteristic of Montana's population. It has been a cycle of movement in, and movement out. Those who left were followed by others moving in, and the process went on. But when the census was taken in 1930, Montana was the nation's only state to have lost more than she had gained.

During the thirties over 45,000 people moved in, and by 1940 she had a net gain of almost 22,000. But three years later nearly 90,000 others had left, and the state had fewer people than she had in 1920. In the years immediately following World War II, some of these returned, yet the U. S. Census report of July 1, 1948, showed that while all other Rocky Mountain states had gained in population, Montana had lost 8.6 per cent of her people, leaving her population still less than in 1920.

Montana has lived through a fast-moving history, a history of rapidly changing conditions with extreme fluctuations from abnormal prosperity to severe depression, and back again. If the state has not developed a strong cultural consciousness it is partly because men have been too busy seeking fortunes and adjusting themselves to the ever-changing frontier. But it has retarded the development of stable communities. Most Montanans are no longer there to get rich and get out, though that philosophy is far from extinct, and many are still indifferent to cultural advance and social welfare, for modern thinking has been conditioned by the forces of a recent history.

Diverse in her landscape, rich in her natural resources, dynamic in her history—she has been as changeable as her own weather. From the dry bunch grass range of the Northern Great Plains, her boundaries reach across nearly 147,000 square miles into virgin forests of the Rocky Mountains. Nowhere is there a land more beautiful. And despite the exploitation of the past her natural resources have not been exhausted. Her fabulous mineral deposits, her fertile valleys, her irrigated farms, her potential cheap hydroelectric power, have made Montana a land of unheralded opportunity, yet she has inherited a disease of instability.

This has been the story of Montana.

2

Melby's Dream

Out of the events of history rises the thinking of today. And to those who would change that thinking, conflict is the natural reward.

This was the destiny of Ernest O. Melby when in July, 1943, he became chancellor of the University of Montana. For here was a man who would change a pattern of thinking that had been established by the events of history. But out of the impending conflict was to come a new adventure in democracy, another episode in the struggle of life in Montana, and a prelude to action that could become a movement for millions—a movement through which many of America's most crucial problems might be solved.

Had Melby been more cooperative with Montana's policymakers, had he been content to let the University continue its simple role of turning out young people in the usual routine, there would have been no need for conflict. But Ernest Melby was no ordinary educator—to him the University deserved a better place than that. His was a vision that saw in the University a great program for humanity through which common men could gain the spirit, the knowledge, and the willingness to work for a more perfect society. A program to endow the people with a deeper devotion to the welfare of their state and their country. A program not limited to the ivory towers of campus courtyards, but an objective means of extending the cultural and educational services of the University into every town, village, and farm, helping men and women to improve the quality of living in their own communities and homes. This was the dream of Ernest O. Melby, but it was far in advance of the ideas toward education then accepted in Montana.

But old ideas could be changed. And Ernest Melby set out to change them. Strong in his convictions, intense in his emotions, and fearless in what he said, Melby would kowtow to no one, and in the ensuing months he was destined to win devoted friends and bitter enemies.

As the exploitation of Montana moved forward, the development of stable communities lagged further behind. Young people said there was not enough opportunity to earn a living in Montana, and over half the women students then attending the State University had stated they had no intention of staying in Montana upon graduation. They said that even if they found economic opportunity, the state presented little outlet for social and cultural expression. Montana was spotted with ghost towns. Small communities from one end of the state to the other were drying up, their very physical appearance a reminder of blasted hopes and thwarted ambitions. Historically, the frontier was gone; socially and culturally it remained to be conquered.

In Montana Melby saw in condensed form some of the serious forces of social decay that for more than two generations have been spreading through America, and which he saw as a potential threat to the democratic way of life.

Here was a man who believed that if intelligently employed for the satisfaction of human needs, the world's productive resources could maintain the entire human family in comfort, security, and happiness.

"Technology," he said, "has given us the tools to meet the needs of all humanity, but it has given human beings neither the disposition toward each other, nor the social direction by which these goals can be reached. We have given nurture to a science which has remade the productive world, but we have not equipped men to live in that world. We have given wings to the mind of man without putting beauty and love in his heart."

As Melby dreamed of ways to meet these human needs he looked again at the natural heritage of Montana. Here there was enough industrial potential to make prosperity for countless generations. Here were the wide open spaces, the ranges of snow-covered peaks, the clear lakes and sparkling streams, the ancient forests and secluded valleys, the wild game and the fish to lure the outdoorsman. He felt the call of the frontier that had drawn adventurous people to develop new opportunities and new ways of living, the spirit of human friendliness and hospitality that in times of emergency had brought pioneers together. In Montana's violent past he saw a treasure of historical tradition, and in her present and future he saw a great living culture.

Yet it was only through common awareness of this heritage, through intelligent understanding of its meaning, that the people of Montana could fully appreciate the opportunities it offered. And if this deeper understanding could somehow be developed, then, thought Melby, there would come concerted action by the people themselves to help youth find more opportunity at home, to pull the state out of her colonial status, and to improve the quality of living in Montana.

Having once set before himself these broad objectives, Melby was now ready for the details. And this is where his troubles began.

Actually, the University of Montana was not one university, but six. State University at Missoula, State College at Bozeman, State School of Mines at Butte, State Normal College at Dillon, Eastern State Normal School at Billings, and Northern Montana College at Havre— together these six units comprised the University of Montana, all under a State Board of Education which had responsibility for control, but no power or authority save that which could be squeezed from a niggardly legislature, usually subject to partisan interests. The chancellor, whose office was in Helena, was appointed by the Board of Education, but his salary could not be paid without a special act of the legislature. Though theoretically he was chief executive of the six units, he had virtually no authority in their administration, and for ten years before Melby accepted the office there had been no chancellor.

There were six presidents, six independent executive boards. Each unit prepared its own budget for the legislature, and there was no over-all budgetary control. It was a loose system of six autonomous institutions, all jealous and distrustful of each other, competing for students, quarreling for legislative favors, overlapping in their duties and programs, yet all part of the same university. It was an expensive luxury for Montana—a state whose population was less than that of San Francisco. And for purposes of political jockeying it was a beautiful setup.

For nearly two years before Melby became chancellor he had been president of one of these six units—the State University in Missoula. Before that he had been dean of education at Northwestern University. But in his new position neither of these former posts was a notable asset. Five autonomous units were now fearful that he would turn favors toward the Missoula unit. His enemies called him a foreigner to Montana.

And Melby did win enemies.

To those who prospered through maintenance of the colonial economy his stand for a free and more liberal education designed to enlighten people on the Montana facts of life made him a dangerous character. To the academics who resented his attempts to liberalize the curriculum of the University, he was a foolish visionary.

But Melby was the crusadinist' educator this state had ever seen. Yet the program he had envisioned to improve the quality of living in Montana was blocked by one barrier that even he could not surmount—a lack of money.

Then one day not long after he became chancellor, he attended a faculty meeting at the State College in Bozeman, and there met the man who was to make this program of his dreams financially possible—David H. Stevens, Director of the Humanities Division for the Rockefeller Foundation.

The State College had developed a project known as "Northern Plains in a World of Change," a cooperative affair between the College and other plains institutions including the University of Manitoba in Canada, but with Montana State College in the role of chief entrepreneur.

The Rockefeller Foundation had granted enough money to finance publication of a book entitled *The Northern Plains in a World of Change,* the purpose being to describe the Northern Plains region, enumerate its problems and possible solutions. The book, written chiefly by Carl F. Kraenzel, State College sociologist, was published in Canada in October, 1942. It was an excellent treatise and the most concrete result of the Northern Plains project. With that the Foundation's support ended. But to the State College it was only a small beginning. College staff members had various ideas as to the final goal of their project, some thinking in terms of enlarged educational possibilities directed toward fuller development of the Plains region, others thinkings in terms of specific programs for their own departments such as research in veterinary science, while still others were seeking a new library. But regardless of their differences, all were united in the one hope of more Rockefeller money for Montana State College. And now in the summer of 1943 they had as their guest

David H. Stevens, who, it was hoped, would make that money available.

Then came Ernest Melby, now chancellor, but recently president of Montana State University, the school that had always been the chief rival of the College. What was he looking for?

Melby, at this time, was still in the exploratory stage, the ideas for his new program not yet having crystallized in his mind. He only knew that it had some relation to a form of education designed to improve the quality of living in Montana. There were several aspects of this "Northern Plains in a World of Change" that appealed to him, and at the faculty meeting with Stevens, Melby began talking about these aspects. Bozeman men were gratified with Melby's approval and no doubt heaved a sigh of relief, all thinking he would support their plea for Rockefeller funds to be used at the Bozeman unit.

Melby himself, however, was merely exploring ideas. As yet he was not supporting any special program. But it was this meeting in Bozeman that led to a series of conferences between Melby and Stevens.

David Stevens was still interested in Montana, but he assured Melby the Foundation had gone as far as it was willing to go with the Northern Plains project. If Melby could offer them another proposal within the province of their Humanities Division, they might do business. Melby's big opportunity had come, and Melby was not a man to shun opportunity.

Certainly, he had a program Stevens could finance. It was rather nebulous, but its objective was to improve the quality of living in Montana. Now he had only to reduce it to definite form, though dreams are not always definite.

On October 5, 1943, John Marshall, Stevens' associate, wrote Melby saying, ". . . As I see it your interests . . . point . . . to a more detailed definition of what the present and emerging needs of Montana are. In other words, an interpretation of those needs in terms of what the state could do in meeting them . . ."

Marshall again raised the question of how the program would be related to the humanities and told Melby that if he would consider it in this light and send in a definite outline they would recommend assistance.

Melby continued the correspondence, meanwhile seeking advice from members of his faculty, but particularly from Merrill G. Burlingame, head of the History Department at the State College, and Harold G. Merriam, head of the Humanities Division at the State University, who had prepared a list of suggested studies. By New Year's Day, 1944, he was nearing an agreement with the Foundation, and a few days later sent his final proposal to New York. It began by saying, "The University of Montana wishes to undertake a research program to determine the contribution of the humanities to a program of higher education designed to improve the quality of living in the State of Montana. . . ." Apparently Melby and officials of the Rockefeller Foundation had come to an understanding. Back came a grant of $25,500 for a three-year project.

Melby's dream was in. But "Northern Plains in a World of Change" was out. And the grant was issued to the entire University of Montana —not the Bozeman unit. Through misunderstanding, and partially from internal rivalry in Montana's university system, a schism had been created; eventually it was to widen. But an experiment in American democracy was about to be born.

3

Preparing for Action

Programs for human progress do not evolve from a moment's thought. Although Melby knew in general the kind of program he wanted, it was only after months of thought and discussion that his new project began taking form.

He remembered his boyhood on a Minnesota farm where people had known the meaning of freedom because they owned their own farms, their own stores, and their own small businesses. For years he had been alarmed because in America so many had grown away from that feeling of independence. In the drift toward cities, the development of mass production, and the extension of absentee ownership into rural areas, people had in large measure lost their opportunity for individual enterprise. During his thirteen years in Chicago, Melby had seen people become dependent on others for jobs and political opinions. He had seen this movement into the cities accentuated by war, with still more loss of independence in political and social thought. And then when he thought of Montana's wide open spaces and its remote communities, it occurred to him that if the program of which he had dreamed could make life more interesting in these rural areas perhaps they could restore to American life some of the independence that people had known when he was a boy on the farm.

In those years of 1943–44, Melby realized that when the guns of World War II ceased firing, America would be in a crucial and strategic position—she would be the world's leading exponent of private enterprise and free institutions. But America would be thrown into conflict with Russia, which would be the leading exponent of state collectivism and communism, and if America failed, the world would say democracy does not work. Melby was therefore convinced that if America could take her heritage of freedom and translate it into reality for the common man, she would not only insure the success of her own institutions, but would keep alive the lamp of freedom for all humanity.

"Democracy," said Melby, "is not something which is in Washington —it is in our own hearts, minds, homes, communities. If it lives there it will live in the big lights, and if it dies in our communities it will die in the world."

If, then, the University of Montana could do something in that far western state to help people in its towns and rural areas to live more fully, more richly, and more creatively—then, thought Melby, Montana would not only improve its own life, but might actually introduce a stabilizing influence on the entire nation.

Melby talked of these aspects of his plan to Stevens, and it was because of this kind of thinking that the two planners turned for advice to Baker Brownell, professor of philosophy of Northwestern University.

An outstanding authority on the problems of rural life, an experienced editor and newspaperman, author of numerous books, such as *Art Is Action* and *The Philosopher in Chaos*, and one of America's leading philosophers, Baker Brownell is one who believes that culture can be found in the potbellied-stove bull session of a country store just as easily as in the intellectual atmosphere of a college classroom. Sophisticated theorizing or academic pursuits that are held aloof from the course of ordinary living have no place in the make-up of Baker Brownell. He is a man who believes that traditional American democracy finds its richest environment in the small communities and rural areas where people meet each other as neighbors, where they have a sense of belonging, and a feeling of personal responsibility toward each other. And it is his belief that if these small-town neighborhoods are allowed to decay, democracy will decay with them.

Yet today these communities are declining, and America is changing from a country of small democratic communities to a nation of great industrialized centers, where people don't speak to their next-door neighbor, where political intrigue, crime, insanity, divorce, and other consequences of human instability are mounting daily. Over fifty-one per cent of the counties in the United States, all rural, are being depopulated. To Baker Brownell this is one of the most critical problems in America, and he has devoted his life to its solution. It was not, therefore, unnatural that when funds were granted for Melby's project in Montana, he should then turn with David Stevens to a man like Baker Brownell.

On the 28th day of April, 1944, these three men met for a luncheon engagement in Chicago's Drake Hotel and there laid the foundation for a new program to be known as The Montana Study—an experiment in human relations destined to become a significant achievement in modern education, the ideas of which would some day spread into other states from New York to California, into Canada, India, Denmark, and Brazil.

The primary problem of The Montana Study was to "find ways to enrich the quality of living in Montana." Rough plans were outlined and approved at the meeting in Chicago, and to Baker Brownell went the job of formulating specific objectives, devising means of carrying them out, and directing the program.

As the planning got under way, the first specific objective was "to get the University off the campus." This did not mean doing away with the University, as certain people who misunderstood the Study later charged. It did mean that through this program, educational services of the University would be extended out from the campus and brought directly to the people in their own home towns, so that people in small communities all over Montana could better utilize the services of their University. As it was, Montana was realizing a poor return on its investment in higher education. Only a tiny fraction of its people ever attended the University, and since about half of those who did left the state after graduation, much of the money spent for the University yielded larger returns to other states than it did to Montana.

This objective of getting the University off the campus was based also upon the belief that while American colleges have been highly successful in training students for professional careers, they have not notably improved the quality of living in the small towns and communities from which many of their students are taken. The general effect of college life is to withdraw American youth from their home communities, train them for a specialized, individual-centered career as contrasted to a family-centered or community-centered life, and send them off into the impersonal crowds of a great city. Little, if any, effort is made to promote in the student a feeling of responsibility for the welfare of his home town. And the result is a further weakening of those neighborhood communities which are the backbone of American democracy.

"This situation," said Baker Brownell, "must be met by expanding liberal education to include persons of all ages all through life, by extending the locale to the home community, and by reorienting the instructional approach with these changes in mind."

The second objective of The Montana Study was to "find ways to stabilize the family and small community." This called for an effort to improve the standard of living in small communities, an effort to help these communities lift themselves up by their own bootstraps to strengthen their local economy, and to create new sources of income so that people would not be forced out of them to earn a living.

"This problem is critical," said Brownell, "because a society based on the human values inherent in a democratic way of life depends upon maintaining small communities as a major form of social organization. A rapid decline in the culture and security of America will take place if measures are not taken educationally, socially, and economically to stabilize our families and small communities."

Closely related to the first two objectives was the third: "To study ways to raise the appreciative and spiritual standard of living of the people of the state and thus keep a larger number of able young people in their home communities," or in other words, to help people in small towns make their own lives more interesting, more exciting, and more worth while. This called for the development of activities within the home community through which people could gain a deeper knowledge and appreciation of their own culture and their historical traditions, the development of creative recreation whereby people could become participants instead of spectators.

By "spiritual standard of living" The Montana Study was not designed to infringe upon the work of the churches as one hostile news editor alleged, but was to cooperate with them as well as with other agencies, in order to help create that quality of life which presents a challenge to young men and young women. It meant, in short, the elimination of decadence, and of dullness and monotony from the small town.

The Montana Study was to be a research project in the humanities, to find out how the humanities could contribute to improving the lives of people in small communities. By "humanities" they were not referring to a special body of subject matter such as the arts, literature, the languages, history, philosophy, and the purely appreciative and intellectual interests in general, but to any worth while human activity which falls within the course of day-by-day living. From this point of view all phases of human life were to be considered together as one integrated whole. It was, indeed, a point of view that interpreted the word "humanities" to mean anything from which human value can be derived. This was not to be merely another piece of theoretical study conducted by scholars in college libraries, but an energized experiment which would put the plan into actual operation in the small communities where ordinary Americans could themselves participate.

There would be no attempt to tell others how to run their communities or how to organize their lives. It was not a case of the teacher standing up in front telling students what they should think and what they should do, but was to be the work of people participating with one another, studying and discussing their own community with a view toward improvement. This was the general method by which it was hoped to "find ways to enrich the quality of living in Montana." And if the program proved successful the methods and techniques developed could be used in small communities anywhere in America.

April 28, 1944, had brought cause for jubilance to Ernest O. Melby. In David H. Stevens he had found the man who could make his dream financially possible, and in Baker Brownell he had found the man who could develop a specific program of operations.

Melby returned to Montana to set the stage for action.

4

The Experiment Begins

Long before The Montana Study was conceived, its most powerful enemy had already grown to tremendous proportions. That enemy was indifference toward any program of community welfare. It had been born in a swift historical past.

From the earliest days, Montana's experience in community planning and group thinking for the general welfare had been thin indeed. And now, before The Montana Study could begin action, other opposition more positive in nature was coming into fruition. It was as though the infant plan were predestined to be a victim of circumstances, for most of its enemies were the product of events that had no relation to The Montana Study.

Ernest Melby had accepted the chancellorship because the State Board of Education had asked him while he was still president of the State University in Missoula if he would assume the chancellor's duties to synchronize the six units, build up the system, and increase its efficiency. He was warned of the political barriers. He was told that sectional jealousies, and the autonomy of each unit, intensified by a ten-year vacancy in the office of chancellor, would make the job difficult, perhaps impossible. With these warnings in mind he had accepted the job, but on one condition—that if, after a year's trial, he was not satisfied with his accomplishments, he would resign.

And from the day he took over, antagonism was the dominant reaction to nearly all that he attempted. Every University unit, and every section of the state that claimed one of those units, was afraid of losing something to another unit—irrespective of the educational benefits that would accrue to Montana as a whole.

Every politician from legislator to local official who saw the six-way split favorable to his special purposes rose up in defiance. Many thought only of the possible increase in taxes if Melby obtained greater support for education, and they were against him too. From the six presidents he got little support, from partisan interests he won denunciation, from a large segment of Montana's press he won hostility. And from the North Dakota border to the Idaho line, he was in conflict with that intangible foe, lethargy.

In January, 1944, six months after Melby became chancellor, the State Board appointed a commission of nineteen representative citizens to make an independent study of the university system and recommend improvements. In June, 1944, this commission submitted its report, recommending clarification of the Board's powers designed to make possible an efficient administration unhampered by sectional jealousies, unification of the six units as to educational program and budget, and elimination of duplication. The commission's report was approved by the Board and action was taken to effect necessary legislation. Melby was in complete accord, for these were reforms he considered basic. But the six units were not so well satisfied.

Meanwhile, factional hostility had increased to such an extent that it was obvious the reforms were—as one of the six presidents put it— "a legislative impossibility."

"The most discouraging feature of the entire situation," said Melby, "is the utter refusal of the partisans of the individual units of the university system to face the facts in regard to the organization and cost of higher education in Montana. . . .

"In the long run it is the young people of Montana who must suffer for the selfishness and local partisanship of educational leaders and their supporters."

By the time his trial year had finished Melby was convinced that he was getting nowhere. He was willing to fight for his convictions, but there was no purpose in pursuing a line of futility. As of July 1, 1944, he resigned the chancellorship.

"This year of study and experience," he said, "has convinced me that the difficulties are deeply rooted in the existing legislative strait jacket under which the Board operates, and in the educational structure the Board is seeking to administer. The legislature has not given the State Board the powers it needs for efficient administration. The establishment of the various units as fiscally independent makes any attempt at unified administration a mere mockery. It makes of the chancellor an overhead administrative officer whose concerns are political and financial rather than educational. I think it is very questionable whether a chancellor can retain his position in the face of political, constitutional, and personal jealousies. Until the position of the State Board is clarified, the educational program of the University is unified, and provision made for a unified budget, the position of the chancellor is untenable, and in my judgment the expenditure for the office is unjustified."

The State Board accepted his resignation, but immediately reappointed him president of Montana State University; he had thereby taken a voluntary salary cut of $2,000.

But on July 1, 1944, Montana was without a chancellor. And on that same day funds from the Rockefeller Foundation became available to the chancellor's office for The Montana Study. Who was to administer it? It was not made out to the State University, or to any one of the six units, but to the University of Montana as a whole.

Melby had promoted the grant. He had attended the meeting in Chicago. He had worked with David Stevens to get Baker Brownell as director. And so the State Board appointed Melby to be responsible for the program. The Board also designated him its chief executive officer, and he served as chairman of the Executive Council—the council of six presidents. Melby was now in a bad position. He was no longer chancellor, yet he was considerably more than just another one of the six presidents. And he had control of the Rockefeller grant —money that had been given to all six units.

If Rockefeller money was to be spent for the university system, Montana State College wanted part of it. It also wanted to revive its project, "Northern Plains in a World of Change."

And there were four other units of the University who wanted a slice, and who felt they were not being given an opportunity to participate in the spending of this gift. After all, Melby was president at Missoula, and that, to five units, meant Missoula would get something they wouldn't have. The fact that Melby intended The Montana Study to utilize all six units, and serve all Montana, was of no consequence. The feeling toward him was not pleasant. And there was no great love for The Montana Study. An important segment of the opposition to follow had now emerged, although Baker Brownell had yet to appear, and The Montana Study was yet to be organized.

Enlisted to work with Brownell was Joseph Kinsey Howard of Great Falls, Montana. Howard was one of the greatest assets The Montana Study had, but with him came a whole new array of enemies.

Author of the book *Montana: High, Wide, and Handsome,* and news editor of the *Great Falls Leader,* Howard was one of the best-known citizens in Montana. He was especially famous for writing the truth exactly as he saw it regardless of whose wrath he incurred. And this, for Montana, was rare. In lucid and beautiful prose he had hammered at the injustice of Montana's colonial economy, and because of his love for Montana and its people he had uncompromisingly attacked the pressure groups and corporate interests who dominate the state's economic and political life. His number-one target was the Company—Anaconda Copper and Montana Power. In Montana's top political and financial circles Howard was about as popular as a rattlesnake at a lawn party, but there was perhaps no one in the state who knew the character of Montana better than he did.

In a memorandum of general information written in connection with launching The Montana Study, Howard commented, "Montana economic conditions have been such that there is both conscious and unconscious hostility toward really free education, toward any movement which seems to come 'from outside,' and in certain circles toward two individuals connected with the project—Dr. Melby and myself."

From the Rockefeller Foundation Brownell obtained an additional grant for Howard's compensation on a half-time basis, and in August, 1944, Howard left for Northwestern to join in the planning.

Paul Meadows, a Northwestern University sociologist, became the third staff member, and for him Brownell obtained another grant. These three—Brownell, Howard, and Meadows—comprised the entire staff of The Montana Study, and because of limited funds two of them—Howard and Meadows—were employed for half-time only. Meadows was to teach half-time at Montana State University and Howard was to devote the other half of his time to writing. The staff was small, but potent. Yet it was hoped that by enlisting the help of faculty members at the six University units The Montana Study would be able to enlarge its operations far beyond what the small staff could do personally.

Brownell and his two associates spent the next few weeks in the Middle West gathering information in the fields of rural life, community drama, adult education, extension work, regional arts, and other fields pertinent to their program. From prominent authorities at such institutions as the Kellogg Foundation, the Universities of Wisconsin, Chicago, Michigan, and Minnesota, they gained valuable advice.

Upon Brownell's suggestion, Melby established offices for The Montana Study on the State University campus at Missoula. And that did it. Resentment in the other five units toward Melby's power, and the feeling that his control of the Rockefeller grant would give the State University an advantage they did not have, had already created a schism. Now it was widened.

But The Montana Study was moving toward the beginning of its operation.

Early in September, 1944, Howard returned to Montana. A few days later Paul Meadows came west. Then on a bright autumn day in mid-September, after a long drive out from Chicago, Baker Brownell arrived with his family on the campus of Montana State University, and a new program designed to lift the level of human living in the small communities of a great western state was ready to begin.

One of the first moves in launching the new program was the formation of a state-wide advisory group called the Montana Committee to assist in developing special projects, and to provide people and organizations throughout the state an opportunity to participate in this important work. In order to keep the program objective and to prevent being identified with any special faction, it was hoped that a good cross section of representative citizens—housewives, farmers, merchants, professional men, labor officials, and top leaders in management—could be enlisted to serve on this committee, including at least one representative of the state's major private enterprises, Anaconda Copper and Montana Power.

But the same month The Montana Study opened for business in its Missoula headquarters, September, 1944, an article appeared in *Harper's Magazine*, entitled "The Montana Twins in Trouble?" Its author was Joseph Kinsey Howard.

The article opened with these words: "For almost a generation a pair of fat boys like Tweedledum and Tweedledee, an arm of each flung chummily across the other's shoulders, have been running the show in Montana. . . . The twins—Anaconda Copper and Montana Power. . . . In the dialect of the Treasure State . . . are 'the Company.' "

The article continued: "The first question asked about a political candidate, whether he seeks a seat on a county school board or a seat in the United States Senate, is always, 'Is he a Company man?' And if someone suggests a major community venture in any of the principal cities—sometimes even in farm villages—everyone else wants to know, 'How does the Company stand on it?' Because if the twins dislike candidate or project, the chances of either usually have been very slim indeed. Have been, up to now; but something is happening in Montana."

From that point the article described how the Federal Power Commission's investigators in March, 1944, had exposed approximately $50,000,000 excess capitalization, or "water," in Montana Power books, and suggested that as a result of this action, and other blows by the federal government, "political control may yet be wrested from the dominant twins."

"Montana . . . comes by such knowledge with considerable difficulty," wrote Howard, "since the twins control seven of the state's fourteen daily or almost daily newspapers and appear to have the Indian sign on some of the 'independents.' Of the eight newspapers in the five principal cities . . . all save Great Falls' two are Company-controlled."

In explaining the hostile attitude shown by Montana's press toward this important F.P.C. proceeding, Howard pointed out that two Montana weeklies were the state's only two papers to make any consistent effort to present the F.P.C. side of the case. In short, "The Montana Twins in Trouble?" put the Company in a decidedly unfavorable light. It was another of Howard's many blows. *Harper's Magazine* had barely hit the streets when virtually every copy in the state was bought out. But just to insure good circulation on this juicy story, *The People's Voice*, a Helena weekly representing labor and the Farmers Educational and Cooperative Union of America, reprinted thousands of extra copies of the article and spread it all over Montana. The Company had been dealt what it considered a foul blow.

In October, the next month after Howard's "The Montana Twins in Trouble?" was released to the public, Baker Brownell made a tour of the six units of the University. While in Butte to visit the School of Mines, he decided also to explain the purposes of his program to officials of the Anaconda Copper Mining Company, and to then invite a company official to serve on The Montana Study's state-wide advisory committee. He thereupon went to the company's offices and during the course of the conversation was asked if Joseph Kinsey Howard was not also helping to organize the Study. Brownell unhesitatingly replied that he was. Then came considerable apology concerning the pressure of company business, and Brownell's invitation to serve on the Montana committee was politely rejected.

This was the first and last official contact between The Montana Study and the Company. The latter has denied any opposition to the Study, though there are people in Montana who claim reason to think otherwise. In any case, The Montana Study received no active cooperation from Montana's "twins."

Meanwhile, the Study was getting little of the help its founders had expected. Academics argued with its techniques because it did not conform to established convention. Some people wanted to know what the Rockefellers wanted in Montana. Some accused the Foundation of squandering its money. Others were suspicious because the program was directed by an out-of-stater. About the only hope now was to demonstrate the project's true motives by proving what it could do for the people in small communities. And in this Brownell and his two associates were confident.

During the ensuing weeks they traveled the state explaining their objectives. They enlisted sixty people for the state-wide advisory committee. They collected voluminous material on Montana life and traditions. And they wrote a 50,000-word study guide, entitled *Life in Montana*, to provide the basis of a ten-week study course in community analysis for people in small towns.

As the work progressed they began developing special projects along several lines, but the largest and most important part of their program was the work planned for community study groups to be organized in small towns where people requested them. Brownell made it a strict policy never to go into a community to organize a study group without first being invited. And this policy was never violated.

Patterned along the lines of an old New England town meeting, the community study group was designed as a technique to help people find out exactly what made their town tick—or what kept it from ticking. It would be strictly nonpartisan, and nonpolitical. It was not to support or condemn any political issue, and it was to include a cross section of all the people in the community. Following the carefully worked out course of community self-analysis, this democratic group of people would sit down together around a large table once each week to study and discuss in an objective way the economic, social, and cultural problems of their own community as they affect day-by-day living. Key objectives of the study group would be to bring about a common understanding of community problems, to find ways of stabilizing and improving the local economy, and to help people make life in their town more enjoyable and more secure. This was not to be an action group, but the fun of getting together to study their own problems and the causes behind them would stimulate new interest in the town and prepare the people for intelligent action on their own initiative after the study was finished.

The idea of community study groups was based on the belief that frank and friendly discussion by the people themselves is the best way to get at community problems, and that so long as people will talk together as neighbors in the communities of America the democratic way of life will endure.

Despite rebuffs, skepticism, opposition, and lack of cooperation, Baker Brownell and his two half-time associates moved forward with the launching of their program.

Christmas of 1944 found them waiting for the big move toward which all their efforts had been pointed—the actual starting of a community study group.

5

Lonepine Leads the Way

In January, 1945, after weeks of planning and preparation, the big moment had arrived. By invitation from the little dirt-road community of Lonepine, The Montana Study was due for its first venture into the field. It had all looked good in theory, but now the big question was to be answered. How would the plan work in actual operation?

Here in this open farm community of about ninety families scattered over forty miles of a broad isolated valley in the mountainous country northwest of Missoula, Baker Brownell was to put the new program on trial. He knew that critical eyes would be watching this initial operation, and if Lonepine failed to respond to the experiment, it would be a major setback.

There was nothing new or unusual about adult study groups. There had been thousands of reading clubs, public forums, and many varieties of community-betterment groups designed to clean up the town, bring in new industry, and take other forms of local action. But never before had an American university undertaken a program of community-centered education in the humanities as interpreted by The Montana Study. Never before had community study groups been used as a technique for gathering information on human values by which a university might better adjust its program to the needs of people.

Traditionally, education at a university has been designed for individual students on the campus, the purpose being to help those individuals improve their lives and thus raise the general level of knowledge. The Montana Study was another form of education designed for communities rather than individuals, and instead of specializing in a certain subject as the student does in college, it was to cover a general study of human life as it goes on from day-to-day in the small American community. Thus, by study and research, a community would become educated in the various aspects of its own life, and, by virtue of this education, would become a better community. Improvement might come in the form of new sources of income developed by inspired local initiative, it might involve town beautification, projects in community recreation, adult hobby groups, efforts to solve specific local problems such as juvenile delinquency, a need for better medical facilities, or any other form of community improvement. Or it could result simply in a richer and more enjoyable community life, creating greater local pride, enlightened attitudes of mind, and giving each local citizen the recognition and feeling of personal dignity to which all human beings are entitled. But whatever form this improvement might take, The Montana Study had to begin its program with a group study of the local community by home-town people.

Hub of community life in Lonepine is a general store, reached over two miles of dirt road leading off the main highway some eight miles north of the resort town of Hot Springs. Most of the men and women in Lonepine are pioneers who staked out homesteads during the months of 1910 and '11 when Congress threw open the Flathead Indian Reservation to settlement. They are people of divergent backgrounds who risked everything they had on the future of this windswept country. From Kansas, from Missouri, from Iowa, and from states as far away as Virginia, they came—merchants, farmers, musicians, lawyers, bankers, preachers, Jacks-of-all-trades. They had never irrigated a foot of soil in their lives, but the government had offered them free land and promised them irrigation if they would come to this Indian country in the Little Bitter Root Valley.

For Montana, this was a most unusual community. Unlike the pioneers of Alder Gulch and those who exploited the forests, these people came to stay—they came to build homes, to transform the wilderness into a settled community. And the difference in the motive that drove them has reflected itself in a sense of permanence and future security from the earliest days, and in a remarkable community spirit.

They say that Bill Whiteside, Lonepine's first storekeeper, and the biggest storyteller ever to cross the Little Bitter Root, gave the place its name. It seems that old Bill unloaded his wagon beside a lone pine tree standing out of the sagebrush and announced that he was starting a post office. When asked what he intended to call it, Bill, who could name anything, looked at the big tree and dubbed the place "Lonepine." The name stuck, though Bill long since departed for the wilds of Canada and has now gone to the great beyond.

But the government did not come through with its promised irrigation nearly as fast as Bill Whiteside came through with a name for the community, and before long the novelty of homesteading had worn off. The Little Bitter Root Valley was a beautiful place and the mountain ranges to the east and west inspired a lot of patience, but it was still a long way from the nearest railroad, and there was no place to get a job when the homesteader reached into empty pockets for money to buy his family provisions.

Winds whipped through the tarpaper shacks, and tents were not too comfortable. On the high bench lands there was good bunch grass for cattle but the homesteaders had very few cattle, and their valley farms grew better sagebrush than they did vegetables. The droughts were bad, but the 'hoppers were worse and what few crops they had failed more often than they succeeded. Drinking water had to be hauled in barrels because wells were not much use unless drilled to three hundred feet, and few homesteaders could afford a three hundred-foot well. Interest on bank loans ran ten, twelve per cent. But somehow, despite all their troubles and hollow government promises, they proved up and stuck it out.

Lonepine people say the government may take a mighty long time, but if you can stand the wait, it always comes through. In 1916, after six years of prodding from the homesteaders, Uncle Sam broke down and started construction on the first irrigation canal. Then the canal was not built right; the homesteaders tried to make water run uphill and failed, and it was not until 1927 that irrigation was anywhere near adequate. By this time many of the homesteaders had decided they loved their former trades back home more than they did homesteading, and had given up. Only the most persistent were left.

As irrigation became a reality the homesteaders diversified their operations. Families began raising their own food. Poultry and egg production increased, they began growing hay, and developed a healthy dairy industry. New homes were built and during the thirties while thousands of farmers in other parts of Montana—and all over America, for that matter—were going through mortgage foreclosures, not one Lonepine homesteader lost his place. Lonepine had set an example of achievement through working together for the common good.

Every year since 1913 each family had brought food to a community Thanksgiving dinner where they joined together to reaffirm their faith. Each spring they all turned out to clean up the community cemetery where neighbors who died young from the strenuous living were laid to rest.

It was this spirit of cooperation for the common good, and their desire to make a home from the first days when they began pitching tents in the sagebrush, that made Lonepine different from other frontier communities. Now the early settlers were growing old. If the community was to survive, its young people would have to carry on.

But it was losing its youth to distant cities from New York to San Francisco. Bars at Hot Springs, Polson, and Missoula were more enticing than the Grange and Ladies' Aid. Modern highways were taking people away for shopping and amusements. They had more money than before and there was not much to spend it on at home. Even canned food was being purchased from the outside. The trend had been reversed—wealth and people were beginning to flow out, instead of into, Lonepine, and with this change people were beginning to lose their community spirit. Slipping away was that quality of living that Vern Dondanville, one of their greatest booster citizens, called "simple contentment."

Then came World War II. To the armed forces went nearly every young man in the community. Young and old departed for war industries. Retired men, mothers, and daughters went to work in the fields. Lonepine was not what it used to be.

For nearly a year before this community ever heard of The Montana Study, a young preacher named Harvey Baty, who directed religious activities at Montana State University, had been coming up for Sunday services. Harvey, as he was known in Lonepine, just had an idea that Baker Brownell would make a hit up there. So in November, 1944, Harvey asked if he could bring Brownell and his family up for the community Thanksgiving dinner. Nothing in this world is easier than getting invited to dinner in Lonepine, and the Brownells had the feast of their lives.

That evening Free Halverson, Lonepine's postmaster and store-keeper, had the Brownells and some other folks in at his homestead drinking coffee. Conversation drifted to The Montana Study.

"That sounds like something Lonepine could use," said Free. "Why don't you make us your guinea pig?"

Brownell, already in love with the people, was more than willing. Free advertised it in his *Hub News*, a weekly bulletin he mimeographs to announce community events. Brownell said he thought thirty-five or forty people would be about the right number because a much larger group would be a mass meeting instead of a discussion.

Free was anxious to oblige so he nailed people as they came into his general store until he had about the number Brownell suggested. That part was simple. But just how long they would keep coming was something else again. Free had come through a lot of hard times with Lonepine, having homesteaded there in 1910. He and Irene, the girl he married, raised three children there, and they knew the people about as well as anybody. The old Lonepine spirit that built their community was far from dead, but in later years Free, along with others like Vern Dondanville and Scrubby Howser, had seen that spirit slipping. In the last ten years Lonepine had been excited about other ideas, only then to lose enthusiasm. So even though Free liked the looks of Baker Brownell, he was about dead certain that after two or three meetings folks would cool off and that would be that. Any-way, it was worth trying.

When Brownell, Howard, and Meadows arrived in Lonepine on that night in January, 1945, they found a store building and post office, a country school, a small community house, a Presbyterian mission church, and a frozen plain stretching off into the distant mountains. But inside the schoolhouse they found a warm group of country folks to greet them.

Free Halverson had done his job well and the people of Lonepine had responded. There was Vern Dondanville and his wife Elsie, the schoolteacher. Next to them was Vern's sister Elizabeth, with her husband Scrubby Howser. And there was Jim Howser, the bachelor, with his sister Klonda, from the same family as Scrubby. Frank Hillman, who came to Lonepine as the first county agent and then twenty-six years ago went to farming, was there with Jessie, his wife. Roy and Lucille Bras, two of the best-loved folks in Lonepine—they

were there. And Chet and Martha Taylor, who built the first homestead shack; and old Von, that's W. W. Von Segen who built the
first chicken house in the valley and lived in it until his chickens
arrived—he's always been a leader in Lonepine—he was there, and
his son Kent with his wife Dorothy; and there were plenty of others
there waiting to see what The Montana Study had to offer—forty of
them in all, including several good-looking high school girls like Verla
Bras and Esther Halverson.

Baker Brownell stepped into the lighted schoolroom and looked into
the faces of these Lonepine people. Something in their eyes told him
he was among friends, yet he knew that after thirty-five years of
homesteading these people were stark realists. They had no desire to
go backward though there was a certain quality about the past that
many wanted to revive—indeed must revive if Lonepine were to
remain a virile community. That's why they were there now, part of
them seated around a table and the rest crammed in behind under-
sized school desks. But it was no time for sentimental theories; unless
Brownell could reduce The Montana Study to cold practicality this
first test would fail. Brownell and his two partners shook hands with
the folks nearest them and sat down.

Free Halverson was the first to speak.

"We're here to organize a community study group that's to be a
kind of guinea pig for The Montana Study, which is something I
think can do us a lot of good.

"But now I want to introduce Mr. Brownell, the man you all met
at our last Thanksgiving dinner, who will tell you what it's all about."

Brownell told them how glad he was to be there, spoke briefly
about The Montana Study, and introduced the members of his staff.
Paul Meadows was a stranger to Montana, but that didn't make any
difference to people in Lonepine. They were glad to make his ac-
quaintance. Everybody knew about Howard. He was author of *Montana: High, Wide, and Handsome*, a book that made a big hit in
Lonepine. What's more, Howard was a Montanan who had become
famous and that made him a feature attraction. Harvey Baty, who had
come along as a guest, was already so well known in Lonepine he
didn't need an introduction. And now they were ready for business.

"We live in a time," said Brownell, "when small communities all
over America are losing the significant place they once held in our

national life. Our universities are training young people for careers in the large city, almost to the exclusion of small communities. Big business and swank places of entertainment are drawing people into the cities more than ever before. Yet we don't think that mass city life is conducive to real American democracy. And since the rates of insanity, crime, divorce, and other human maladjustments are far greater in our large cities than in rural communities, we don't think that city life produces the best conditions for wholesome living. We of The Montana Study believe that vigorous small communities as America once knew them, provide the only atmosphere in which democracy can thrive and remain a powerful force in our country. We therefore believe that preservation of the American family and the small community as vital elements in our national life is of paramount importance to our country."

Brownell paused. He looked more closely into the faces watching him. Strenuous years had caused many of those faces to become grooved with deep lines and furrows. They were tanned. And some of the men were not smoothly shaven. Not all of them wore suits. Some were dressed in overalls, and several women were wearing cotton print dresses. But there were youthful faces, too. There were high school girls. And everybody was intent. They liked what Brownell was saying. And they were thinking about Lonepine, the community they loved because it was home. They felt no resentment because these men were outsiders. They had all been outsiders once themselves, and now there was something in their hearts that told them these men had come as friends.

Brownell continued.

"Upon the invitation of Mr. Halverson we have come here to help you organize a Lonepine study group, in which you may analyze and look into the problems of your community. We are not thinking in terms of an action committee, but a group that will uncover whatever problems exist, study their underlying causes and effects, and engage in objective, friendly discussion with a view toward solving them."

He told them about the study guide, *Life in Montana,* which had been mimeographed, and said they hoped to take the humanities, interpreted as anything of value to human beings, to bedrock. That included everything from having a good time to making a living, and Brownell said he thought that even making a living ought to be something people can enjoy.

The study guide was planned in a series of ten sections with the thought that one weekly meeting would be devoted to each section, although Brownell asked the group to alter the course to suit their desires if they saw fit.

"This is our first study group," he said, "and we hope to learn as much as anybody. Your criticisms of the guide will help to improve it."

Organization of the study group was simple. It called for a chairman and secretary, the chairman to assume general responsibility, and the secretary to keep minutes of the discussions and a file for reports. This would help keep track of the information they gathered, and the minutes showing subjects discussed and what various members said would make a useful record.

Each week the chairman was to appoint a discussion leader and question committees to make advance preparation for the questions asked in the next section of the study guide. Besides these questions, intended to help analyze various phases of community life, the study guide also contained four research problems which called for temporary research committees to be appointed once every two weeks. The research problems were a further means of gathering facts and information about the community.

"This thing really sounds all right to me," said Vern Dondanville, looking around at the others.

"By gosh, it strikes me that way," Scrubby Howser agreed.

Copies of the guide had been passed out by this time and everybody was talking and thumbing through the sheets.

"Look at that," Vern whispered to Scrubby, "even the high school kids are interested."

Brownell suggested that everyone should try to come regularly for the full ten weeks.

"Regular attendance of the same people will give the work continuity," he said. "Unless we have that continuity it won't be possible for the discussion to proceed on the basis of what was studied the week before."

They all assured him they could be counted on for regular attendance, and what's more they agreed to open and close every meeting on time. This, they felt, was important because everybody had early morning chores and some people might not be able to keep coming if they stayed up too late.

Brownell said he wanted the group to be completely informal, so they refrained from a regular election of officers and everyone just decided to make Free Halverson chairman.

They decided that big John McCoy, their school superintendent, was a natural-born secretary, so somebody got John a pencil and paper and told him to start keeping minutes.

Free Halverson started things off. He was to read aloud from the study guide and people were to interrupt whenever they wished.

First question was, "Who and what are we?"

The guide gave an analysis of people in Montana generally. Eighty-eight per cent have parents born in America, about thirty per cent of those above fifty years old came from another country. Four per cent of the people in Montana are Indians. One out of five people in the state belongs to a church, about half are Protestant and half are Catholic. Thirty per cent finished high school, about five per cent finished college. In proportion of college graduates Montana is exceeded by only fourteen states.

The guide gave the average number of children per family, the number of people living on farms and in various sized towns, the per capita income, the occupational distribution, the number of people who own cars, who have electricity, telephones, and the fact that in national elections during the previous sixteen years about sixty per cent were Democrats and forty per cent Republicans.

"This is the picture of the average Montana family and community," Free read from the guide. "Does our community differ greatly from this average?"

Not much in these respects, they decided, except that about eighty per cent of those present were born in America, twenty per cent in Montana, and forty-five per cent were high school graduates.

They discussed why they were living in their community. Most of them agreed it was by choice. Some thought Lonepine had a higher standard of living than other communities, but others were too modest to agree with that.

They talked about how Lonepine had changed in the last few years in population, wealth, occupations, ages of its people, ways of living, and patterns of thinking, and they discussed what they could do to make farming more attractive to young people.

Everybody agreed with Free that well-established farms, people they liked, and a healthy community spirit would keep folks in Lonepine.

Vern said, "A lot of people who left Lonepine in the past came back because during hard times they could make a living here easier than they could in the city."

The discussion was only in general terms that first night. Just enough to get people started thinking about the basic elements that make their community what it is, get them in an objective frame of mind, and stimulate interest in the more detailed analysis yet to come.

Time passed so quickly they forgot to notice it, and all of a sudden it was nearly midnight.

"We've got to close earlier than this," said Free.

Everybody was agreeable to the idea, but they had no complaints. Already they were having a good time with The Montana Study.

Free quickly appointed question committees for the next week and committees for the first research problem.

This problem asked for the preparation of several histories of the Lonepine community. Mrs. W. W. Von Segen agreed to write the history of their churches, John McCoy would take the schools, Vern Dondanville, their one-man chamber of commerce, the business and economic history, and Jim Howser, the bachelor farmer, would write up significant men and women in the life of Lonepine. These histories were all the guide asked for, and they were to be ready for presentation to the group two weeks hence.

But they decided that just to make sure nothing was overlooked they'd add a few histories of their own, so Frank Hillman agreed to write the history of Lonepine irrigation, showing its effects on local customs and agriculture, and Edna Gannaway, editor of *The Camas Hot Springs Exchange,* was appointed to write the history of newspapers in the Lonepine region. Edna actually lives in Hot Springs, eight miles south, but Lonepine folks have a strong claim on her. And just because Edna liked doing things she also volunteered to write a report on "The Indian As We Have Known Him in the Little Bitter Root Valley."

As Free closed the meeting he was beginning to think he'd been wrong about people cooling off on this project.

It was after one o'clock before Baker Brownell, Joseph Howard, Paul Meadows, and Harvey Baty left Halverson's homestead where Free took them for coffee after the meeting adjourned.

"Well," said Howard, heading the car toward Missoula, ninety miles southeast, "it looks as if we've got a study group."

"And what a group!" said Paul Meadows. "There wasn't a dull moment."

"I told you so," Harvey remarked, as though he were talking about his own home town.

Brownell was sure he'd never seen such fine people in all his life.

After all their troubles getting started, The Montana Study was at last being tested—and the chances of success looked good.

The enthusiasm shown that first night never slackened. And work was not limited to weekly meetings in the schoolhouse. For ten weeks lights in the homesteads burned just a little later as question committees and homemade researchers, young and old, gathered to assemble data for factual reports to be discussed pro and con by the whole group.

You would have thought Lonepine was preparing to print a section in *The World Almanac*. How many families do we have? What is the average number of children per family? Compare modern families with those of our grandparents. How many single people do we have by sex, and how many in the various age groups?

How many families have been here ten years or more? How many of our families were started here? List all the people who have left our community within the last three years to stay. Tabulate the reasons for their leaving.

What proportion of the goods and services used in Lonepine are produced here? Consider groceries, clothing, butchering, mechanical work, entertainment.

Enumerate practical ways to increase local production for local use. What about goods produced for consumption in the home itself? Prepare a table showing all our different work activities at different times of the year. Consider both work in the fields and work in the home. What opportunities for earning a living do we have to offer our young men? What new small industries could profitably be started in Lonepine?

What are our seasonal activities in recreation and culture? How could these activities be increased?

To what extent is our school linked with our community in an effort to raise the level of education and cultural life for all our people? How about the church in this respect?

These, and hundreds of other questions were given detailed consideration. Almost no phase of community life escaped attention—

past, present, and future. And with the same care they studied Lonepine in relation to their state, and their state in relation to their nation.

No matter how serious they became, they never forgot their sense of humor. In his comprehensive report on "The Economic and Business Development of Lonepine," Vern Dondanville, describing the early-day practice of medicine in their community, wrote, "The first to pose as a doctor was a bewhiskered gentleman who probably carried more germs in his whiskers than pills in his case, and only a couple of the latter was he capable of using, a sedative and a laxative. It was reported that he was at one time a veterinarian, but people no longer trusted their livestock in his care so he took up the treatment of humans. It was in this man's care that the health of the local Indians was entrusted, which probably helps to account for the rapid decrease of Indian life in our neighborhood."

As they drew near the end of their tenth week they began considering what they had accomplished. It had been fun. Everybody agreed on that. They had dug into the history of Lonepine to create their own literature. They had recorded anecdotes and information about their own past that otherwise would have been lost. To them, this was of immeasurable value. They had carefully studied the social, economic, and recreational problems that could make life empty in their community, or could make it abundant. And from working together to analyze and understand these problems they had recaptured that spirit of "simple contentment" which made Lonepine a community of neighbors where down-to-earth American democracy is a living reality. Perhaps their greatest accomplishment was what they had done to their attitudes of mind. This, to be sure, was pretty intangible, but it was terribly significant, for it had given them a deeper understanding of themselves and a more conscious appreciation of life in their community.

Their group had not been organized specifically as an action committee, but you just can't study your community as thoroughly as these folks did and not be stirred to start some action. The fact that Lonepine had no library was a problem that had never really occurred to them before, but during their study they found that more people would read books if they had books. And so they decided it was high time they established a library.

Like all such projects the idea had to grow. At first they gathered up a few books and put them in one corner of Free Halverson's store, but that didn't prove too successful. There was no regular librarian and the books merely gathered dust on a shelf.

Then the project was assigned to the Lonepine Women's Club, which organized a permanent library committee consisting of Ruth McHenry, Dorothy Von Segen, and May Page. Jack Erkkila, one of their high school teachers, suggested they take over a storeroom in the schoolhouse, and with Jack's help, and with brooms and scrub brushes, the women went to work. Husbands built shelves, and wives did the painting. Wide appeals were made for books. Free advertised it in his *Hub News*. And books came from all directions. Now Lonepine has a community library. With more than 600 books so far, and the committee planning new shelf space, they have fifty-seven card holders, mostly young people, and every library card is in regular use. When you figure that Mom and Pop and everybody else in the family all check books on the same card, and that Lonepine has only ninety families, this is a record few cities can equal. So far the cost has been $10.50 for shelves, and $25.00 for cataloguing. Every Tuesday afternoon the library is open and a member of the committee is on hand to check out books.

In April, 1945, the Lonepine Study Group put on a big community "feed" (the women objected to calling it a "banquet") to celebrate completion of their ten-week study course.

Jessie Hillman expressed the feeling of all. "Our discussions," she said, "have helped us to live richer, fuller lives, and by combining work with pleasure we have had a wonderful time doing something really worth while for Lonepine."

Speaking for The Montana Study staff, Paul Meadows said, "Lonepine has given us a better conception of what education can do for people in a real life situation."

And what Meadows said was exactly right, for Lonepine had made suggestions that helped improve the study guide, which Brownell now called *Life in Montana: As Seen in Lonepine, a Small Community*, and had printed in the form of a book. By their cooperation the people of this small community had helped create a working technique that other small communities could use to help solve their problems.

As part of the effort to find ways of enriching community life it was considered important to create something of broad local interest that would provide further means of community self-expression in the strictly cultural and appreciative aspects of American life. For this purpose Brownell, in the fall of 1945, invited Bert B. Hansen, an expert in community dramatics from the State College at Bozeman, to join in the work of The Montana Study. Hansen was a veteran college teacher and though he had achieved prominence in his field, he had a big western smile that made you more apt to call him Bert than Professor Hansen. Hansen and The Montana Study just naturally fit together, for this was a program in which he could spend part of his time off the campus helping men and women to enrich their everyday lives right in the communities where they lived.

Late in 1946, after helping with dramatic programs in other communities where other Montana study groups were started, Hansen came to Lonepine. And with his help they began work on a series of historical plays.

Meeting now for the sole purpose of writing plays about themselves and their community, study group members began living the life of Lonepine all over again.

"That reminds me of the time we went hunting and got snowed in," said Scrubby Howser, as they started reminiscing.

The whole group laughed so hard they could hardly talk, and before Scrubby could finish, Doke McHenry had one. Ted Vander Ende added another, and then everybody had one to tell. The women had yarns too, but they could hardly find an opening.

"Remember how Reverend Murray used to drive his Model-T over the irrigation ditches?"

Just the mere thought brought another barrage of laughter.

Bewildered by the antics of their parents, who they never realized could have such fun, the young people just sat taking it all in. Lonepine was participating in a form of culture that certain intellectuals might not appreciate, but to these people it meant more than tea at the Metropolitan or a course in the classical works of art.

After weeks of telling tales, writing them into dialogue, casting, and rehearsing, the "Lonepine Historical Drama" was ready for production. It was a drama of real life—a story by the people of Lonepine, about themselves and their community, beginning in 1909 just before their first homesteads were staked out in the sagebrush. The show was written with a prologue and four episodes, linked together by a narrator who pretended to flash his audience back into intimate events of the past through which Lonepine had lived. It was work and fun all wrapped together. And the teen-agers came in for as much work as anybody, since recreation for young people was one of the principal reasons for doing the plays. But they loved it. They had already learned from the earlier discussions that matching wits with the older folks was a lot of fun, and any shyness they may have had about participating with the "old fogies" had long since vanished.

Altogether sixty Lonepine people took part in writing and producing the drama, which was presented before capacity crowds on two successive evenings in the Lonepine Community Hall. Nearly six hundred people from points as far away as Spokane, Washington, witnessed the performances, and the second night was topped off with a supper and old-fashioned community dance. The gross receipts were nearly $500. To this they added approximately $600 which had been donated for community recreation, and made some much-needed improvements in the community hall.

But if you ask people in Lonepine what were the principal accomplishments of their Study Group, the answer you'll get most often will be that it crystallized their own history in the minds of the people and gave them a better understanding and greater appreciation of their own community. It taught them to think objectively—to look first for the facts, and then form conclusions without regard to politics.

War workers and veterans have returned, some with wives from as far away as Boston and distant England.

"And," said Vern Dondanville, "as a result of our Study Group we've noticed a big difference in the part young people are playing in our Grange."

"That's right," said Free Halverson, "we really mixed 'em up—all the way from Frank Lee who's past seventy, to high school sophomores, including my own daughter, Esther."

The Montana Study had passed its first operational test.

6

Darby

Back in the early part of this century a young man in Pennsylvania, answering the call of Horace Greeley to "Go West," bade his sweetheart farewell and struck out for the frontier. After weeks of travel, he arrived at the little woods settlement of Darby, deep in the mountains of Montana's Bitter Root Valley. He looked at the natural beauty he had found, and then, kneeling down in the road, lifted his face to the heavens and repeated after Brigham Young, "This is the place."

This young man was destined to become one of the most unusual lumberjacks in the history of American logging for he was interested not only in cutting trees for gold, but in creating a permanent and stable place to live where a man could raise a family without fear of insecurity. His name has never made headlines and outside his own valley he is unknown. But wrapped up in his life is the story of a community, for he is a living symbol of the grassroot common people who make America. His name is Denny Gray.

Darby was a typical one-street logging town where the clang of silver dollars was heard nightly in local saloons. Most of the inhabitants made their living by cutting trees, or by selling flour and whiskey to the woodsmen. It was a land of wooden gold, for out of Darby's forests thousands of feet of logs moved daily from the lumberjack's saw to the mills of distant cities. But it was a society that could not last, for it was built on the false notion that forests are inexhaustible.

Here Denny went to work in the woods and learned the code of the lumberjacks, yet he was different from those who lived in the camps. Shortly after arriving in this mountain village he established a home, sent for his Philadelphia sweetheart, and was married. Together they raised seven children, and as years passed their little town grew to a community of five hundred people. But each succeeding year the lumberjacks cut deeper into the forest. Their absentee employers were not interested in Darby as a community. Their policy, like that which had always dominated the frontier, was strictly cut out and get out. And by 1944, Darby's large private timber holdings had virtually passed into history. It had been another American boom town—settled in a flush of pioneer enthusiasm, boomed to main-street size, and then left to molder and die, as more and more the nation's life concentrated around large industrial centers. Now in the midst of wartime prosperity Darby was on the verge of becoming another ghost town.

In the mountains around Darby great forests still remained, but they belonged to the United States, and could be logged only on the basis of sustained yield. This meant that only about one-third as much timber could be cut each year as had been cut before. The last big logging operator had employed more than a hundred men. Now he was moving out. And a substantial percentage of Darby's 173 families faced the possibility of no income.

Already there were empty buildings along Main Street, and the town's dilapidated appearance sent strangers hurriedly on their way. Destructive logging had reduced taxable valuation to sixty-seven per cent below its 1930 depression level. The support of public education had become critical. Young people graduating from high school found no opportunities in Darby and seventy-five per cent of them were leaving.

"But Darby had something worth saving," said Denny.

Here people were more than just a crowd. They were Jimmy, or Mary, or Joe, or somebody else you knew real well. They kind of felt like they belonged there. When a neighbor's house burned down the town threw a dance to help build a new one. Once when a widow's little boy had to be taken to the hospital in Helena, her neighbors quietly chipped in a hundred dollars for the trip. Hardly a day passed without most folks seeing each other because every morning they stood around the post office "chewing the fat" while waiting for the mail to come in. They had no local newspaper, but a bulletin board on Main Street served the purpose. Most folks didn't have much money but they loved Darby because it was their home. They did a lot of hunting and fishing in their Bitter Root primitive area—and that was something for which dudes from New York would pay hundreds of dollars.

"Yep, that's Darby," said one of Denny's friends, "a swell place to live, but a tough place to make a living."

Denny had long been worried about their vanishing forests and since most of his neighbors had made their living in the woods, he decided that saving the forest and saving the town were both parts of the same problem. When he thought about the thousands of logs he himself had cut, he felt a sort of personal guilt.

Most folks were against regulated cutting because they were individualists. It was in their heredity. But Denny knew that only by selective logging could Darby's remaining forests be permanently productive. Yet he was no great community leader. He was just an unpretentious lumberjack. He knew that alone he could hardly make a dent in the big job of saving Darby. But at least he could do his share. And that's why, years before, he quit logging and began working for the Forest Service. To him it was a kind of moral duty. He even worked on his own time without pay. He planted trees on cut-over mountains. He burned brush to reduce the hazard of forest fire. He built erosion controls in old logging trails where rich top soil was being washed away, and water needed by ranchers in the valley below was being lost. In town he helped with community projects. He became active in the P.T.A. and helped improve hot lunch facilities for the children at school.

But in 1944, Denny was not alone in his desire for Darby's survival —there were a lot of others. People like Mrs. Ford, the woman with a big dude ranch on the hill south of town. She had come out from the East and made Darby her home because she loved the people and the mountains they lived in, and the people loved her. No one knows how many community enterprises she has made possible. There was her daughter Phyllis, who met Harry Twogood when he was packing mules through the mountains. They married and settled on a cattle ranch because Phil said, "So help me Hannah, the city's no place to raise kids." There was white-haired Arden Cole, the town's dignified school superintendent, who came to Darby with his wife Lydia in 1922. Next to their own dads the kids thought he was about the best guy on earth. He had taught readin', writin', and 'rithmetic to about every young person in town, and somehow kept the whole thing going on half enough money. The Coles raised five daughters and one son in Darby. Now they've all finished school there, gone to Montana State University, and scattered all over the world. The oldest married a Yale psychologist. And there was Abbie Osborne who knew more about Darby than anybody in town because she was their telephone operator. From her they learned when a new baby was born. She was the one who told them when the P.T.A. postponed its meeting, and relayed messages for folks who had no telephone. Darby never could have paid for the service Abbie rendered. And there was Fred Printz who came to Darby in the spring of 1880 when nobody but Indians lived there, and his son Bob who could always be counted on for help in any community affair. And there were people like Sam Billings and Les Robinson, the two local forest rangers, and their wives, and Charlie West, one of their most progressive ranchers. Yes, there were a lot of folks who wanted to keep Darby going, but they just couldn't get together behind a common effort to change things.

Then one day in the winter of 1945, news came to Darby about The Montana Study, and what was happening in Lonepine, 150 miles north. Some people scoffed at the idea of letting a strange professor use them as guinea pigs, but Denny Gray and some other folks decided they'd like to know more about this plan to prevent ghost towns, and they urged Brownell to come to Darby.

Baker Brownell talked in straightforward language that Darby people understood. In his quiet way he challenged them to forget petty differences and tackle their problems as one man. His Darby listeners were inspired and his challenge was accepted. On the evening of April 23, 1945, almost one year to the day after that eventful meeting in Chicago's Drake Hotel, the Darby Study Group was organized.

Champ Hannon was made chairman, and Pauline Bibler secretary. In addition to the weekly question committees and temporary research committees called for in the study guide which Lonepine helped improve, it was now suggested that two or three standing committees be appointed to investigate the community's major long-range problems. Thus, the group established committees on small industries, local taxation, and Darby education and recreation. Denny Gray was appointed chairman of the small industries committee. With him were Luther Donica, Isobel Satterlee, and Jake Prinz, but actually the entire group worked together on this problem, for unless folks could earn a living without leaving their community, Darby was finished.

For thirteen consecutive weeks nearly thirty resolute citizens gathered around a table in their community hall and, stretching the study guide into three extra meetings, sized up the problems of their town. When Denny's committee began investigating Darby's economic problems they started with a strange situation that folks had always known about but just taken for granted. Here in the heart of this logging country you couldn't buy a stick of finished lumber. Every frame house in town had been built with lumber shipped in from the outside. Absentee operators, mostly contractors for Anaconda Copper, had always shipped Darby's logs away in the raw state to be milled into finished lumber somewhere else. And the more they thought about it, the more obvious became the first step toward solving their problem. Why couldn't somebody in Darby build a local planing mill? There had always been a few small sawmills, but these only sawed logs into rough lumber. What they needed was a mill that could go still further and remanufacture rough lumber into finished products.

With his committee Denny went to the Forest Service for advice. They checked freight rates with the Northern Pacific that runs a spur into Darby from Missoula. They figured the cost of shipping by truck over Lost Trail Pass, south into Idaho. They found that a good part of their lumber could be sold locally, and to ranchers along the Bitter Root River. There were markets in Missoula, western Montana's shipping point for the East and Mid-West, where the surplus could be sold. Home milling and remanufacturing were not only sound financially—it would mean that for every lumberjack in the woods about three men could be employed in town. And that spelled new incomes for Darby's families.

But if small mills were established how could they be sure that a big operator from the outside wouldn't some day come in and outbid them for logs on the National Forest? If that happened their source of raw material would dry up, local industry would go broke, and Darby would be right back where it was before. In the process of making their study the answer to this hazard was found.

Back in 1941 while carloads of logs were still rolling daily out of Darby, the U. S. Forest Service had foreseen the disappearance of private timber upon which this community depended, and in the interests of preserving the community had established a policy giving the forest supervisor the right to reject all bids for timber on the Bitter Root National Forest, "the acceptance of which would involve milling

. . . outside the Bitter Root Valley." Written into Forest Service management plans was the statement, "Remanufacturing within the working circle is to be encouraged," and further, "small mills, locally owned and operated, are to be encouraged." Yet regardless of how well-meaning the Forest Service may have been, its policy was worthless to Darby unless local initiative took advantage of it. And it is doubtful that any official efforts by the Forest Service could have ever persuaded people to take this initiative. The effort necessary to make that policy effective had to come first from the people. The community had to get behind it. The people had to learn about it for themselves, they had to appreciate its value. And that's what Study Group members were doing. By their efforts they were generating local interest in a real home industry, and they had discovered for themselves a guarantee that enough timber could be cut on a sustained-yield basis to make it permanent.

Denny and his committee kept working, until eventually they had information showing that fourteen new enterprises could be successfully operated in Darby.

But The Montana Study called for more than just the means of making a living.

"To hold its own," said Brownell, "a town needs to be interesting. People need to play together as well as work together. For unless a community can produce the cultural and artistic activities that make life enjoyable many of its people will move to places where those things are produced."

Darby was pretty well isolated down there in the Bitter Root Valley, and most folks had never given much thought to such things as cultural activities. But in their group discussions they decided that such things did count after all, especially to their young people who went away to college and never came back. By following the study guide they devoted considerable attention to the relation of Darby's future to its people, the cultural and appreciative sides of life, and the need for making their town more attractive.

This was not just a commercialized community betterment campaign, and there was no effort to dodge unpleasant facts. They were dealing with the fundamentals of community life. And if action was to follow it would be upon the basis of those fundamentals.

To help demonstrate what they meant by creating their own cultural activities, and at the same time tell the whole town what they had learned about Darby's social and economic problems, they decided to stage a community pageant that would dramatize not only the humorous and personal sides of life, but the moral and economic aspects of Darby's past, present, and future. This suggestion came from Bert Hansen, the community dramatist whose efforts were chiefly responsible for developing this aspect of the experimental program. The Study Group took quickly to Hansen's idea, and with his help the greatest stage production in Darby's history was in the making.

Darby folks proved you don't have to be a playwright to write a play, for in six weeks they had written their own story. It was a kind of modern morality show depicting the conflict between traditional practices of wastefully exploiting natural resources, and the modern scientific use of resources by careful planning.

Director of the pageant-drama was Mrs. Arden Cole, versatile wife of Darby's school superintendent. Had it not been for her persistence in rounding up the cast and holding it together through ten strenuous weeks of writing and rehearsing, the show might never have gone on. In Darby, you don't just board a subway and go downtown. Many of these people came in from ranches and woods camps, some as far as twenty miles through blizzards—to work on something they often said would never be done.

But on the evening of December 7, 1945, the pageant-drama, "Darby Looks at Itself," was produced. And it was indeed a community drama, for it had a cast of 125 people, plus members of the high school orchestra—more than one-fifth of Darby's total population. The cast ranged from children of three to grandparents of seventy-nine. It was so large the actors had to sit with the audience while they were off stage. This gave the show a kind of Olsen and Johnson touch for all through the performance a stream of people moved from the audience to the stage and back again. Nobody but a Darbyite could tell who was in the show and who wasn't—and there are still rumors in Darby that now and then an innocent spectator got caught in the crowd of actors and suddenly found himself on the stage.

The scene opened in 1895 amid flashes of lightning and rolls of thunder. The Devil, representing outmoded thinking, and played by Bob Printz, was dressed in horns and a long black cape. Leading an off-stage chant, "Beat the land, cut the trees, beat it, beat it . . ." he was driving the lumberjacks to work harder, faster, telling them they could finish the job in a lifetime if they worked hard enough.

Through the various phases of Darby's history the story moved on into the present time. Appearing for the last time in 1945, the Devil laughed loudly as he listened to the young man of 1895, now an old-timer, say, "This here's the last big tree on the last big job. Logging around here is about finished and so am I who logged it."

"Grand, that's just grand," laughed the Devil.

"I've worked these woods for fifty years, bought myself a home, got myself a wife and kids. Lots of friends here and Darby's a fine place to live. But guess I'll have to pack up and get out. Sure hate it, but guess I'll have to," the old-timer replied.

"Wonderful! Wonderful!"

Still the Devil wasn't satisfied. Now he wanted his destructive methods extended to the National Forest. But that was going too far. Denny Gray, playing the role of the old-timer was leading the opposition.

"Our logging jobs are shot," shouted the old lumberjack, "because fifty years ago, twenty-five years ago, ten years ago, we listened to men like this devil here instead of men of vision who saw then a simple truth that is so pathetically clear now—that you can't cut all the timber from our Bitter Root forests and still have forests."

A wave of restlessness went through the mob of woodsmen. They moved forward against the Devil and hurled him from the stage.

For three hours the people of this little community played together as the story of Darby, its forests, its ranches, its industries, and its citizens unfolded. In this way the people saw how soil, timber, and wildlife conservation affected their daily lives. By dramatic action they felt the intimate problems of themselves, and the spiritual qualities inherent in their little town by which human lives might be enriched.

As part of the drama the Mayor and board of aldermen conducted an official meeting on the stage and voiced wholehearted support of the Darby Study Group. The movie house and both saloons closed for this big community event, and over eighty per cent of Darby's people crowded into the high school auditorium to see it. After the show they had a community dance with doughnuts and coffee for everybody. With all the volunteer help the actual cost of producing the drama was five dollars—the cost of mimeographing programs.

It was nearly dawn before Darby folks went to sleep that night, but they had a clearer vision of themselves and their town. On a purely technical basis their show didn't measure up to Broadway standards, but they were not concerned with commercial excellence. This was recreation in the purest form—for in one way or another nearly every family in town had participated. The mere process of so many people of divergent opinions working together for the success of a difficult common project had given their community a new spirit of unity. Their show, conceived, written, and produced by themselves, dealing with the contemporary problems of their town, was the biggest show in the history of Darby.

There was a unanimous feeling of pride, and rightly so—for in one night Darby had advanced in community democracy perhaps twenty years ahead of many other towns in America. Now they were ready for action.

People no longer talked about Darby as a dying community. Instead Main Street buzzed with talk of new home industries, town beautification, improvements in recreational facilities, and more tax support for local schools.

One of the loudest voices demanding home manufacture of Darby's timber was Denny Gray.

"Why should some outside company get the profits from our timber?" he demanded. "Why can't we finish our own lumber?"

They could. Ray Flightner, a local lumberman, formed a corporation to build a planing mill. Tall, lean, and rugged, Flightner had just turned forty. He had spent most of his life in the logging game and was a man who cared about what happened to his community. Ray had wanted to start a Darby planing mill for a long time, but with all the logs being shipped out Darby offered no dependable supply. Then with the town looking as if it were about to fold up, he had been afraid to risk it. Now things were different. Ray knew the community was behind him. And he lost no time getting started.

Soon the pounding of hammers was heard in Darby's south side as Ray Flightner and his crew went to work building the new mill. This was a real Darby business, representing an original investment of $40,000. In April, 1946, he began ordering machinery, and seven months later went into operation with seventeen men employed. By June, 1947, the mill's production was up to 12,000 feet of finished lumber daily, and was providing steady employment for twenty-six men with a pay roll of over $5,000 monthly, plus a crew of lumber-jacks in the woods. But Ray didn't stop there. In 1948 he built a rail-road spur into the plant and began rebuilding and enlarging the mill. Since then more up-to-date machinery has been added, and a modern storage shed to handle 50,000 feet of dried lumber and to better accommodate local trade has been built. Now his bills are paid, he's operating on the black side of the ledger, and the mill is still growing.

What's more Ray didn't forget the need for conservation.

"Out of our Study Group," he said, "we have learned that we've got to submit to regulated cutting of our timber if we're going to continue having enough pay rolls for our community."

And that's why from the very start Ray installed a band saw instead of a circular saw. It was a lot more expensive, but the added efficiency makes more boards and less sawdust, and in the long run it pays off in dollars and cents.

Outside Darby there are a lot of people who wouldn't understand Ray Flightner's attitude. For in most places, especially along the West Coast, operators of small mills usually resent the restrictions of sus-tained-yield logging, and they would rather use their old-fashioned circular saws, regardless of the waste, than spend more money for modern band saws. But the people in Darby have advanced a long way, and it's men like Ray Flightner who will keep them moving ahead.

Three more local men laid plans for a post treating plant to utilize lodgepole pine, a supposedly worthless species covering thousands of acres around Darby. This scheme didn't look very promising at first because necessary equipment appeared unavailable.

"But we have ways of doing things in Darby," said Walt Griggs, one of the three promoters.

They found tanks that would do for treating-vats in an abandoned C.C.C. camp, they acquired a second-hand boiler from an old logging camp, and, after scratching around, found everything they needed except enough pipe to connect the vats with the heating plant.

"You couldn't buy pipe for any amount of money," said Walt. "So we had to go to the graveyard to get it!"

In the cemetery they found pipe being used for fencing. Town offi-cials agreed to swap pipe for wire, and Darby had a new plant, em-ploying twelve men, which turned out treated fence posts guaranteed not to rot for twenty-five years. Before this Darby ranchers had shipped in cedar posts that often needed resetting within three years.

It wasn't long before new enterprises began popping out all over Darby. Luther Brechbill started a machine shop to service tractors and heavy lumber equipment; Ralph Keyser started a well drilling outfit; Ted Border blossomed out with a sporting goods and gunsmith shop; Orville Eastman, a returned veteran, established a small planing mill in partnership with Walt Griggs, manufacturing moldings, window casings, and door sills from waste edgings that would otherwise be burned as scrap. Mrs. A. J. Ellis started a modern dress shop that has since changed hands and been expanded to include men's and boys' apparel and now carries a full line of paintings by Ernie Peterson, a Bitter Root Valley artist. Melvin Damon started a cabinet shop, and Charlie West brought Darby a modern dairy and pasteurizing plant.

They used to have a sleepy little store in Darby where you could buy pop and bus tickets, but when thirty-one-year-old Lyle Barringer was seized by the town's newborn enthusiasm this spot came to life and the chain of events that followed has been typical of Darby's new growth. Lyle first converted it into a luncheonette and in the same room opened an electrical repair shop. He then added a full line of home appliances from refrigerators to waffle irons—a service Darby had never had before. But business grew so fast Lyle couldn't handle it all, so he sold the electrical service to Ed Waugh who greatly enlarged it and installed more merchandise. With the help of Mike Baird and Ed Waldon, two more Darby citizens, Lyle acquired a Quonset hut from war surplus and rebuilt it into an attractive restaurant. The result is that Darby now has a modern appliance store in what was once a run-down pop stand, and a new building on Main Street with a full-sized going restaurant.

Said Barringer, "Four years ago it looked like Darby was about done for but now we've got a real future."

George Miles, one of Darby's earliest pioneers, put up a building in 1888 that was the most elegant structure in town. But in 1945 it was only a crumbling landmark scarring the face of Main Street. George had long since passed on and everybody thought the old building was ready to collapse. Then Jake and Ellen Prinz, both pressing sixty, had an idea.

"Our Study Group gave us a lot of ideas," said Ellen. "And I just figured that with Jakie's ingenuity and my ability to work, we could do something with that building."

A year's work and Jake had the old building rehabilitated. Now it houses a sparkling modern store offering Darby everything in groceries. In the north end of the renovated structure Darby has a farmers' trading center where you can swap anything from hay and cattle to furniture and farm machinery. Upstairs Jake is building ten tourist rooms, and behind the building they are planning an elaborate rose garden and tourist park with twenty modern cabins, and public rest rooms for Darby shoppers.

In conjunction with the food store Hans Andersen opened a new butcher shop equipped with a quick-freeze plant and two hundred individual cold storage lockers featuring a complete service for processing wild meat, so that after killing an elk or deer in Darby's nearby primitive area, a New York hunter may leave the rest to Hans, and within two weeks the animal will be delivered at the hunter's Manhattan doorstep, butchered, frozen, and ready for eating.

The Bitter Root-Selway wilderness has always been a popular hunting ground for sportsmen from all over the country. But it wasn't until the town's awakening that folks fully realized the importance of wild game as a natural resource and began providing accommodations to make hunting a dependable business.

Returning from the Navy, Cliff Shockley, son of Darby's Mayor, had plans for going into business near Long Beach, California, but when he saw the change in Darby's complexion he decided there was no place like home. He teamed up with twenty-eight-year-old Keith Daw and bought the old Darby Mercantile. When the boys finished face-lifting this ancient store Darby didn't know it for the same place. Now they have a modern grocery and meat market with 328 freezing lockers, and, like Hans Andersen, are equipped to handle wild meat for the hunters. In the other half of the building they induced Lowell and Oscar Honey to install a new Gamble Store—for the first time offering Darby a complete line of dry goods, clothing, and hardware. Having sold a successful business in Los Angeles because they were tired of city life, the Honey brothers were looking for a good opportunity in a small community where they could settle down and stay. When they saw what was happening in Darby it didn't take much convincing.

"And," said Lowell, "people here have proved that Darby has what it takes."

Mrs. Ford, one of the Study Group's most vigorous personalities, never lets a guest leave her dude ranch without explaining about Darby's progress. Now she has been influential in bringing two more businesses to Darby. Charles Belknap from Ohio is developing a registered cattle ranch, and Miss Edna Skinner, a New York actress, is establishing another dude ranch to help accommodate the increased number of vacationists wanting to visit Darby's mountains.

"If we make our town attractive," said Mrs. Ford, "new people will come here and put more money into circulation."

And that's exactly what's happening. The Morris brothers, three young veterans from Idaho, in May, 1947, bought an old dilapidated garage and turned it into a well-equipped service center. Hank Redlaczyk has come to Darby with a new carpenter service. J. G. Roberts sold his John Deere implement business in Iowa to become a Darby citizen, and early in 1947 erected a $30,000 local saw mill with a weekly pay roll of nearly $1,000.

"Progress" has become the most talked-of word in town, and Darby folks have plenty of concrete results to prove it.

Recently the men got together and hauled away an old railroad car that for more years than most folks can remember had been an eyesore parked beside the community hall.

"When they did that," said blonde Phil Twogood, "I knew Darby was really moving."

Now more than half the houses in town are sporting fresh coats of paint. As Mrs. Ford puts it, "There's hardly a woman in town who doesn't wield the brush." Lawns have been improved, and nearly everybody is growing flowers. Margaret Shockley, the town's first lady, and ex-mayor herself, said, "Why, it seems like everybody is trying to outdo his neighbors."

But they didn't stop with town beautification and new ways of earning a living. From their study of local history and the relation of their town to their state, and of their state to their nation, people became aware in a manner that had never occurred to them before that Darby was not only their community, but was a part of the larger community of Montana and of the still larger community of forty-eight states that make America a great country. Gradually Darby developed a new consciousness toward the democratic privileges. And they even have a local group worrying over the fact that some folks don't get out to vote on election day.

On June 23, 1947, the determined populace turned out en masse and put Darby's education on a sounder foundation than it had been in years, by voting three to one for a twenty mill increase in school taxes. Later that summer a Darby delegation traveled over 350 miles to Billings, Montana, to sit in on Congressional hearings concerning land use. In Darby they say this all adds up to one conclusion—the home folks have become aroused to issues concerning good government.

Things don't have to be spectacular to rate as significant with Darby folks. In their Study Group people developed a desire for the ability to express themselves better. Charlie West, one of their leading members, had taken considerable training in this subject and frequently helped out by teaching in the high school. So they asked Charlie to organize a class in public speaking, and for ten weeks he devoted his time free to this work. It was all done just because people wanted to have a better usage of the English language. And in Darby they still count Charlie's course among the outstanding results of their Study Group.

In the spring of 1947 twelve businessmen bought uniforms for a local baseball team. Ted Border built the Boy Scouts up from eight boys to a flourishing troop, and in June, 1947, the boys made $200 for their treasury by selling pop at Darby's record rodeo attendance. In the community hall Abbie Osborne, one of Darby's top citizens, organized weekly folk dancing groups. First objective of the dancing was to take up some of the leisure time during which young people go delinquent, but before long it became so popular that entire families were participating and they say that as a result modern dancing is strictly second choice in Darby today.

Social welfare agencies, such as the county health service, are beginning to find that because of the general awareness of community needs, they now have a whole host of people to help carry on their work, and social workers themselves say they never saw such cooperation as they get from the Darby end of the Bitter Root Valley.

In 1947 this alertness toward community improvement had grown to such proportions that local citizens arranged for Montana's State University to send in a group of experts to lead a ten-week forum on family relations. And because the citizens themselves went to the University and insisted upon it, the forum was conducted along the same lines as their Montana Study Group. There's no doubt that people in Darby have learned how to use the democratic group process for getting at community needs.

"We never dreamed," said Phil Twogood, "that our Study Group would lead to so many wonderful things for our community."

But the fact is that the Study Group has led to so many different things which have in turn led to other things, that people in Darby are finding it more and more difficult to say where it will all end. Already they can't always tell where the direct influence of the Study Group left off, and where the influence of things it started began. But that's the way Baker Brownell intended it—not an action group, but a study group to help people understand and become aware of their community needs. Once that had been accomplished it was a pretty sure bet that people in most communities would take the necessary action on their own initiative. And each bit of action started leads in turn to more action. The whole secret is getting people started to think in terms of community needs and local opportunities, for thinking is a powerful force that once set in motion among ordinary Americans keeps reaching out in ever-widening circles.

And by that process most Darby folks agree that their community will be feeling the results of their Study Group for many years after The Montana Study is forgotten—though many of them like Denny Gray say The Montana Study will never be forgotten.

7

Politics Can Be Dangerous

The people of Lonepine and Darby had shown by vivid demonstrations the purpose of The Montana Study and what it could do for America's small communities. In Darby the results had been more spectacular because the problems requiring solution were more spectacular. But the more intangible, though equally important, educational values had flourished in both places.

Yet because no two communities are alike each study group resulted in different achievements, and this was the Study's chief claim of service. It had been designed as a master plan that could be used in any community, for no matter what a community's needs might be— whether economic, social, cultural, or all three—the study group program was intended to ferret them out, apply the stimulus of education to their solution, and enrich the quality of human living.

But as Brownell and his associates proceeded with their experimental operations and as more study groups were being launched, The Montana Study as an organization of the university system was inheriting new enemies on a state-wide level. And again, these enemies were coming from a battle in which The Montana Study had no part.

At the time the Study began its operations there was perhaps no issue in Montana involving more intense political controversy than the proposed Missouri Valley Authority, providing for the development of electric power and other natural resources by a government agency patterned in general after the T.V.A. In western Montana the same controversy had developed over the proposed Columbia Valley Authority, though in general the principles of M.V.A. and C.V.A.

were identical, and in effect the two proposals were merely different parts of the same controversy.

The controversy had become a violent struggle in which all contenders firmly believed in the virtue of their respective causes. Lines of battle had been sharply drawn and both sides had declared open season on each other. There were no rules, no restrictions in this conflict, and neither side would rest until victory had been won. From the opponents came bitter allegations of "socialism, communism, super-state," and from the M.V.A. supporters came stinging charges of "falsehood spreading, power monopolies, plunderbunds."

According to Montana's Senator James E. Murray, all the state's newspapers under the control of Anaconda Copper and Montana Power were against M.V.A. while most of the independents were for it. And the controversy was punctuated by some real old-fashioned journalistic slugging.

Some of the arguments of the opponents were that an M.V.A. would infringe on state's rights, that it would function without adequate controls, that it was not necessary, would delay instead of hasten development of resources, that states would lose tax revenues from land taken over by the Authority and that it would put the federal government in the power business. M.V.A. supporters bitterly opposed these arguments, contending that if the measure were enacted it would ensure a prosperous and secure future to all the people of the Missouri Valley. West of the Continental Divide the same arguments were applied to the Columbia Valley.

Regardless of what is right and what is wrong about an M.V.A., the issue was red hot and about the quickest way to pick a good fight in Montana was to just choose one side or the other and begin talking.

On frequent occasions members of the community study groups would bring the question of valley authorities up for discussion, as they did most other important controversies, and when they did both sides came in for thorough airing. But it wasn't long before people outside these groups were alleging that a major purpose of The Montana Study was to promote M.V.A. or C.V.A.

Early in 1945, while protests were still being heard against Joseph Kinsey Howard's "The Montana Twins In Trouble?" Howard was assigned by *Harper's Magazine* to do an article on the M.V.A. controversy. Howard, who at this time was neutral on M.V.A., employed that portion of his time which he was not required to devote to The Montana Study, and set out to gather data and write the article.

From Montana to St. Louis he called on nearly everybody he could find who had competent information, including people on both sides of the controversy. He read back issues of newspapers, studied government records, examined all aspects of the M.V.A. proposal, and made a personal inspection of the Tennessee Valley. After weeks of intensive study he wrote up his story. In it he related the facts as he saw them, and although it was to some extent critical of the M.V.A. bill then pending, it concluded that M.V.A. was the best answer to the valley's problems. The article, "Golden River," appeared in *Harper's Magazine* in May, 1945, and immediately cries of protest rose from his traditional enemies. Again Howard had hit them where it hurt, and he had injured the feelings of every M.V.A. opponent in Montana, including the Governor, Sam C. Ford.

They were still sizzling from this blow when a few months later Howard was requested to appear in Washington before a committee hearing of the United States Senate to tell what he knew about M.V.A. Howard testified for the bill and at the same hearing Governor Ford appeared in opposition. If there was ever any doubt about where either of the two men stood their positions were now made public. Howard's enemies grew more hostile, and although he had made it clear to the committee that he spoke solely as a citizen of Montana interested in what he believed to be the welfare of his state, not as a representative of any organization, his presence in The Montana Study was again drawing the attention of unfriendly eyes.

But Howard had lived in Montana since 1918; he was practically a native, was better known as an author than as a staff member of The Montana Study, and in all probability the Study would have escaped involvement in the M.V.A. controversy had it not been for the even more conspicuous actions of its third staff member, Paul Meadows from Northwestern University.

Having given up an earlier study for the ministry to become a sociologist, Meadows had set one of the most brilliant records in the history of Northwestern, completed his doctorate, and entered the teaching ranks. When Baker Brownell invited him to do research for The Montana Study he was just past thirty and eager for experience. Though he had as yet had little opportunity to express himself publicly he was liberal in political opinion, a close student of every issue, and superbly qualified as a debater. And, being a student of no mean ability, he had no difficulty acquiring a wide knowledge of Montana and quickly made up his mind on local political issues. With him, it was not merely a matter of ambition, it was ideological. So in his hard-driving fashion Paul Meadows set out on a personal campaign of liberalism, and within less than one year became one of the most controversial figures on the campus of Montana State University.

He was employed half-time as an associate professor of sociology in the State University and half-time as a research specialist for The Montana Study, but since it was the latter that brought him to Montana it was the Study that inherited all the hostility he created.

Meadows wasn't afraid of anybody or anything. From his classroom he preached the gospel of liberalism, he attacked Anaconda Copper and Montana Power by name, at faculty meetings and student convocations he gave 'em hell, and in campus conversations he made no secret of his opinion. He became the talk of the University. And then he began an open campaign for valley authorities.

His campaign started with a broadcast over KGVO in Missoula within less than three months after The Montana Study opened for business, and rapidly gained momentum. In December, 1944, he presented the M.V.A. argument at a forum sponsored by the State University School of Journalism, and later that month was again heard over KGVO in a debate on M.V.A. with Professor J. Howard Toelle of the University Law School, Meadows taking the affirmative. On February 4, 1945, in a speech entitled "Some Democratic Aspects of T.V.A.," delivered in the capital city of Helena, he addressed the Montana M.V.A. Association. The speech, which was actually an argument for M.V.A., was published five days later in *The People's Voice,* the Farmers Union organ thoroughly hated by the Company and every M.V.A. or C.V.A. opponent in Montana. Meadows was now acquiring a state-wide reputation—and so was The Montana Study. On February 16, 1945, he held forth on behalf of M.V.A. in a speech at Stevensville, where one of the community study groups was to be organized only a short time later.

Meanwhile, he continued his campaign on the Missoula campus, and on March 24, 1945, at Kalispell, Montana, made what was perhaps his most conspicuous appearance. By invitation from E. A. Atkinson, then head of the State University Extension Department, he appeared before a public meeting of the Montana Labor Relations Council and debated the affirmative case for C.V.A. His opponent was again J. Howard Toelle, University law professor. The occasion was a memorable one for among the crowd was a Kalispell attorney by the name of Charles Baldwin, a bitter opponent of C.V.A., M.V.A., T.V.A., and all other valley authorities, and a member of the State Board of Education, which held final authority over The Montana Study. Baldwin was furious, as was every other member of the crowd who opposed valley authorities—and apparently the crowd was full of them. Meadows was alleged to be a communist. He was accused of preaching state socialism, and The Montana Study was said to be a "red front" for valley authorities.

But Meadows was not deterred. About a month later he presented his case for C.V.A. to the Missoula Kiwanis. The next month saw him again debating the issue with Toelle at Thompson Falls, Montana. The campaign continued all summer, and on November 30, 1945, he began publishing a series of articles in *The People's Voice*. The articles were the written counterpart of his verbal campaign, most of them concerning the M.V.A. under such headings as "The Primer of the Montana Negatives," which attacked the position of all M.V.A. opponents from the Company and Governor Ford on down. Not all these articles concerned M.V.A. There was one, for example, "It is Time for Tax Reform in Montana!" directed against the Company and Governor Ford on another score. The Governor was ex-officio chairman of the State Board of Education.

Meadows became famous in Montana education, but with his fame came countless enemies. And they trailed him right to the door of The Montana Study.

Meadows' campaign was direct and pointed. There was no doubt about where he stood, or whom he was against. Then came the counterattack.

Typical was that made through an editorial in the *Missoula County Times*: "The University of Montana has suffered many afflictions in the past 10 years. We seem to catch the crackpots, the communists and the chautauqua speakers in the faculty net. . . . Now comes Paul Meadows. . . . Who is this feather-footed, wild-eyed sociology professor? Who is this recent arrival in Montana? Who is he to attempt to dictate our political and economic policies? His chosen profession is the teaching of sociology. No organization or college has pinned any roses on him for success in his chosen profession. Yet, he is the type who can tell all Montana where to head in, who to elect to public office and how to live. . . ."

Then his opponents trained their counterattack directly on The Montana Study. After hurling a dig or two at Meadows personally, and attempting to discredit Howard, the *Miles City Daily Star* put it this way, "One of the major projects of 'The Montana Study' would seem to have been to sell the Missouri Valley Authority scheme, with all of its socialistic trappings, to the unsuspecting people of this state." Referring to the Study's first progress report, the *Star* said, ". . . we learn that thirty-three study-group sessions were held in certain communities of the state. Four of the sessions were led by Meadows. . . . What chance did the 'spiritual level' have in those meetings. . . ."

Like all other organizations labeled M.V.A., the reputation of The Montana Study automatically assumed a reddish hue, and the less people knew about it the more extreme became their epithets—not barring the most malignant of all—"communist front."

Among those who were influenced by these charges was the secretary of one of Montana's larger chambers of commerce who replied, when asked what he knew of The Montana Study, "Nothing, absolutely nothing, except—you know," he spoke now in hushed tones, "it's a communist organization." This individual professed having no evidence to back up his assertion, and when told that his questioner was writing a book about The Montana Study quickly retracted his remarks and added, "For heaven's sake don't quote me!"

Meanwhile, Montana's known communists made their own public denunciation of the Study, calling it "neo-fascist" because they said it urged strengthening of rural culture and economy, thus conflicting with the communists' desires for increased urbanization and mass thinking.

The attacks kept mounting. After listening to the Meadows-Toelle debate at Kalispell one influential citizen held that since Meadows was a University professor he had no right to speak at all on a controversial issue; this citizen's remarks did not include Professor Toelle. A prominent Montana stockman denounced the experiment because he said it was stirring up the people. Another said it had been organized for the deliberate purpose of turning the people of Montana against each other and promoting class struggle. And when one of The Montana Study's supporters, attempting to defend Meadows at a meeting of the State Board of Education, said, "Ignorance rather than knowledge is the thing really to be feared," the governor's reply as quoted by the *Great Falls Tribune* was, "Would you extend that to teaching Communism?"

Then the *Kaimin,* Montana State University student newspaper took this position: "A serious charge, unwarranted in our estimation, was made in Helena Monday against one of the most popular and capable instructors on the campus by the governor of Montana. . . . The governor implied that Mr. Meadows is teaching Communism."

The student paper continued, "Especially since the instigation of the purge of Communists from government and educational circles, an unjustified accusation that a man is connected with Communism is a serious offense. When the stigma is applied by a man in high office, the result can be very detrimental to the accused person.

"It seems that as soon as a person voices a criticism of the status quo in Montana he is roundly rebuffed—and often finds employment outside of the state. We hardly think the governor meant to associate Mr. Meadows with the Communist party. His opposition to the MSU instructor, which has been voiced before, could quite possibly be predicated on the fact that the two men have antithetical views on such locally pertinent issues as M.V.A.

"Perhaps we don't agree with all the views of Mr. Meadows, or other persons within the state, but a man who has made a serious study of our social problems should have the right to speak his mind without being subjected to unjustified name-calling."

Mountaineer, a State University magazine, compared the attack against Meadows and The Montana Study to the hillbilly who takes a pot shot at all strangers, and remarked, "The cartoon mountaineer saves himself from the effort of stirring to meet a new idea, but he never gets further than the front stoop."

But in spite of all this, it must be recognized that when a man identifies himself with one side of a political issue he must expect certain consequences, just or unjust, even though it can mean serious damage to an innocent program with which he is associated.

Actually no part of Meadows' campaign was either sponsored or financed by The Montana Study, nor did it mean that this program was designed to promote M.V.A. whether it was or wasn't a worthy proposal. Howard's "Golden River" was merely a report of facts as he saw them in his capacity as a free-lance writer and was written at the instance of *Harper's Magazine*, to which he had been a previous contributor, and which does not dictate the political opinion expressed by its authors. Howard, as in the case of Meadows, was with the Study only half-time, the remainder of his time being devoted to his occupation of writing. His appearance before a committee in Washington was at the request of the United States Senate. And for this he paid his own expenses. The debate at Kalispell, as were all other Meadows-Toelle debates, was a project of the State University Extension Department, and had no connection with The Montana Study, financial or otherwise. In September, 1945, three months *before* his articles began appearing in *The People's Voice*, Meadows resigned from The Montana Study to become a full-time teacher in the State University, though an editor's note preceding the first of these articles described him as, "Dr. Paul Meadows of the State University and Montana Study."

In answer to a letter which Baker Brownell wrote to Governor Ford explaining that The Montana Study had nothing to do with the campaign for M.V.A., Governor Ford wrote on December 28, 1945, "There is some criticism of The Study, or perhaps I should say of some of the personnel who are going about the State trying to sell State Socialism . . . you must realize that when these men go out and speak on such subjects, it is mighty hard for the average citizen to draw a fine line of distinction and determine where Montana Study ends and the individual's views begin."

Brownell had repeatedly emphasized the importance of not allowing the Study's program to become identified with either side of a political controversy. In the study guide he had written, "Group thinking on any problem is constructive and worth while only when it is objective." Moreover, no program, regardless of how worth while, can have too many enemies and survive.

Most of the community study groups were not affected by the hostility; some were greatly hampered. Later this hostility was to prove a serious handicap to the Study itself as an official project of the university system.

8

Stevensville

About thirty-five miles north of Darby on the main highway through the Bitter Root Valley is a large billboard with an arrow pointing to a side road leading off toward the east. The sign, long overdue for painting, reads, "Stevensville, Historic Fort Owen & St. Mary's Mission." Spanning the Bitter Root River over a squeaky one-way bridge, the road winds through green hay fields into the historic settlement.

Stevensville was larger than Darby or Lonepine, though essentially it was still a country town. In a letter to the editor of the local newspaper in May, 1945, an irate subscriber complained, "Some people persist in tying their cows to stakes close to sidewalks. Very true, the grass seems better there. But, why mess up the sidewalks? They are for people to walk on, not cows. . . ."

This was once a county seat and the metropolis of western Montana, but somewhere in the passing years these distinctions were lost to more progressive places, and by 1945 Stevensville was a languid town of 700 inhabitants. Main Street with its assortment of antiquated buildings and vacant lots had long since been engulfed by a stiff wave of inertia. And under a canopy of cottonwoods along streets reaching out from this center stood the time-worn dwellings of a dignified people.

It was within the borders of this quiet world that The Montana Study met its first real operational difficulties.

Actually, Stevensville was only part of a larger community of farmers in the surrounding countryside—an area which brought the total population up to around 2500. Although it was the oldest community in western Montana, seventy-five per cent of its families had lived there less than ten years and in 1940 the town proper had ninety-six fewer people than in 1910. By gradual processes the old place had lost its vitality.

In common with most of Montana, the area around Stevensville had gone through a period of intense exploitation. Situated in the same valley as Darby, though at the opposite end, Stevensville was completely dependent upon what was produced from the land in its immediate vicinity. Yet abusive land practices had been the pattern of history.

Heavy cutting without regard for the future had long since depleted the saw timber that once grew around Stevensville, and logging as an occupation had virtually disappeared. Largely because of a strong spirit of individualism inherited from this policy of clean up and get out, which often causes people to rebel against anything that even smells of outside authority, the findings of scientific research in the fields of forestry and agriculture had often been rejected, and people had thereby deprived themselves of a more stable economy.

Through overgrazing much of the remaining private forest land was deteriorating. Mismanagement had reduced most of the once productive grazing lands to inferior cheat grass ranges; yet, on the whole, local stockmen refused to accept corrective measures, especially when it was a government expert who warned them. Only a third of all land in the valley received needed irrigation, and according to the National Resources Planning Board about half this acreage was inadequately supplied. However, with proper facilities and scientific management which cooperative efforts could bring about, adequate water supplies would have been readily available. Nature had made this one of the finest areas in the country for producing fruits and vegetables, yet because of high-pressure speculators who in the nineteen hundreds had promoted an artificial land boom, and because proper marketing facilities had not been created, thousands of fruit growers had gone broke. And from an unwillingness to change the established pattern of exploitative land practices, one out of every thirty-five acres in the county was being retired each year from cultivation—this despite the fact that seventy-two per cent of the people in this community lived on farms, and agriculture was the only occupation preventing Stevensville from becoming a ghost town.

Stevensville had no vision for the future, and with the exception of a few old-timers, no interest in the past—a history full of color dating back to 1841 when Father DeSmet arrived with his small party of "Black Robes" to establish St. Mary's Mission. Historic Fort Owen, which could have been preserved as a tourist attraction and a living monument to one of the West's famous trading posts, was now just a broken-down adobe shack overrun with weeds. With high mountains, miles of trout streams, thousands of acres of wilderness thriving with big game, and a delightfully mild climate Stevensville was a natural vacation center, yet virtually no effort was made to attract tourists.

Potentially, the resources upon which a stable economy and thriving future could be built were still there. Cooperation, objective analysis of their problems, and a willingness to work together for the community welfare could insure that future. But through years of living by a philosophy of extreme individualism, such cooperation had been impossible and gradually Stevensville was split into competitive factions. In 1945 there was one organization for every eight families in the community holding regular meetings and pursuing individual ends. The Grange and the Farmers Union were at odds, and because of the conflict in economic philosophy between the usual forms of business organization and the farmers' cooperatives, there was lack of unity between people in town and those on the farms. Since Stevensville did not have the community spirit of Lonepine, and since there was no immediate emergency such as that which had threatened Darby, few people even recognized their plight. People had adopted an attitude of "it can't be done," and any effort to promote progress was likely to die against open hostility or cold indifference. Yet there was nothing unusual in this condition; it is a community disease that has afflicted hundreds of small towns from one end of America to the other.

On November 1, 1945, a small group of people assembled with Baker Brownell to organize the Stevensville Study Group. There was one businessman, one schoolteacher, a nurse, a dentist, the Catholic priest, the Methodist minister, a forest ranger, and some of the community's housewives and leading farmers. Although it was a small group they were people who did not hesitate to speak out on any issue, and they were all anxious to gain a better understanding of their community.

One of the important conditions that Brownell had laid down for a successful study group was that it should represent a good cross section of the entire community, and in order to insure airing of all sides of a question it should include people whose opinions differ. The Stevensville Study Group had nine Republicans and nine Democrats, so in one respect it had satisfied that condition. Yet most of those who participated were farmers, chiefly members of the Farmers Educational and Cooperative Union of America, known commonly as the Farmers Union. Townspeople were notably disinterested, an unfortunate situation, for the group's chances of achievement would have been much greater had it been more representative of town and country alike. But for this no one was to blame except those who refused to come.

Charlie McDonald, the forest ranger, who was one of the few people in Stevensville not content to sit while the old town slept, was the "leg man" who deserves credit for bringing The Montana Study to this community. After hearing Brownell speak one night in Hamilton and feeling the depth of his personality, Mac went to Missoula to discuss the proposition of a study group for Stevensville. Brownell expressed willingness only if there were a nucleus of interested people willing to come regularly and make a good study. Mac then put the idea up to his fellow citizens and, on behalf of those who expressed interest, invited Brownell to come in and help organize the new Study Group.

In Stevensville—this community of individualists—Mac was not just another citizen. He was a United States forest ranger, a symbol of government authority—though nobody could have been less authoritative and more genuinely interested in community welfare than Mac. But in this community where history even up to the present time has been dominated by a lack of interest in community welfare, that was against him too. He had preached good management of natural resources for so long that people were sick of listening. For him, scientific land management which he felt was vital to the security of his community was probably a lost cause, yet he never quit trying. Maybe tomorrow people would understand. That's how it was with Mac—always tomorrow.

But when he went out to look for people to participate in The Montana Study, he figured, "After all, this is just a project in education —the school will be interested in that."

So he tried Stevensville's school superintendent. He wasn't interested.

"Gosh, that's funny," thought Mac, "but the businessmen will be interested in improving Stevensville."

So he made the rounds.

You would have thought Mac was selling "hot" merchandise.

"Sorry, can't spare the time."

"Sounds like a lot of trouble for nothing—better count me out."

"What's in it for me?"

"I don't see anything wrong with Stevensville like it is."

"Why," remarked one influential citizen, "it sounds downright communistic!"

That's how it went up and down Main Street. So he tried the Farmers Union folks. From them the reception was different—but they wanted to make it a Farmers Union project.

"No," said Mac, "this is something for the whole community. We've got to have a cross section of the people."

Why, that would mean mixing up the Grange, the Farmers Union, rich farmers and poor farmers, country people, townspeople, corporation people and co-op people!

Even some of the Farmers Union folks decided to pass it up, but Mac wouldn't quit.

Among those who finally said yes was the man who became the group's chairman—Charles Amos Buck, former Mayor of Stevensville. Charlie had operated the Buck Mercantile Company since 1906, purchased by his father from a French trader in 1876. He was as conservative as a Maine Republican, and he was the only merchant in town who participated in the Study Group.

Mac had done his best. He had extended what seemed like a million invitations, and after Brownell agreed to come he had announced it in the local paper inviting everybody who was interested in a better Stevensville. Eighteen showed up.

That first night Esther McFadgen, a woman with a crusader's heart whom they made secretary, wrote in her minutes, "Mr. Brownell outlined the purpose of a study group—first, that by a representative body of the community, we might discuss the problems of our community as they pertain to ourselves, our children, our state and our nation, with a view toward finding out how living in communities like ours may be made better, more interesting and more secure. . . ."

Just how difficult would be the attainment of these objectives, only time could reveal. But despite a general lack of community interest, no group of people, not even in Lonepine and Darby, showed more enthusiasm than did this small group in Stevensville.

With solemn intent they began the systematic analysis designed to ferret out weaknesses in their community life. Standing committees were appointed to investigate what they considered three of Stevensville's major problems—land utilization, recreation for young people, and community health. And in the study guide they found searching questions leading to the analysis of many other community problems.

"There's only one way of getting the answers to these questions," said Bessie Shrock, a farmer's wife, "that's by asking as many people as possible and drawing conclusions from their replies."

By this method of asking questions, analyzing, and discussing the evidence, they made themselves aware of local problems they had never known existed, and they acquired a knowledge of community needs which they had known about but never really understood. It was a deliberate effort by interested citizens to get at the truth of local conditions. And because their problems were vital, their discussions often became heated—sometimes downright personal. But they were developing in the technique of group thinking and working together for the welfare of their community—a novelty for Stevensville.

Despite their sincerity, they suddenly realized their work was not being appreciated by the community at large. Each week a long story of their meeting and an invitation for the public to attend appeared in the local *Northwest Tribune*. Yet outside the group almost nobody knew what they were doing. And almost nobody cared. This inertia was sometimes discouraging even to the most ardent among them, but what really hurt was the opposition that grew up against them from certain businessmen and from the superintendent of their local schools. For some reason which they could not comprehend they were being called "intellectual communists." Then the "intellectual" was dropped. And the further they probed into fundamental community problems, the more vociferous the opposition became. The name-callers had no idea what the Stevensville Study Group was all about. The presence in the group of such respected men as Father Jensen and the Reverend Mr. Horsell, and of such known conservatives as Charlie Buck and Lawrence McFadgen, the "Wheat King" of Sunset Bench, made no difference. They were just naturally agin' it.

The rumors arising from the controversy over M.V.A. had drifted far away from their original source and were now being reflected in the form of local opposition to a community study group. Indeed, the accusations had been made in Stevensville even while Mac was out seeking members for the new Study Group before its first meeting had been called. In other communities, such as Lonepine, these rumors had only the effect of a good joke. But in conservative, lethargic Stevensville many people were easily victimized. Here, where apathy toward cooperation for community betterment had long been an established attitude, there was already natural resistance to the Study Group's objectives and the rumors that it was communistic simply made its program easier to ignore.

Nothing could have been more truly American—a group of interested citizens evenly divided between Republicans and Democrats sitting down together in nonpartisan relationship to objectively discuss the problems of their community. Yet they were called pink, red, radical. And although the group tried to ignore these charges, like any good Americans they resented the aspersions. Some of them like one leading farmer, as genuine an American who ever banked a five-figure account, just laughed at the hostility.

"Hell," he said, "I didn't give a damn what the businessmen said about us, I could buy out any one of them—and pay cash!"

But others were more sensitive. One of their most articulate workers dropped out because he considered the personal wound too great, although he later named The Montana Study as one of the most constructive movements ever started in Montana.

The group realized they were not an action committee. Their job was only to learn what problems existed and establish pertinent facts. But once having seen and understood their community needs, most of them were no longer satisfied by discussion alone. They wanted action. Yet against such indifference and opposition how could these few people inspire action? How could they roll back the inertia that had so long engulfed Stevensville?

When they came to their tenth meeting to consider what they had accomplished it seemed to some like a dismal accounting, although within their small group they had created a core of enlightened, thinking people. They had differed and quarrelled in the past, but now their awareness of community needs united them all. A tiny but powerful force had been unleashed in Stevensville, and though it was not given to them to see into the future they were determined that the work they had started should not cease.

Then at a meeting in January, 1946, Brownell brought in Bert

Hansen, who only a month before while on leave of absence from his regular position at Montana State College had helped the people of Darby produce their community drama. Maybe an artistic expression of this kind would be worth trying in Stevensville. Art has always united people the world over, and every small town has material for a community pageant of its own. Hansen told them about the success in Darby and said that, because of the human drama in Stevensville's old Fort Owen and St. Mary's Mission, they were especially rich in material for a historical pageant that would not only make them conscious of their own culture but would make a great community enterprise.

An enterprise for the whole community, something that might win unity—and, perhaps, understanding and cooperation from the people of Stevensville. Quick words of approval went through the assembly. Charlie Buck appointed a committee to meet with Hansen then and there, and before the evening was over enthusiasm was running high.

A few weeks later on a cold night in February members of the Study Group met at Al and Bessie Shrock's farmhouse for a definite decision.

"I move we put on the pageant," said Bessie.

The motion was quickly seconded, but before a vote could be taken Charlie Buck jumped to his feet and threw parliamentary rules out the window.

"Now listen here," he said. "I'll admit it's a good idea, but does anybody realize how much work that means?"

Everybody sat still.

"If we have a pageant will you work?" he asked Bessie, shaking his finger in her face.

"Yes, sir!"

Charlie didn't stop until he'd shaken his finger at everybody individually and they had all said "yes."

"Well," said Charlie, "Bert Hansen got us into this. Now I say he ought to come over here and stay in Stevensville until we get out of it."

That sounded fine. But after all, Hansen had just been helping The Montana Study temporarily. He might be able to come back for a meeting or two, but surely they couldn't expect him to move into Stevensville and stay there just because somebody wanted him to help put on a pageant. He had a regular job as professor at the State College in Bozeman, about 250 miles away. Charlie didn't expect him to just up and quit did he? By gosh, they were taxpayers. They'd just write Dr. Renne, the college president, and tell him they wanted some cooperation for their Montana Study Group, and that Stevensville just had to have Hansen. Charlie appointed a committee to frame the letter.

Next day Bessie Shrock and Esther McFadgen went down to borrow Mac's typewriter. Everybody had already seen the letter and approved it except Ed O'Hare, one of their leading members. But that day Ed was in Mac's office to make sure the letter was right. They must have retyped that letter fourteen times, but Ed finally approved it, and that spring Bert Hansen became a resident of Stevensville.

The pageant was one thing that could not be done unless the whole community got behind it. And getting people to participate was only the first of their troubles. As fast as they got people interested others cooled off. But on May 2, 1946, Bill Cochran, editor of the *Northwest Tribune*, printed a front-page story saying that in a recent meeting of townspeople great interest was shown in the pageant and that plans were under way. In June Bert Hansen and Father Jensen described the project to a meeting of the influential Service Club. On August 1st, Bill's headlines read, "Pageant-Drama Production Goes Into Nightly Rehearsals."

That tiny force unleashed in Stevensville weeks before was now beginning to be felt, and the whole community was watching its progress. Yet the big question was still unanswered. Could Stevensville become united enough to make a large community enterprise successful?

The pageant that would soon answer that question was to be a realistic story of what happened to the Flathead Indians between 1841 and 1891 when white men brought civilization to Stevensville. To help recreate the frontier atmosphere the drama was to be staged out of doors almost on the very spot where many of the historic incidents occurred. It called for a cast of more than one hundred people: real Indians from the Flathead Reservation, and for men and women who could convincingly portray the lives of frontier missionaries, hunters, traders, and the pioneers who built the community of Stevensville.

Under the chairmanship of Father Jensen, a writing committee was searching through dusty records, yellowed newspapers, early diaries, and talking to old-timers for authentic information. Charlie McDonald with a large crew of volunteers was bringing hundreds of trees down from the mountains to produce a forest setting. Johnny Gress, as barn boss, was responsible for horses and wagons. Charlie Buck's Aunt Nell headed a committee to outfit the entire cast with early western costumes. For miles around they were pawing through attics and trunks digging out clothes that people had forgotten. One of their discoveries was a formal dress worn at the inauguration of President Arthur. M. W. Bretzke, their local theater manager would see to lighting. Jim Smith and his wife would take care of make-up, including sixty beards. Esther McFadgen, with help from Bill Cochran, was handling publicity. Mrs. James Morrison was designing scenes. Myrtle O'Hare was handling finances, and Lina Taylor was production manager. It just seemed they had a job for everybody.

Charlie Buck had never been more right than he was that night in February when he shook his finger and warned people how much work this pageant would involve. And to stage it outside it had to be done just when the farmers, who comprised much of the cast, were spending their longest hours in the fields.

Then one night when it looked as if they could never get everything done, Bessie Shrock came up with another idea.

"What about music?" she asked.

"Isn't the pageant enough already, do we have to have music?"

"By the Sam Hill," said Charlie, "if Bessie can get music let her go at it."

Bessie sought help from Cora McCormick, wife of old Washington J., the ex-senator, and with her as director, Bessie rounded up a chorus and orchestra.

For three months they worked. As Charlie Buck put it, "We sweat like Sam Hill."

And then there was a technical difficulty. With the acting arena covering more than an acre of ground it would be impossible for people in the grandstand to hear what the actors said. However, Bert Hansen had the answer to that. Action would be done in pantomime while narrators read dialogue over loud speakers, synchronizing their words with the actors' movements.

It would have all been a big job for professionals; for ordinary folks in countrified Stevensville it seemed impossible. Many said it couldn't be done. Others were curious but doubtful. Right up through the last dress rehearsal this attitude prevailed, and even then cast members were still threatening to quit. But when Bert Hansen went home from that last rehearsal something inside him said, "We've got a show."

When sunlight spread over Stevensville on August 18, 1946, the day of the production had arrived. Hours passed quickly as stage crews and cast members hurried through a thousand final details. Then the sun disappeared, shadows lengthened, skies darkened—it was time for the curtain to rise. From Stevensville, Hamilton, Missoula, Darby, from all directions the crowds kept coming until 2500 people had gathered to witness "A Tale of the Bitter Root."

Actors stood ready with horses and covered wagons. A hundred men and women adjusted their costumes. Musicians took their places. Narrators stood at their microphones. Lighting technicians and stage hands checked their equipment. Hansen glanced over the community park. There was the forest setting. Tribal tepees stood among the pines. Smoke curled up from burning campfires as Indians moved about them. And silhouetted against a starlit sky the jagged Bitter Root Mountains rose behind the outdoor stage.

Suddenly the action had started. It was September, 1841.

An Indian on horseback galloped into camp shouting, "The Black Robes are coming!"

Six more riders appeared. Father DeSmet had arrived to establish St. Mary's Mission. The community of Stevensville was being born. And after waiting many moons the Flathead Indians were to learn of the white man's Great Spirit.

Now the drama was moving rapidly. There was the beginning of agriculture by the priests. The arrival of Father Ravalli in 1845, who built a grist mill, started irrigation, and brought medicine and surgery to the valley. It showed how in 1850 the mission was abandoned for lack of funds and sold to Major Owen, who established the fort that today bears his name. There was the Indians' disappointment when the "Black Robes" left, and Father Ravalli's promise to return.

Nearly sixteen years later Father Ravalli kept that promise, but meanwhile new white settlers were beginning to demand that U. S. troops get rid of the Indians. From low whispers the demand grew to thunderous proportions. A treaty bearing Chief Charlot's forged signature was circulated in Washington. In the fourth episode a

colonel arrived with U. S. troops under orders to move the Flatheads
northward into the inferior Jocko Valley.

In the pageant full-blood Indians dressed in native regalia played
the role of their Flathead Tribe. Some of them, as children, had ac-
companied their parents on the tragic march out of their valley.

Then came the colonel's warning. The Indians must leave their
ancestral home. For one last minute the old Chief stood his ground.
He reminded the colonel of how Flathead braves had died defending
white men against hostile tribes.

"Charlot wants white man to live. White man wants Charlot and
his children to die."

But the colonel had orders—Charlot and his people must go.

The Chief called another council of his tribe, and then gave his
answer.

"My women and children are hungry. My men are weakened by
many sicknesses. They can no longer fight. For their sakes I go."

Then as he made ready to depart he said, "I shall never return. The
white chief has taken the land of my fathers away from me and my
people. It is his. Let him do with it what he will."

As this scene was re-enacted at the climax of the pageant the
Indians took down their tepees, extinguished their campfires, and
loaded tribal belongings into wagons. After saying his last bitter farewell, Chief Paul Charlot, playing the role of his own grandfather who
had led the tribe in that historic trek, mounted a pony and led his
people past the grandstand out into the darkness. As the Indians
passed, the audience rose in salute and many spectators wept, for as
youths they had lived through the tragic scene they were witnessing.

Stevensville had done it. In two compelling hours their show had
been produced. And the thousands who watched acclaimed it a tri-
umphant success. But the little group who had promoted it, and those
who had taken part, knew that it was more than a dramatic success.
They had proved in action that the people of Stevensville could work
together for a common community cause.

It had embraced every faction in their community. Working side by
side in the narrator's booth were two Protestant ministers and the
Catholic priest, an official of the Farmers Union and the master of the
Grange. The part of the early Catholic founder of St. Mary's Mission
was played by a prominent Mason and the first trader in Stevensville,
a Protestant, was played by a leading Catholic. It had been written by

people ranging from a day laborer to a Harvard graduate. The cast included people who previously had been only bare acquaintances. The orchestra and chorus supporting the production combined every church choir in town. White men and red men had been courageous enough to re-enact the unvarnished truth of their own bitter experience, and between them they had created a new level of tolerance. In this success of a great community effort the people of Stevensville could be justly proud.

Old-timers say they had never seen anything like the spirit of community good will that prevailed in the weeks that followed. One Stevensville citizen, who had called the Study Group nonessential, made such a complete reversal that he was later instrumental in getting the Grange to endorse The Montana Study on a state-wide basis. The Stevensville Study Group now found itself with a host of new friends. A permanent executive committee was appointed to make the pageant an annual event.

But it was yet to be shown that this unity in a work of art could be turned into an attack on the more basic problems of their community.

Brownell and his staff had outlined a second series of ten study group meetings dealing with regional literature, arts and crafts, and the purely appreciative side of life. But in Stevensville they said, "We have a pageant to take care of the arts." And so turning again to what they considered the most important problem facing their community they put committees to work and wrote their own study guide.

It was an eleven-week course in land utilization with questions ranging from whether the landowner has an obligation to society in how he uses his soil, to the relations between farm people and community institutions such as churches, schools, and social welfare, and the farmer's responsibility toward general improvement of the town. It involved the farmer's responsibility toward social security for his employees, land use policies best suited to their community, and local processing of agricultural products. One objective was to create a closer understanding between farmers and townspeople of mutual community problems. The course in itself was an example of how far these people had progressed in their thinking.

With a dozen new members added to the group, they got under way. But no sooner had they started than the old "red hue and cry" began again. The harmony created by their pageant had made deep penetrations into the years of prejudice and resistance toward group

planning for community welfare. They had promoted a high level of
unity and good will in their community. But the old doctrine of "to
hell with it" toward social and economic problems, had not been
entirely broken. The conditioning effects of history are not destroyed
that easily.

"Radicals, reds, communists," cried the opposition.

The hearsay kept mounting, and then came the eruption.

Before a meeting of the local American Legion Post charges were
brought into the open.

"It is the duty of the Legion," said its Post commander, "to guard
our country against subversive elements. If the Study Group is communistic, it should be stopped; if not, people ought to quit gossiping."

The commander simply wanted to get it into the open. And he did.

That night a young veteran rushed to his mother's home with news
of the Legion's meeting. His mother was one of the Study Group's
most active members. Calls flooded the night switchboard. Charges and
countercharges flew. Court action was threatened. For one black moment Stevensville had plunged from its lofty heights of pageant harmony into the deepest canyon of disunity.

Three of the Study Group's leading members hastened to the Legion
Commander's home with direct information correcting the false
charges. All action was dropped. Stevensville's purge had dried up
overnight.

Some time after these events had become history the Legion commander told the author that he had been misled by false charges and
expressed his regrets over what had happened.

When the Stevensville Study Group completed its second course,
its members had developed a still deeper understanding of local problems, and the group's number had grown still larger. There was a
new attitude in their thinking about land use and community planning, and farmer members were practicing more soil conservation on
their own farms. The participation of people of various religious
denominations in the community, including their ministers, had created a better working relation among Stevensville churches. The
Catholics and Protestants even got together and arranged to bring
children into their vacation church schools in one bus load. Later
Stevensville organized its first Parent Teachers Association, and while
this was not the direct action of the Study Group it was among Study
Group members that the demand for a P.T.A. was started. In the

summer of 1947 their pageant, "A Tale of the Bitter Root," was successfully repeated, with Jim Smith, their former make-up artist, directing the production.

But perhaps the greatest result of the Study Group was the creation of a demand in Stevensville for adult education. As a result of this new desire the Study Group members, with Charlie McDonald again acting as their representative, applied to Montana State University for a formal course entitled "The Conservation of Natural and Human Resources." Joseph W. Severy, head of the Natural Science Department, and Harold Tascher, sociologist, came in answer to that request and with the help of other University faculty members brought the University away from the campus and into Stevensville. Nearly forty people, including some who had been most opposed to the Study Group before, completed the course, and now they are demanding more.

Social progress and community improvement are traditionally slow processes and are sometimes difficult to get started. In all communities this kind of planning must begin from a nucleus of interested people who are willing to keep working until the forces of apathy and resistance to change finally give way to a broad understanding of common goals. The Stevensville Study Group was handicapped from the beginning by a misunderstanding of its purpose and by its failure to start with a broad enough representation of the entire community. Yet in spite of these handicaps The Montana Study had produced a new community spirit that is gradually spreading in Stevensville. Twice this spirit was demonstrated in a great historical pageant by which broad strides were taken toward unification and cultural enrichment of the community. Slowly the wave of inertia is receding and in its place there has come a band of determined people to keep alive the progress that has been started.

One Stevensville woman put it this way. "Before we started our Montana Study Group people in this town were so negative toward community progress you couldn't get them into an educational meeting to see George Washington ride a bicycle.

"But now," she said, "we're demanding that the University give us some courses in adult education to help solve our community needs. And if it hadn't done anything but that, The Montana Study has been worth more to our community than Stevensville will ever realize."

9

Conrad

One Thursday evening in March, 1945, Free Halverson and his neighbors in Lonepine had as their guest an attractive brunette named Miss Ruth Robinson, a schoolteacher from Conrad, Montana, about fifty miles north of Great Falls. She had come to see for herself what The Montana Study was doing.

That summer Ruth and her friend Alicia O'Brien, another Conrad teacher, went to see Baker Brownell in Missoula, and arrangements were made for Conrad to become the scene of the first Montana Study Group without regular staff assistance. And perhaps this was the most important test of all, for unless the plan worked without the presence of staff specialists its value was decidedly limited.

Conrad is like an island in a great sea of wheat on the high plains of northern Montana about fifty miles east of the Continental Divide. Here people brace themselves against freezing winds in January and broil under hot skies in July. Their economy rides with the price of wheat and the narrow margin of rainfall that makes the difference between prosperity and depression. They have seen good crops and bad, but Conrad has always survived to wait for the next harvest.

In most ways it's about like any other American country town—no better and no worse. It has the usual "main drag" with the ordinary cluster of business houses, and the familiar groups of men standing around street corners chewing tobacco and commenting on the girls who pass by. It has its share of taverns and pool rooms, there is an active Lions Club, a weekly newspaper, and a couple of hotel lobbies where middle-aged women like to knit while catching up on the latest gossip. In the shady residential sections where children play cops and robbers, there are homey neighborhood churches and the usual percentage of big brick houses and small frame bungalows. They have a mayor and city council, and the imposing Pondera County Courthouse with its well-clipped lawn and sprinkler system. Population in 1945 was about 1600.

Perhaps it was because people wanted Conrad to go forward instead of backward, or maybe it was just a sense of community pride. At any rate, Ruth Robinson and Alicia O'Brien had little difficulty rounding up enough interested people to form the Conrad Study Group. Besides several teachers and both the county and district school superintendents, it included a tall Irish Catholic priest, and a short Dutch Reform minister, a gas utility executive, a nurse, a probation officer, housewives, practical-minded businessmen, and hard-skinned dry land farmers. They represented seven religious denominations, more than twenty community organizations, and varied in political and economic opinion from stand-off conservatives to outspoken liberals. They were not all too well acquainted at first, and there was good reason to doubt that so diverse a group could ever discuss vital community problems and still hang together. Yet diversity was a quality Brownell considered essential, for without diversity of opinion it might well become just another pressure group where objective discussion is impossible.

Brownell was there with Howard for the first meeting in October, 1945, and after that he did not return. Howard returned for two or three later meetings, but actually the Conrad Study Group was on its own.

Meeting around a large table in the Pondera County courtroom, Father Moroney, the tall Irishman, sat at one end, and the Reverend Mr. Duiker, the short Dutchman, at the other end. Along the two sides sat the others, about twenty-five in all. Formalities were out, and upon Father Moroney's suggestion everybody agreed on Mr. Duiker for chairman.

Then somebody said, "Why not make Ruth Robinson discussion leader, and Veta Marsh secretary?"

And that was that.

Ruth had been their chief organizer and Veta, as clerk of the school district and secretary to Sig Hefty, the district superintendent, was their experienced note-taker.

As they progressed through various sections of the study guide it

developed that Conrad had one major problem overshadowing all
others—community recreation.

Some time back, local citizens had established a place they called
the "Pond," a room in the city hall devoted to young people's recreation. Authority for supervision was divided among civic organizations
and volunteer helpers, and as Father Moroney put it in his Irish
brogue, "Divided authority frequently becomes no one's."

There was nothing particularly evil about the Pond—it merely failed
to serve its purpose. Aside from the Pond, young people could hang
out in bars or drugstores, stand around street corners, or drive out and
park in the country. Or they could take in a movie. And that was
about it.

Conrad was not entirely blind to this problem, though few people
gave it more than a passing thought. But around that big table in the
county courthouse inquiring citizens were now giving the problem a
thorough airing, and for once the old town was taking a beating.

One housewife said that until she joined the Study Group she
considered Conrad about perfect.

"Why," she said, "I was shocked to find that we had such serious
problems!"

Working on the principle that opportunity for earning a living is
not enough to prevent people from deserting the small community,
and that young people especially are not content to live in a dead
country town, the Study Group concluded that unless something were
done to make Conrad more interesting there was no hope of competing
with the big cities. For years Conrad's youth had been leaving home
in uncomfortably large numbers, and in all too many cases veterans and
defense workers were returning for just long enough to say good-bye.
To some, the home town did not offer jobs they wanted, but with
wheat prices up and all the good rains they had been having, this itchy-
feet complex could hardly be explained by economics.

"Jeepers," exclaimed one young lady as she prepared to depart for
San Francisco, "I can't afford to let myself rot!"

The problem was just that urgent, and most people hardly knew it
existed.

"Our problem of recreation," said Mrs. O'Brien, "is not so much for
solving juvenile delinquency, but for keeping our young people here.
Our town has started a trend of becoming a community of retired
farmers."

Father Moroney lifted his glasses. "That's right, but we must not forget the moral aspects."

"And another thing," said Mr. Duiker, "our adults could do with some worth while recreation themselves."

As they continued their diagnosis, carefully fitting the facts together, listening to committee reports, arguing and discussing evidence, they began developing the idea that their problem involved more than just recreation. It also involved education, for if Conrad were to have the richest kind of community life, recreation could not be separated from education.

"In the study guide," Ruth pointed out, "it says that a good community educational system should be designed to enrich the life of the home community and make the relationships among its people fuller, more creative, more worth while.

". . . It will not limit its efforts to young people of certain age levels; but will direct its educational and cultural services towards all the people, of whatever age, in the community."

But just what part did the schools play in Conrad's community life? The chairman called on Mr. Christopher; Chris had been asked to report on this question.

District manager for a gas utility, Chris was one of those cautious fellows who seldom makes errors. And being a natural conservative, he was a good balance against hasty conclusions. His report was blunt, but true.

"This community doesn't ask much from its schools. School appearances in public events are very meager, and the schools are not linked closely to community life. The schools are willing, but the community is lacking."

"Look at our P.T.A.," said Alicia O'Brien, "it has become nothing but a teachers' organization. I sometimes wonder if this town gives a rap what the school does."

They could just as well have added that Conrad was no different in this respect from many small towns from Maine to California, but they had enough to worry about with their own problems.

After four weeks Sig Hefty, chairman of the recreation committee, signaled that he was ready with a progress report. His committee concluded that a good recreational program is the responsibility of every citizen in the community and should be tax supported.

"This program should serve all our people, young and old. It should operate the year round, and include a full-time director, probably working through the school."

To accomplish these objectives, the committee recommended that Conrad build onto the high school an auditorium or new gymnasium, and presented a long list of specific outdoor and indoor activities calling for playground equipment and a swimming pool.

For an instant the group looked stymied. Was the committee dreaming? But it was their business to call facts as they saw them, and awareness of a bad situation naturally leads to recommendations.

Ruth Robinson spoke first. "Would including recreation in the school program make it seem like just school? What about this barrier between the school and the community?"

"This might be one way to break that barrier," Sig Hefty replied. "Maybe if we had space in the school for adult hobbies, discussion groups, and—"

"Adults feel uneasy in schoolrooms," another warned.

"The answer," said another, "is separate rooms set aside specifically for recreational purposes."

Discussion moved faster. Dreams grew larger. And all the time the committee's report seemed less visionary.

At length one member voiced the feeling of everybody. "Our school should be more than just another school, it ought to be a real community center offering adult education through discussion groups, and recreation for everyone."

Slowly a new kind of thinking was emerging in Conrad. Never before had anyone thought of the school as anything but a place where teachers grind out instructions in the three R's.

Howard brought in Kenneth Fowell, director of recreation in Great Falls, one of Montana's largest cities. Fowell added more ideas by describing his city's program of community recreation, and by this time enthusiasm fairly oozed out between the courthouse bricks.

Then, more meetings. Sig Hefty brought in more reports. They chewed over more facts, and they dreamed more dreams. For the first time Conrad citizens were appalled by the inadequacy of their schools even for regular classes, let alone recreation and adult meeting rooms.

Antiquated school buildings were so lacking in space that dozens of children were denied important courses. Shop, and other departments essential to rural areas, were jammed into a third the needed space; home economics looked like a Washington apartment house kitchen being used by six families; indoor sports and physical training were nearly squeezed out of existence; piles of athletic equipment in need of storage space made doorways to the high school's Tom Thumb gym nearly impassable; there was no auditorium; and the stage in the gymnasium resembled a platform built for marionettes. With one of the finest collections of books in Montana, Conrad's public and school library was shoved into one end of the high school study hall, so crowded the public could hardly get in. And yet the Study Group had envisioned their high school as a community center!

By joint study and airing of local facts they had arrived at an impossible situation.

Mrs. O'Brien ventured a suggestion. "Could we float a bond issue of, say—$200,000?"

"Are you asking us to spend $200,000?" said an excited businessman.

Father Moroney cleared his throat. "We should have spent the $200,000 a long time ago to prevent the evils that exist. Then we wouldn't have to be curing them now."

Alicia O'Brien gained courage. "If we don't spend it for education and recreation we'll be spending it later for insane asylums and penal institutions!"

"That's right!" said another.

"Let's launch a drive for money!"

"Sure, we'll build a new high school!"

"That's what we should do, let's organize into a—"

Chris cut the discussion off. "Wait a minute. This is a study group, not an action committee. We'll be into politics if we aren't careful."

What had started out as an innocent study of community life had now led to the place where it hurts. Dollars! Thousands of them!

"Chris is right," one of the members asserted.

Both Reverends agreed.

But the action impulse had gone too far to stop. Discussion surged first one way, then the other. Finally they reached a compromise—but it was a compromise that still envisioned new high school construction, swimming pool, and a sweeping program of community recreation.

The big question now was, how could they proceed and yet remain a study group?

It was true the Study Group had not been organized as an action committee, and its members knew that only by adhering to that policy could they retain independence from politics, pressure groups, and the local entanglements to which direct action would surely lead them. But the same thing that happened in Lonepine, Darby, and Stevensville was now happening in Conrad. From weeks of studying and analyzing life in their community, this little group of people had created within themselves an awareness of community needs so intense they could no longer be content until appropriate action was taken. Yet they were only a few among many. Other people in their community had not been through these weeks of study, and with a few exceptions did not share their enthusiasm.

But even the most cautious realized that unless the community was somehow stirred to action their recommendations were useless. Then came the idea that was to lead them out of the courthouse meeting room and into the streets of Conrad.

"Let's call a general meeting to discuss our educational and recreational needs, and invite delegates from every organization in the community."

"Let's call the meeting immediately."

Others joined the demand for quick action, but again the balance wheels held back.

"Let's not act too hastily," they warned.

"We ought to take plenty of time for planning," said Chris.

The big meeting was set for six weeks ahead—January 30, 1946. Even that didn't allow any too much time, and meanwhile Christmas was upon them. Unanimously they refused to call a holiday halt, and at their next regular meeting, the day after Christmas, the recreation committee reported that letters had gone out to every organization in the community.

Discussion now centered on how they should conduct the meeting and what role the Study Group should play. They had no desire or intention to "steamroller" the meeting or to control the opinions of those present, but somebody had to provide the leadership, and if they didn't who would? They had been the investigators. They had the facts. They would get people together. They would present facts and ideas for discussion, and having done that their responsibility as a study group ended. From there on it was up to the community, but unless the Study Group properly fulfilled its responsibility they could not expect action, for action springs only from ideas.

The plan sounded good, but that night when they went to O'Brien's for coffee they were not at all sure they could make the whole community feel this need for concerted action.

After all, Conrad's recreational and educational needs were nothing new. For more than a decade there had been talk of building a swimming pool. The Lions Club had even saved some money, nearly $2000, toward a pool, though as a whole the town had shown little interest. People had talked about how inadequate their school buildings were, but nothing had been done about it.

Moreover, the Conrad Study Group was not without enemies. Certain people called them "idle dreamers," and others, who had somehow been infected by the same propaganda that threatened the Stevensville Group, referred to them as a "radical element." The fact that such criticism was the product of misunderstanding rendered it no less dangerous, for it was made by intelligent and influential people whose words helped form public opinion.

Fortunately, this opposition never became too serious in Conrad, though it was unmistakably present. As long as the group's efforts were strictly confined to research and study, such misunderstanding was nothing to fear. Now that they were about to submit proposals for community action, there was fear that ill-informed and disinterested citizens might wreck their plans by failure to cooperate. To add credence to their fears, rumors were now beginning to circulate that the Study Group merely wanted to spend money. These were loaded rumors, for standing solidly against any increase in local taxes was a small but influential bloc who concerned themselves with community welfare only when it involved no cost to them.

But now the Study Group was fighting mad—to think that such community needs as recreation and education had been so long neglected. Everywhere they went, in the post office, at public eating places, in homes, on the streets, in church, in stores and shops downtown, they talked up the need for better educational facilities and a program of community recreation. Like Paul Revere sounding the alarm they urged people not to forget January 30th—the night of the public meeting where the big questions would be discussed. In dozens of community organizations of which they themselves were members they spread the news. And just to make sure no group was overlooked they divided among themselves a list of every organization in the community. Each member was responsible for appearing before one or more organizations and reading the recreation committee's letter inviting delegates to the big meeting on January 30th. Front-page stories were carried in the local *Independent-Observer*. Wherever people gathered they heard the reminder, "Don't forget January 30th."

At their meeting the day after New Year's one of Conrad's top war heroes, Colonel LeRoy H. Anderson, recently home from overseas, and his wife Jessie, came for the first time. One of the outstanding wheat ranchers in Pondera County, Anderson had long been known as a leader in community life. Now he was anxious to get back into community affairs, and to him it was a real treat to learn that a program like The Montana Study was at work in his community. Already the Study Group's band wagon was rolling toward its goal of community improvement, but when Anderson climbed aboard it was like picking up the New York delegation at a political convention.

Anderson was chosen to preside at the meeting on January 30th, with specific responsibility for encouraging the freest discussion. Veta Marsh would record names of delegates, organizations represented, and keep a complete record of proceedings to be mimeographed and sent to each delegate for use in reporting back to his organization.

On January 23rd, seven days before the big date, Sig Hefty's recreation committee came out with a detailed eight-point program to meet community recreational needs, including the construction of a modern gymnasium, auditorium, swimming pool, and special rooms suitable for the participation in and enjoyment of arts, crafts, music, and other recreational and educational activities by the public. The program further called for adequate playground equipment, a wading pool, specific improvements of parks, lights for a skating rink, and a full-time recreational director.

Then came the big date—January 30, 1946. As the clock ticked close to eight P.M., delegates began arriving at the courthouse. Every group in the community from Boy Scouts and Girl Scouts to the local fire department, veterans' organizations, farm groups, churches, laborers, merchants, young people, old people—from the town and every country crossroad they came, to unite in action for a greater Conrad.

Pounding of Chairman Anderson's gavel silenced the drone of voices, and the "Conference of Delegates from Community Organizations" was in session.

"We are here for the purpose of discussing a recreation program for our community," said the chairman, "and we feel the discussion should follow these three points."

Quickly he ran through the list: recreation, what is lacking, and what we should have; educational needs, buildings, rooms, and facilities. He pointed out that education and recreation are closely allied and that planning for both should be integrated. Last, taxation and what will the program cost?

Anderson then called on Sig Hefty as chairman of the Montana Study recreation committee, to outline the eight-point program.

Then the discussion broke loose. Whatever doubts there may have been about the community's response were soon forgotten. Everybody talked. In great detail they went over their current needs and what ought to be done. No practical question was overlooked.

Elsie Campbell, their county superintendent, furnished information on school taxation. George Foltz, representing the School Board, got behind the rising tide and went all-out for a complete new high school. Everett Auren, from the Lions Club, placed his crowd squarely behind the recommendation for a community swimming pool and announced that $2000 was available at once.

Without inhibitions they discussed the inadequacy of the Pond. Mr. Duiker, a member of the Pond committee, turned this discussion into a movement for a complete recreational program with full-time director. As one man, the delegates rose behind him. By discussing the needs of both education and recreation the entire assembly had come to accept the idea that education and recreation should not be separated in a community the size of Conrad. Now the feeling for action was beginning to boil. LeRoy Anderson brought it to a head.

"We've been at this discussion for two and a half hours. I believe a recess is in order and after that we can organize our permanent organization. We have only scratched the surface, but we all agree that such an organization is needed."

During recess they gained second wind and when Anderson again declared the meeting open, sentiment for a bond election to raise money was running high.

Then came a motion: That this conference form an association to have a permanent council of nine members with terms varying from one to three years; that the name of the action body be "Conrad Education and Recreation Association"; that each community organization have one vote, but that the association include all delegates of these organizations and anyone else interested. Mrs. Moore, a schoolteacher, made the motion. Dorothy Floerchinger, a Farmers Union member active in the Study Group, seconded it.

The chairman called for discussion.

Suggestions came rapidly. The meeting was moving toward a vote.

"All these suggestions must be considered by the council in drawing up a constitution and future plans for the association."

The chairman pounded his gavel.

"If there is no further discussion we will take a rising vote on the motion."

As the sound of LeRoy Anderson's voice died away, the entire assembly came to its feet.

"The vote is unanimous!"

Without hesitation they elected the council: five members from the Conrad Study Group, and four from the community at large.

It was midnight. The meeting adjourned. January 30th was gone. And Conrad had started its own march of progress.

A few days later LeRoy Anderson was elected chairman of the Conrad Education and Recreation Association, and special committees deployed for action. Their first move was toward constructing a new high school. News stories were published in the *Independent-Observer* relating facts about Conrad's defective school facilities. To furnish expert advice, The Montana Study sent in Howard Beresford from Denver, regional recreational representative for the Federal Security Administration. School officials and the county attorney got busy.

Before a bond issue could be floated a thousand details called for attention. Budgets had to be scrutinized. Statutes had to be looked up. Miles of legal red tape had to be untangled. Finally it was determined that Conrad's high school district could be bonded for $281,000. That was the limit the law allowed. Fred A. Brinkman, one of Montana's best architects, was called in to hear what they wanted—a new high school with gymnasium, swimming pool, library, auditorium, teachers' lounges, and special rooms for recreation and adult education. A mighty big order for $281,000!

Brinkman would do the best he could.

Finally he submitted blueprints. If a bond election were held—and passed—they could have a new building. It wouldn't be all they wanted, but this is what the plans included: A two-story L-shaped structure of modern design with clean-cut lines, simple flat surfaces, square pillars decorating the two front entrances, and arranged to give maximum sunlight to all rooms. Exteriors would be of cream pressed brick, trimmed in white terra cotta. There would be extensive use of glass bricks, and inside the entrances colored plate glass would contrast with interior wall surfaces. Fluorescent lighting would provide illumination throughout. There would be scientifically planned classrooms, a study hall, and laboratories for 350 students—enough to care for future needs—shop room for automobile and Diesel repair, welding, sheet metal, electric wiring, carpentry, painting, and blacksmith classes; a gymnasium three times larger than the old one, with folding doors to provide spaces for boys and girls, a 24 x 48-foot stage for concerts and dramatics, showers and locker rooms, ample storage space, and a seating capacity for 1650 people at athletic events. The gym, in addition to being a place for physical education, was designed as a community center where groups embracing both the town and countryside could engage in a well-rounded program of recreation and adult education. There would be a modern library especially arranged with outside entrance for use by the public as well as the students. Thus, the building was designed to help enrich the total community life.

And they hadn't forgotten the auditorium and swimming pool. Brinkman had drawn his plans to permit easy additions of other facilities later on, including a 20 x 60-foot indoor pool with special dressing rooms and showers for students and public, an auditorium with orchestra pit, projection booth, a full-sized stage completely equipped, and other additions not then foreseen.

All this, excluding the pool, auditorium, and other facilities to be added later, they could have for $284,000, only $3000 over the legal bondage limit. They'd take it—and worry about the $3000. But there was one joker. They were still living in the days of extreme shortage following World War II. Where would they get building materials?

Well, they'd worry about that too. If bonds were sold immediately they could take advantage of prevailing low interest rates, and who knew what the future might bring?

CONRAD 99

The bond election was set for May 18th. On May 2nd, Brinkman's drawing of the new building appeared with front-page headlines in the *Independent-Observer*.

But $281,000 is still more than a quarter of a million, and while that may seem small enough to a big city, the Conrad high school district, including the whole countryside, had only 700 qualified voters. Under Montana law only property owners are eligible to vote in a bond election, and unless forty per cent show up at the polls the election is void. Other Montana towns had called two and three school bond elections without getting the required percentage out to cast a ballot. Of course, these towns hadn't had Montana Study groups to focus attention on community needs, but nearly all of them were richer than Conrad.

And even Conrad wasn't entirely free of inertia—that old torpor that makes voting too much trouble to bother with. If only forty per cent turned out, twenty-one per cent could defeat the measure, and if only thirty-nine per cent turned out it was dead regardless. But there was yet a more direct threat—that small though powerful bloc of businessmen opposing any increase in taxes. They were actually urging people not to vote.

Anderson and his backers knew what they were up against. On May 13th they held an important meeting. That night, delegates divided themselves into seven groups to get out the voters. On May 16th, only two days to go, local headlines read, "All Urged to Vote Saturday on High School Bond Issue."

The opposition fought hard, but on May 18th over fifty per cent of the qualified voters marched to the polls and by a three-to-one majority passed the $281,000 bond issue for a new Conrad High School.

Almost before X's cooled on the ballots the entire issue was sold to a Minneapolis investment firm, and without touching one penny of that money, the School Board provided funds for purchasing a building site. Water lines were installed and work was moving ahead on an athletic field. The fact that a national shortage of building materials delayed construction of the new building was no discredit to Conrad. Money was in the bank. Blueprints were ready for use. The home folks had done their job. And now they were content to pay off their bonds while waiting for building materials.

Meanwhile, the Conrad Education and Recreation Association, with cooperation from the School Board, City Council, and other local organizations, instituted a general improvement program for the Pond, including redecoration and the hiring of two paid chaperones. A daily outdoor recreational program was launched for young people with a full-time director for summer months. Swings, slides, and other playground equipment were installed in the City Park. A ball field was graded and the American Legion started community softball. The high school expanded its dramatics program, and by securing Bert Skakoon, a talented musical leader, developed a community chorus and one of the best young people's musical programs in the state.

The Study Group organized country dancing, with Dorothy Hoylman and Veta Marsh directing. This continued all summer, and today folk dancing is a major attraction to Conrad's youth. Later, The Montana Study sent in an expert named Frank Smith, under whose guidance about fifty people participated in a program of arts and crafts, resulting in a big community show where young and old displayed their hobbies.

Unwilling to wait for their indoor pool to provide Conrad with a good swimming hole, a group of local businessmen formed a special committee, the Pondera Swimming Pool Association. With subscriptions totaling over $25,000, and volunteer labor from what seemed like half the town's able-bodied males working spare time by day and under flood lights by night, the people of Conrad built themselves a 42 x 100-foot outdoor concrete swimming pool and modern bathhouse. At this writing they are working on a wading pool, and new plans for more community recreation are still under way. Conrad has become a community of united people determined to make their town second to none. More young people are sticking around, and population has climbed from 1600 to over 2000 people.

But the action to solve community needs in education and recreation was not all that grew from the Conrad Study Group. Back in October, 1945, Harold Dolliver, a successful businessman, was named chairman of a small industries committee. As the price of wheat kept rising and rains kept falling, this question did not develop into the major problem people had feared. Yet they had not forgotten the drought, grasshoppers, and twenty-five cent wheat of the 'thirties. That's why Dolliver's committee was formed. From that committee came a list of thirty-three new enterprises for which there were openings in Conrad.

Then, to have practical information ready for returning veterans on financing a business, they brought in a government official from Great Falls to explain the G. I. Bill at a round-table discussion, and invited all interested organizations in town. Eight of the suggested small industries have since gone into successful operation, and information concerning the others is still available as a kind of insurance against possible breaks in Conrad's present economy.

The Study Group had generated such enthusiasm for community analysis that they decided to continue as a public forum.

"Our country is in a dangerous state," said Mr. Christopher, "because our destiny is too often governed by pressure groups. A group like ours is a bulwark against that danger."

And besides that, it had been fun.

"We couldn't even bear to recess for the Christmas holidays," said Clara Withee.

In 1946 seventy-five citizens attended a community dinner given by the Conrad Study Group to celebrate its achievements.

The next fall they began an analysis of Montana school laws, and later when a state-wide committee of parents and teachers was organized at Helena in 1948 to overhaul Montana's secondary school laws, people asked why that bunch in Pondera County was so far ahead of others in their ability to discuss and understand school problems.

"Well," said Dorothy Floerchinger, local delegate to the state-wide committee, "I just told them we were accustomed to discussion and that we had already studied these problems."

They had experienced the thrill of seeing action grow from their aspirations. By the democratic process of people with conflicting opinions sitting down together to study life in their own community, they had become better Americans—more tolerant, more understanding. They had learned how to free themselves from emotional prejudices that grow from political controversy. And they had given proof to Baker Brownell's belief that a small community can, by self-analysis, lift itself to fuller, happier living, without the presence of expert leaders from the outside.

"This is the heart of Christianity," said Father Moroney. "It is only through groups of this kind that transcend differences among people that we can cure the evils of the world—not by laws and political speeches."

10

Lewistown

The Montana Study had been designed for small communities of 2500 or less, and its possibilities as a means of enriching the lives of people in towns of this size had been demonstrated. But Lewistown, where one of the study groups was now to be organized, is a city of 6000 people. To those who live and have grown up in America's large industrial centers, Lewistown, Montana, may seem small indeed. Yet there is a great difference between communities of 2500 or less and one of 6000.

With its staunch old county courthouse, library and hospital, its grade schools, parochial school, and large junior and county high school buildings, its thirteen churches and numerous civic organizations such as Jaycees, Kiwanis, and Rotary, its downtown business houses and thriving commercial life including many retail stores, eleven hotels, and two banks, and with its thirty miles of paved streets neatly laid out between long rows of shade trees, Lewistown had all the elements of a well-established urban center.

This was a far different atmosphere from that which prevailed in Lonepine, Darby, Stevensville, or Conrad. Here Brownell knew that it would be difficult to get a good cross section of people from the whole community who knew each other as neighbors. Yet many were anxious to learn what the program of The Montana Study could do as an educational experience for a group of people living in a town of this size.

It all started on a night in October, 1945, while Brownell and Howard were on a long trip into eastern Montana. The sun had disappeared, darkness was coming fast. Howard was at the wheel heading southwest from Glasgow where they had attended a conference of schoolteachers. It was a hazardous road across the badlands of the Missouri far from the main-traveled highway, but if they could get through, it was a shortcut into the Judith Basin country of central Montana where Lewistown is located.

Suddenly Howard brought the car to a stop. The road beyond was impassable. They would have to turn back and drive 300 miles around by Great Falls. But in developing The Montana Study this was just another incident. At eleven o'clock that night they rolled into Lewistown. Three hours later the new Study Group had closed its first meeting and Brownell and Howard were on their way back to Great Falls, 107 miles west.

Betty Attwell, a Lewistown native, and attractive organizer of the group, was about as persistent a young woman as Montana ever produced. Trained in dramatics and speech art, she had come out of college full of energy and idealism, spent four years teaching school, and then began looking for some kind of work in community development. It was just about this time that Betty heard of The Montana Study. Then the war ended, her husband Al returned from overseas to teach art in Lewistown's high school, and with his help Betty began looking for people to organize a Montana Study group. She asked Brownell to help them get started, and though he was a bit hesitant because of the town's size, Betty didn't give up until he arrived with Howard on that night in October.

Consisting largely of young married couples, though with all of the town's elder citizens included who wanted to be, the new group met around at each other's homes, ending their discussions over cups of coffee.

"And each time everybody went away amazed at all we had learned," said Trudy Saxtorph, one of their most active members.

"You just felt loaded with information," added Betty enthusiastically, "and you felt stimulated."

"The group wasn't much accustomed to this kind of research," said Henrik, Trudy's husband, "but we all liked it, that's shown by our keeping each meeting going till midnight."

They had begun, as did all other Montana Study groups, with the analysis of their community, its physical, cultural, economic, and social structure, and the region in which they lived. For those who participated, all agreed that it was an enlightening educational experience, but in this case the ten weeks study did not have the community-wide results that might have been expected.

The Montana Study was designed for the community as a whole, and this Study Group, which averaged about twenty members, did not represent a good cross section of the entire community. Thus it had failed to meet one of the requirements that Brownell had laid down as essential for what he considered a true *community* study group. The members of this group were not lacking in enthusiasm or individual initiative. Occupationally speaking they were well represented. But they did not have enough of the town's influential business and professional leaders to give their group the prestige that was needed in this town of 6000 to initiate successful community-wide action, though action was the natural sequel to a Montana Study group. Members of the group, however, vigorously insist that these difficulties could have been overcome had it not been for a combination of two handicaps which prevented them from obtaining community-wide support.

The first was natural human apathy toward any program involving adult education and social change, and this handicap was intensified by the second. From the very beginning of their study there had been certain business leaders outside the group and opposed to an M.V.A., who accused The Montana Study of being communistic. One of these individuals told the author that the Study had been organized for the sole purpose of spreading strife and class hatred among the people of Montana. Rumors were widely circulated through the city, and as a result the Lewistown Study Group fell heir to a campaign of vilification that frequently brought personal attacks upon the members themselves.

One of these rumors is reported to have grown in this fashion: A certain farmer belonging to the Study Group was hauling some farm machinery and had attached a red danger signal to the part that protruded over the end of his truck. On this same day a prominent businessman happened to be driving past the farmer's home and upon returning to town reported that he had seen this farmer flying a red flag. As the story was told and retold around town they added a hammer and sickle, and in time this member of the group was accused of actually flying a Russian flag from the top of his barn.

Against that kind of opposition the members of this small group were virtually powerless to initiate any broad program of action, which would have provided an outlet for the enthusiasm they had generated. And it would seem that herein lay an operational weakness of The Montana Study.

In attempting to extend the experimental program into as many communities as possible the Study undertook to do more than its small staff could adequately handle. In this case Brownell and Howard came in hurriedly for the first meeting and were soon on their way to keep other engagements. They did not have time to stay in Lewistown long enough to make personal inquiries throughout the community as to "who's who and what's what," they did not have time to make themselves personally acquainted with the town's business and professional leaders, or to address advance community meetings that might have been sponsored by established local organizations, or to fully explain the purpose of their program until it had community-wide acceptance. Had they been able to carry out these preorganizational operations, including advance publicity and adequate coverage by local newspapers, perhaps opposition to the Lewistown Study Group could have been avoided. Indeed the opponents themselves might well have become members of the group.

One of the principles of this experiment was that a community study group should not have less than twelve members, and not more than forty.

"Beyond these limits in either direction," Brownell wrote in *State Government*, "it becomes difficult to get flexible and representative discussion. If for any reason the group should grow larger than about forty," he continued, "it is better to organize another group than to have mass meetings where speeches take the place of discussions."

Had the Study's staff been able to conduct adequate advance operations Lewistown might well have presented an opportunity to experiment with several study groups in the same community.

But this small staff had neither the time nor the facilities for such operations, and extensive follow-up activities were physically impossible. It takes from early morning to late at night to cross Montana by train, and without funds sufficient for a larger staff, and without larger travel budgets for the staff it had, The Montana Study was of necessity limited in most of its operations to a relatively small radius around its Missoula headquarters.

In the study guide there was material for a powerful program in community education, advancement, and improvement, but it was of no use whatever unless people were persuaded to take advantage of it.

Yet despite all their difficulties, the Lewistown Study Group had created within the minds of those who participated a new desire for community improvement and a deeper realization of their responsibility as citizens.

In their minutes Almeda Weiser, the group's secretary, wrote, "From our study . . . we have come to see that our problems are many and very probably cannot be remedied in the immediate future but we realize that they are possible of solution through greater and fuller education of adults over a long period of years. We must not despair of their solution."

By spring they were so inspired from all they had learned, that action was taken to organize a Citizens' Committee which for two months worked nights and week ends printing up circulars and typing post cards urging people to vote in the general election. From the draft board they obtained a list of returned veterans and they got the names of other eligible voters from the courthouse.

"We didn't try to tell anybody how to vote," said Al Attwell, "we just wanted to make sure everybody voted."

When it was all over the Citizen's Committee had cost them $60 for supplies and printing, and no one would dare estimate how much in time and labor. Yet nobody seemed to mind, for somehow the satisfaction they derived from just being alert citizens made all the trouble seem worth it.

"It's a cinch," said one of them, "that democracy won't run by itself."

They continued all summer, holding picnics and more discussions, and they planned to start that fall with another series of meetings devoted to what Brownell called the appreciative aspects of life.

Many alternatives were open to the community study groups after completing the first ten weeks outlined in the guide. They could continue with the social and cultural analysis of their town, or the study could lead to a permanent community action group, as in Conrad, proceeding by the methods of group study and research. But to be stimulating and enriching, the study group didn't have to result in new buildings or new industrial enterprises. Indeed, from the standpoint of the individual at least, it may well be sufficient to measure the results of a community study group in terms of changed mental attitude and genuine satisfaction.

In Stevensville people had found a rich kind of personal satisfaction from expressing themselves through community dramatics. It was this sense of satisfaction, or perhaps a sense of local significance, derived from community cultural expressions to which Brownell referred when he talked about the appreciative aspects of life. And it was for this purpose that he had proposed a second series of meetings designed to encourage creative recreation through such activities as folk dancing, studies in the human side of regional history, arts and crafts using local materials, music groups, and all those cultural activities that make living in any town more enjoyable.

"However," said Brownell, "these expressive activities should not be started until after the study group has completed its community analysis. For if the people first gain a thorough knowledge of local conditions, understand their needs and capacities, they will then be better fitted to appreciate the manner in which these cultural interests can enrich their community life."

The Lewistown Study Group was just waiting to begin this second-year program when one night during a September rainstorm Al Attwell got a telephone call.

His caller was Frank H. Smith, just arrived in town and staying at the Calvert Hotel. Smith was a specialist in community recreation, came from Kentucky where he had done a lot of work along this line for Berea College and the Kentucky Extension Service. Now The Montana Study, in its third year of operation, had managed to bring him to Lewistown to help out with the cultural and recreational aspects of its experimental program. He spoke with a southern accent, was easy to get acquainted with, and was endowed with all the energy his specialty required.

Al got dressed for rough weather and went off through the rain to meet Frank Smith in the Calvert Hotel.

After the usual formalities, Smith told Al again why he was there, mentioned the recreational program he had in mind, and asked if the group would be interested.

"We're just waiting to get started," said Al. And then he began to describe what had been accomplished through their first series of studies. He pointed out how all members of the group had grown in their capacity to appreciate local needs because they had gained a factual understanding of the conditions out of which these needs arose. He told how they had learned to think objectively and to apply the methods of research and education to the solution of their problems, how they had acquired a deeper feeling for the human values inherent in their own community, and how it had made better citizens of them all.

Smith had never seen a Montana Study group in action, but as he listened to Al Attwell tell what their group had done, he began to feel what it really meant to those who had participated. As Al said, it wasn't something you could put your finger on; it was too deep for that. It was something you had to feel inside.

In the minutes of their tenth meeting Almeda Weiser had put it this way, ". . . self analysis . . . has made us formulate more clearly what we want and expect from life. We feel that we now have a background for the appreciative aspects of our heritage."

It had quit raining by the time Al finished his story and the hour was getting late. Smith outlined his proposals for a second year's work in the cultural and recreational phases of community life, and after discussing their plans Al said good night and went home, leaving Frank Smith with the feeling that the Lewistown Study Group would not only enjoy the program of community expression, but had developed a philosophy by which it could be appreciated.

Smith spent the next few days getting organized. Clarence G. Manning, Lewistown's school superintendent who had been of great assistance to The Montana Study, loaned him an office.

In order to give people as wide a choice of expression as possible, this phase of the program was organized into a folk dancing group, an arts and crafts group, and a folklore group; many people took part in all three activities.

Early in October the second year's program got under way with a barn dance at Asgar Mikkelson's farm a few miles out of town, and then began meeting weekly in the Junior High School.

As the group became better known it grew rapidly in size. Housewives, insurance salesmen, bankers, farmers, men and women of all occupations and all ages from high school youth to past sixty joined in for the fun.

"Anybody who can walk can do folk dancing," said Hazel Finnan, one of their main enthusiasts. Like a lot of people who grew up on country dancing, Mrs. Finnan hadn't been in a place for a long time where she could fall into the swing of a good old schottische.

"I always felt clumsy and awkward at parties where I didn't know people," remarked a Lewistown newcomer, "but after five minutes of this you're really among friends."

Muscles that hadn't seen use for twenty years were limbered up. Shy, self-conscious folks came out of their shells. Red-faced boys forgot their embarrassment. Stiff-backed men and women forgot their dignity. Strangers forgot they were strangers. Political differences, social prestige, economic levels melted away, and people became united in a common enterprise. Frowns, pains, prejudices, and personal dislikes were lost somewhere in the promenade. Young people and old people found fun in each other. There were no individuals, there were no couples, there was only one big group of people. Nothing like this had happened in Lewistown for many years.

Few of these people had ever done a folk dance, and at first it all seemed so complicated. But they were all learning together, and Smith showed them just how to move each foot, where to put their hands, and how to swing their bodies. They looked at diagrams, they watched Mr. and Mrs. Smith, and they tried it again. If you made a mistake nobody cared. They just showed you how again and the dance went on.

They ran the gauntlet of American folk dances, and learned about foreign nationalities by doing their dances—Irish, Scotch, Spanish, Croatian, German, Scandinavian, and all the rest.

In one of his many informal invitations to join in the dancing, Smith wrote, "An educational project of The Montana Study has been inaugurated to introduce in Lewistown the national cultures of different racial groups in America. The folk dance group gives everyone an opportunity to participate; and in its own way, is promoting world friendship, and making this world a healthier and more delightful place to live."

In the arts and crafts work about sixty people met on a drop-in basis in the Lewistown Junior High School, and learned how to do textile painting, linoleum block printing, sketching, and other creative activities.

The folklore group was organized to study and collect anecdotes about pioneer days from the old-timers of central Montana. Everybody was responsible for bringing in as many stories as he could dig up, and several old-timers like Elizabeth Swan, whose family has many Indian ancestors, joined in with tales they had experienced themselves. Several of the group's members had come to Lewistown on the immigrant trains of homestead days, and many stories from the past were recorded that in a few years would have been lost forever.

But there was something more to these Montana Study recreational groups than just dancing or arts and crafts and telling stories. For by their actions these people were providing others with an example of how a community can be enriched and made a more interesting and satisfying place in which to live.

It was part of The Montana Study's philosophy that one of the disintegrating forces of modern society has been the separation of the processes of production from the processes of consumption. And this philosophy was particularly applicable to recreation.

"Too many people," wrote Brownell in *School and Society,* "buy their music at two dollars a seat or take it ready-made from the phonograph or radio, instead of participating, even unskillfully in the productive act of making it themselves. Too many look at pictures in museums, sit through hours at the movies or theater, listen to lectures or take docile notes in the classroom, or absorb their sports only as spectators, instead of contributing actively, as best they can, in the creation of good conversation, interesting action, valued graphic expression."

"No matter how amateurish his efforts may be," said Brownell, "the participant experiences a kind of abundant living the spectator can never know."

In her report on a question in the study guide pertaining to the community's resources in the arts, Betty Attwell had written that every person is a potential creator of art forms. "People have been educated to believe that few possess greatness in art, but this is not necessarily so," she said. "To fully appreciate art forms one must participate. There are a few very gifted artists but that does not mean others do not have a capacity for expression.

"To be creative," she said, "one must be constantly growing in new experiences and degree of sensitivity to all situations. Self-expression to many may seem inadequate at first but with guided adult education in the arts it will come to really express the lives of Montanans."

Then Betty read from her report, "We shall look at a Van Gogh and we shall know why his composition was so arranged . . . we shall hear a symphony and we shall know which instruments are being played . . . we shall read a poem and we shall hear a song—all these things we shall appreciate truly because we have written a poem, played in our little symphony, painted a picture, sung a song and played grandma in our own play."

Thus there was a philosophy underlying the organization of these groups which gave them a certain depth of satisfaction.

In February, 1947, Frank Smith and his folk dancers gained county-wide reputation by demonstrating their art before a large crowd at the annual Fergus County Farm and Home Week. Meanwhile, Smith extended the folk dancing and handicraft work to Lewistown's Junior High boys and girls, the Girl Scouts, two troops of Cub Scouts, and the nearby rural communities of Glengarry, Brooks, Deerfield, and Hilger.

But the members of Lewistown's Montana Study weren't satisfied by merely demonstrating their dancing at the Farm and Home Week, and in order to provide further outlet for their action spirit they decided to put on an all-day folk festival. An executive committee was organized to take charge of arrangements, and three months in advance all members began working toward this big community event. Dancers polished up their waltzes and quadrilles, amateur artists and craftsmen prepared their products for exhibit. With advice and guidance from the folklore group, Tom Moore and Annabelle Zook began work on two full-length plays.

"Echoes From the Eighties," by Tom Moore, was a simple account of human interest out of his own early-day experiences, showing the cowboys, the girls, and the ordinary events of a Montana frontier community. In it were the character types familiar to all people of this region, their daily lives, their romances, and their evenings of recreation. In the preface to this play Frank Smith wrote, "I should like to say that Mr. Moore, who is nearly eighty-two years old, has actively shared in most of the activities of The Montana Study in Lewistown. His reminiscences of early days have given us delight. He is an ardent dancer . . . attends the old-time dances of The Montana Study . . . and . . . Tom Moore will, I hope, be seen swinging the ladies with youthful energy for many years to come."

In "Homestead and Busted," a life story through which thousands of Montanans had passed, Annabelle Zook based her account on the pioneer experiences of her own family, when as a girl she came west with her homesteading parents. During the writing of the play her aged mother suddenly died, leaving Mrs. Zook to write the last two scenes depicting the early life in which her mother had played so prominent a part, with the day of the festival less than three weeks away. It was almost as though the hardships of her pioneer past had now returned to plague the telling of this tale. Mrs. Zook worked faithfully at her task, though the days through which she was passing made it impossible to express on paper what she had in mind. Had it not been for her daughter, Betty Attwell, who helped her finish the writing that was yet to be done, "Homestead and Busted" might never have been produced. From experiences narrated by her mother Betty finished the story and though part of it was still in the process of being written as the actors went into final rehearsal, the production was ready when May 31, 1947, the day of the Central Montana Folk Festival, arrived.

The festival began at eleven-thirty in the morning with a community lunch, and continued until after midnight. Large arts and crafts displays were spread out in the Fergus County High School, there was an afternoon Punch and Judy show, folk dancing by children, "Echoes From the Eighties," "Homestead and Busted," and music by the Lewistown Civic Orchestra. In the evening more folk dances were demonstrated by people from the outlying communities where Smith had helped revive this art, and it was all topped off with a session of dancing to the early tunes by the nearly five hundred people who participated in this all-day folk festival.

Today there are no buildings or new industries to mark the initial efforts of the Lewistown Study Group. There are no tangible signs to reflect the results of the ten-week community analysis. Many are unaware that such a study was ever made. But according to those who participated in that study, there has been left the permanent results of a rich educational experience that has better equipped them to analyze and understand the significant social and political issues that face the community and the nation in which they live. For these people there is a new community consciousness, an articulate awareness to the need for an alert American citizenry. Through their program in the arts and crafts they had found new outlets for self-expression which have embraced many others who did not participate in the initial study. And now more than a year after Frank Smith left Lewistown, this program of creative expression is still expanding. Each week they put into action their philosophy of recreation.

> Roll down your pant legs
> Turn up your collar
> Grab up a girl like ya'd grab
> A silver dollar
> Skip around the corner
> Fly down the middle
> Dance like the grease
> On a red hot griddle.
> —Betty Attwell

"All join hands and go to the middle . . . swing on the corner and promenade all. . . ."

The Lewistown folk dancers are now in session. Sedate businessmen from Main Street have shed their coats and ties, farmers from the countryside have left their cows and chores, housewives have come out from their kitchens, and high school youth have joined with their vigor in this evening of fun.

Chairs and desks have been pushed aside, a large room in the Junior High now filled with gay music from "Turkey in the Straw," has become a hall for dancing. Sets of couples take their places and the evening goes on. They allemande left, they allemande right, they all join hands and swing in the circle, the first two forward and swing in the center, they grand right and left, they all promenade. And in between dances two young ladies step forward to sing a ditty one of the group wrote while someone else swings on the ivories a tune of her own.

This is one of the action counterparts of Baker Brownell's philosophy of creative recreation in which all can participate. It was a vital part of the experimental program for community enrichment; it was demonstrated in Lewistown, Montana. And despite all mistakes in early organization and the hostility that followed, who can say that in this town of 6000 The Montana Study did not find an important place in the life of the community?

11

A Three-Way Cross

Genetically speaking, The Montana Study was a three-way cross, for within its program were the qualities of research, education, and action all rolled into one, and all operating at the same time.

Undoubtedly Baker Brownell could have done a more expert job of research had he gone into the small communities with his staff of specialists and made the usual professional surveys to determine community needs, written up some high-sounding scholarly reports, and let it go at that. But the results would have had little influence on people living in the communities, and like most expert surveys would have wound up in a dusty filing cabinet of the University.

The community study groups were a form of research in which the people most concerned could for once participate. It was their research. They did the investigating, they discovered their own needs, they became self-educated by studying those needs, and by thus making themselves aware of their own problems they inspired themselves to formulate and prosecute the action necessary to deal with those needs. It didn't make any difference whether their reports were written in professional two-bit words or the jargon of Luke McGluke who never went to college. If their reports never found their way to a university filing cabinet that was all right too—they had served their purpose when they helped ordinary men and women build a more vital community life. And that was worth more to the future of America than a whole room full of doctors' theses.

Thus, by actual operations, Baker Brownell and his tiny staff had developed an effective means of community-centered education. But this was only part of the project that had been envisioned on that day in April, 1944, when Brownell, Melby, and Stevens had had lunch together in Chicago's Drake Hotel.

Besides the work accomplished through community study groups, they had planned a general study of Montana as a cultural region in order to determine the conditions necessary to the best kind of human living in that state. And out of this research, together with that made by the people themselves through community study groups, it was hoped that the University of Montana could provide America with an example of a state educational program based upon careful study of the peculiar geographic, social, economic, and cultural conditions existing in that state. The same kind of program could be developed in Kansas or Maine, or in any other state, and education could then be more accurately directed toward the actual needs of the people.

"We have stressed the importance of education to democracy," said Melby. "But we should stress with equal fervor the importance of democracy to education."

"The crucial problems of our society," he said, "lie in the areas of human living and human relationships. And they will be solved largely as the universities of our country identify themselves with the life of the state and the nation."

The three planners knew from the beginning that Baker Brownell and two half-time assistants could not do all this alone. But when Melby first dreamed of The Montana Study he thought of it as a project in which the resources of all six institutions of the University of Montana would be mobilized to accomplish the job together.

Included in these plans were many special projects, all designed to accomplish the high goals that had been set. There was, for example, a productive home project, in which experts at the State College were to study practical ways for Montana farm homes to produce more of the goods they used, thus making these families more stable and self-sufficient. Studies were planned to determine how it would be practical for Montana to process more of her raw materials locally, rather than shipping them away to be manufactured into finished products somewhere else as Darby had always done with her logs, and to determine what products would be economically suited to home manufacture.

Brownell had hoped to encourage development of a Montana regional style architecture adapted to local climate, designed to utilize native materials, and to meet the need for attractive low-cost housing.

Plans were laid out for projects in agricultural production for processing and consumption within the region, projects in community health, home arts and crafts, community play and state-wide dramatics and recreational programs, community choruses and other musical programs in which people without special training could participate, literary groups, special studies in regional folk history, and decentralized education through local forums and classes conducted by professors traveling out to small communities throughout the state. Research was to be conducted in laboratories and classrooms at the six University units in community organization and the relation of the small community to modern production methods and technology. These, and many other such projects, were to be carried out by staff experts in the University of Montana, and by any other agencies wishing to cooperate. There was work for churches, farm organizations, labor groups, service clubs; in short, something for every group in the state that wanted to have a hand in this joint effort to make human life a richer, fuller, and more creative experience. The projects they could undertake were endless.

Brownell realized that it would be necessary to adjust these special projects to the wishes and facilities of the different University units and various other agencies cooperating, and for that reason they would be diverse and not always closely connected. But they were all designed to help achieve the basic objective of The Montana Study—to improve the quality of human living. And The Montana Study, through its state-wide advisory committee established during the early months of organization, would act as a center of coordination. This was what might be called the "special project phase" of the experiment, and behind it was a three-way purpose. As information from the various projects became available it could be passed on to the people through their community study groups, it would enable the University to provide Montana with broader educational services, and later it could be used in planning formal courses designed to help the people further develop and improve their state.

The third aspect of the program was that of training teachers and leaders for the community work being done through local study groups so that this kind of work could be made continuous through years to come. For this Brownell proposed faculty seminars in the six University units, short courses for selected leaders who would come to the campus for periods of training, and eventually a regular training course for teachers in small communities and for other leaders interested in community betterment.

In these three ways—community field work or community study groups, special research projects, and teacher training—The Montana Study was to develop a new and significant kind of education designed to supplement the professional training for individual careers already being given in American colleges.

It was all quite an idea. Yet because of one difficulty the special project phase and the leadership training part of the program did not develop to the extent that had been hoped. The Study's founders and organizers had expected to utilize the resources of all six units of the university system in one great effort. In theory or in broad outline Melby had explained this to the unit heads and on general principles everybody promised to cooperate. But when it came down to specific details of exactly what services each unit would be responsible for, exactly who would assume these responsibilities and to what extent, there appears to be a gap in the planning. The result was that although Melby felt thoroughly confident of the needed cooperation, actually no advance assurance had been given that it would materialize once the plans had been completed and the action was ready to begin. According to deans and administrators in Montana's university system they never had too clear an idea of just what these plans were, or of just what was intended by the word "cooperation."

Like most American institutions of higher learning, the University of Montana was at this time suffering from a shortage of instructors and was hard pressed by the government's urgent training programs to help defeat Germany and Japan. As time went on and these programs ended, the University was confronted by rapidly expanding veteran enrollments, and in the face of this task all six units were approaching a state of financial starvation from years of inadequate budget appropriations by the state legislature. Instructors were straining under heavy teaching loads, classrooms were jammed full and overflowing.

From the point of view of The Montana Study these conditions were made worse by the fact that the Study involved a kind of education the faculty members of Montana's university system had never heard of. It was based on a philosophy that had no precedent in the University, and because of its experimental nature it was launched without a detailed statement of operational procedure.

In commenting on the origin of the program at the organizational meeting of the Study's state-wide advisory committee in Bozeman on February 2, 1945, Melby said, "After a lot of tries we finally shaped up a study, and the idea of the study was to find out what contribution the humanities can make to the improvement of life in Montana. . . . Since The Montana Study got under way, it has gone through a great many metamorphoses."

It is apparent that somewhere in the process of these metamorphoses many professors, busy with their own classwork, became confused as to what was going on. And to the six units of the university system, all involved in problems of their own administration, Brownell's requests for assistance in a program they did not understand sounded impractical.

Many of the difficulties of The Montana Study were inevitable. Here was a new idea, a dream, based on a series of thoughts that were stirring around in the minds of Melby and Brownell, one a great educator, the other a great philosopher. Even in their minds the details of carrying it into reality had not fully crystallized when the time came to begin operations, and these details could only evolve from experimentation and further thought. Meanwhile, they had the problem of persuading other men, perhaps lacking in vision, but practical in administrative procedure, to lend cooperation and assistance on virtually nothing but their word that by so doing this program would yield desirable results. Here was being repeated the age-old story of the idealists, impatient with administrative details, absorbed in the ultimate objectives of a great philosophy for the advancement of mankind. And, as this story has always worked out in the course of history, these men of vision had come into conflict with the practical executives, concerned first with administrative details, and unwilling to accept an untested idea until its value had been proved and the mechanics of operation had been clearly established.

Thus, the expected mobilization of University resources in this effort to improve the quality of living in Montana never occurred. Yet as time went on and the Study's program became more and more definite these difficulties could have perhaps been resolved had it not been for other important factors which also contributed heavily to this lack of institutional assistance. The six units of the University, all scrapping among themselves, made little concerted effort to cooperate even to the extent that many professors in accord with the Study's objectives felt would have been possible.

On the campus of Montana State College was the Agricultural Extension Service, which, unlike this service in most states, demonstrated little sympathy for the objectives of The Montana Study. Perhaps this may be partly attributed to what informed Montanans have described as favored treatment shown by the Extension Service toward élite operators engaged in farming on a large commercial scale, many of them out-of-state corporations controlling hundreds of thousands of acres of Montana farm land and wielding great influence in state political circles which have an important voice in determining the College budget.

Baker Brownell's first interest in efficient land utilization was based on what it can do in terms of human values for the families who live on their own farms and the small communities dependent upon agriculture for their continued existence, and it was his belief that if properly utilized, technical efficiency can itself become an instrument for the preservation of these human values. Within the specialized limits of their technical training and their apparent emphasis on large-scale agricultural efficiency, the extension experts then in charge of the Bozeman service evidently did not appreciate Brownell's philosophy.

When they first heard of The Montana Study as a project in the humanities it failed to impress them. Then, as the program got under way and it became evident that it was dealing in the humanities as interpreted to mean anything of human value, agricultural and economic activities included, the Bozeman experts began to take notice. They had no objection to a program that went into communities to put on plays, organize recreation, and form reading clubs, but when it started dealing in land use, that was something else again. Then it was invading Extension Service territory!

When this feeling on the part of the Agricultural Extension Service, an agency which exercised major influence on the Bozeman campus, was added to the traditional rivalry between Montana State College and the State University, and the early established feeling that Melby had robbed Bozeman of Rockefeller Foundation support for its project, "Northern Plains in a World of Change," plus the fact that this unit had problems of its own, it is not difficult to understand why the State College administration was none too friendly toward The Montana Study.

The four smaller schools in Butte, Dillon, Havre, and Billings merely assumed that once the Study was located at the State University, it was no affair of theirs and more or less let it go at that. Brownell visited them as often as possible, but with only two half-time assistants and the many places he had to go in a state that is larger than all New England plus New York, Delaware, and West Virginia, such visits were too rare to make much impression, and the four schools had neither the facilities nor the inclination to exert any great effort for a project regarded as a function of another institution.

If having The Montana Study located at the State University was any special advantage, apparently that institution did not know it. Since the Study had been designed as a state-wide program and not an exclusive function of any one unit, Melby was careful to keep it independent of local administration at the State University. As a result, Missoula faculty members did not recognize it as even a loosely connected part of their unit and, having no voice in its policy, the majority simply ignored it entirely or made little effort to understand its work. The small and hard-pressed staff of The Montana Study did not have time to engage in the campus diplomacy that would have been necessary to overcome this lack of understanding, and consequently it not only failed to win support from the five units that were rivals of Missoula, it failed also to win what was regarded as Melby's own institution.

Thus, a strange office grew up on the campus of Montana State University, and although the deans and professors knew it was there, few of them knew what went on inside, and few took the trouble to find out. These were strenuous years and men were too busy with work of their own to give time to something they did not understand. Brownell got little of the cooperation he needed, and after awhile he gave up asking. As time went on the State University and The Montana Study grew farther and farther apart.

It would be unfair to assume that Brownell's office received no cooperation at all from the six units of the university system, for some departments rendered assistance through special projects and surveys conducted in cooperation with the Study's staff. Faculty members such as Walter A. Anderson, then dean of education, and Edmund L. Freeman, professor of English, at Missoula; Merrill G. Burlingame, historian, and Carl F. Kraenzel, sociologist, at Bozeman; and many others who could be named, honestly and loyally supported the program. Some faculty members went to great personal inconvenience to meet with community study groups and to lend their assistance in other important ways, whenever such assistance could be sandwiched in with heavy teaching loads. In all six schools the Study had friends. But, officially, there was little definite provision for regular faculty assistance or for adequate coordination of the program with the established work of the university system. And on the whole, The Montana Study received only a small fraction of the institutional support needed to achieve the broad objectives envisioned by its founders. It was thus denied the institutional prestige which would have given it strength with state policy-makers who held the educational purse strings in Montana, and who were later to determine its destiny.

"This," said one of Montana's professors, "was simply another instance in the long story of history where an effort of great vision for the advancement of mankind was hampered by the inability of human beings to appreciate the high opportunities it offered."

Perhaps part of the explanation for this lack of institutional cooperation can be found in the story of Montana, for the events of that story have been more conducive to sectional and individual rivalry than to any state-wide effort for the common welfare. But in any event the failure of The Montana Study to achieve as brilliant a record with the special project phase of its operation and its leadership training program as it did with its community study groups, can be chiefly attributed to its lack of coordination with the six administrations of the University of Montana.

12

The Loss of a Champion

Baker Brownell found his tiny organization beset by hostility and misunderstanding. It had inherited a batch of enemies from the fight over M.V.A. and it had failed to gain adequate support from its institutional sponsor.

But standing squarely between the Montana Study and its enemies was the powerful figure of Ernest O. Melby. Melby was chairman of the Presidents' Executive Council, representing all six units of the University, he was idolized by thousands, and because of his dynamic leadership he commanded support from the State Board of Education. Men could deny the Study their cooperation, they could slander its program and its personnel, yet as long as Melby remained in Montana they could not tamper with its operations.

However, Melby, in his efforts to reorganize the university system, eliminate inefficiency, unify the six units, and revise the State University curriculum, was engaged in a major battle of his own. The state-wide commission on higher education had studied his program of reorganization and recommended its approval, and it had complete support from the State Board of Education. But under Montana law it could not become effective without ratification by the state legislature, and if this sanction were to be obtained it was up to Melby to obtain it.

Although The Montana Study and the proposed University reorganization were separate and distinct programs, it was Melby who had initiated them both, and since he had become the recognized champion of educational reform in Montana, which included The Montana Study as well as University reorganization, both programs were irrevocably attached to his name, and his enemies simply lumped the whole thing together under the general heading of "Melby's program," and opened fire. Once more The Montana Study had inherited enemies from a battle in which it had no part. If Melby were defeated it would not only mean the end of his plans for unification of the six units, it would be a major disaster for The Montana Study. If he won, however, many of the Study's problems would be solved, for it would be much simpler to coordinate its program with a unified system than with six autonomous units. It was a desperate gamble, and Melby knew it. Defeat was unthinkable. He had to make others understand.

And so, in the hard-driving manner that was part of his nature, the great educator had carried his fight to the people. Within the boundaries of this western state he had traveled enough miles to carry him around the world. He had talked himself hoarse in hundreds of speeches, caught brief hours of sleep in dingy hotel rooms, stayed long night hours at his desk, and then, red-eyed and exhausted, climbed aboard early morning trains to attend more conferences and make more speeches at distant points. He had been misquoted by Company papers, discredited by sectional politicians, hampered by jealous college administrators, and cheered by crowds of admirers. He had known despair, he had seen hopes of success. But he was tired. The physical strain that finally overtakes all men who drive themselves for humanity was beginning to tell. Yet he would not slow down. Time was precious, and until he had finished his job he could not rest.

Then on December 18, 1944, the State Board of Education called him to Helena to discuss plans for recommending his program to the Montana State Legislature, due to open less than three weeks later. Preparations were now under way for the climax of his battle. The Board drew up a formal statement of policy showing its full approval of the recommendations. It had now come to Melby to pilot the program through the legislature.

During the three weeks before the legislature opened its twenty-ninth session, Melby worked feverishly perfecting the proposed legislation, while other college administrators, the very men from whom he felt he should have had strongest support, worked just as hard with sectional pressure groups to prepare the opposition. Then on January

5, 1945, his crucial hour had arrived. On that day Melby presented to each member of the legislature a copy of the Board's statement of policy, embracing in detail the reforms for which he had been fighting. And all hell broke loose. Splitting into groups representing each section where a unit of the University was located, the competing factions tore into Melby like wounded lions and ripped his proposals to shreds.

"He can't do that to us," shouted the delegates of each faction, all claiming that if the proposals were adopted, the school in their section would lose prestige, be out part of its program, and, what was saddest of all, local business would lose student trade.

Actually the controversy was all out of proportion to the effect the proposals would have had on any one school, for while each unit was slated to lose something, it was also slated to gain something. In essence Melby simply wanted to get each educational department, such as business administration or home economics, located in one place so that a concentrated effort could be made toward building strong departments instead of having them scattered through six separate schools, all drawing on financial support which was enough for one but not for six. And he wanted to utilize what money was available in a single budget for a unified system instead of having it broken up into six separate budgets for autonomous administrations. From these fundamental changes in organization Melby proceeded to show how Montana could bring its educational system up to higher standards and achieve a more effective utilization of the money available.

The proposals should have at least been subject to peaceful discussion, but life in Montana is always vigorous whether it concerns politics, gold mining, or weather conditions. And the factional politicians were less concerned about the state as a whole than they were about their local sections. The old characteristics of individualism and sectional rivalry inherited from frontier days were again asserting themselves.

Meanwhile, The Montana Study was advancing toward the second year of its program to improve the quality of living in rural areas, and the people engaged in community study groups were making great progress. But as the political fight against University reorganization grew in intensity, the Study's prestige in the higher echelon of state policy-makers was losing ground.

In a letter to David Stevens dated January 20, 1945, Brownell wrote, ". . . Just now the legislature in Helena is boiling with the problems of the reorganization of the university system which President Melby is pushing. Nobody knows how it will come out, but in any case important issues are being presented to the people of Montana which may have its effect later. Because of the explosive situation in the state I am planning the work of The Montana Study on a year to year basis so that we shall at least have something accomplished at the end of each year even though the next may not be as had originally been planned. . . ."

After local factions in the state legislature had each had their turn at Melby, they all joined forces and attacked him together. It may have been logrolling politics, though for once Montana had seen cooperation among local interests, and in the face of this opposition Melby went down to defeat.

Despite the roar of controversy Melby had, by skillful planning, managed to obtain a substantial increase in funds for the university system, and a bill was passed directing the Board of Education to appoint a new chancellor with nominally increased powers to fill the position Melby had left vacant when he retired to the presidency of the University unit in Missoula. The bill also directed the State Board to "prevent unnecessary duplication of courses of instruction in the various educational units of the University of Montana," though provided for the six presidents to retain "the immediate direction, management, and control of their respective institutions." Thus the principle of the plan for unification was accepted, but it was nullified by leaving the six units in full control of their individual budgets, and in effect the heart of Melby's proposal was rejected cold.

Reporting to the Board on his defeat Melby wrote, "After three decades of controversy and discussion the problem of organizing higher education in Montana thus still remains acute. Common-sense thinking on the part of most informed citizens of the state leads to a recognition of the soundness of the proposals made in the last legislature by the Board of Education. Localism in the various towns in which the units of the university system are located is, however, so strong that it seems to preclude an open-minded consideration of the most obvious facts. . . ."

The *Great Falls Tribune*, largest independent daily in the state, said, ". . . The impression of the board members seemed to be that the board had gained little from the 1945 lawmakers. . . ."

Later the *Tribune* reported, "It has been evident for some time, however, that members of the board are becoming more and more concerned over the asserted power of the executive council—the presidents of the six university units—to influence the ultimate policies of the system even though the state board of education is the constitutional policy-making body. . . . In the 1945 legislature, members of the board began to appreciate more than ever before the conflict between a policy of having a single university system as opposed to separate institutions—statewide interest versus local interest."

It seemed to Melby that his long hard fight for better education in Montana had come to naught. The Board was still solidly behind him, out through the state thousands of people recognized his efforts and were grateful, and in the university system itself he had the loyalty of many faculty members. But as an educator he had no previous political experience. He was not versed in trick maneuvers. The only way he knew how to do business was to tell people plain out what was wrong and how it could be remedied. And that he had already done. He felt that in his fight over unification he had destroyed his usefulness to Montana. He had loved this western state like his native Minnesota, its people, its mountains, its plains, but he was so constituted that he could never be satisfied without that feeling of accomplishment that nurtures the soul of an idealist. And in Montana he felt he could no longer perform that kind of service.

Then a few weeks later he was asked to become dean of education at New York University, and though he could have stayed on in Montana, he accepted the offer. Members of the Montana Board pleaded with him to stay, they wanted him to return to his old job as chancellor, hundreds of friends asked him not to go, but Melby's mind was made up. He wanted only to do what seemed best for Montana, and to him that meant a fresh start with a new chancellor, a new president for the Missoula institution. On June 1, 1945, his resignation was made public, and three months later he took up his new duties in New York.

Still angered from the battle that Melby had waged, his newspaper opponents released a barrage of criticism. In Havre, the home of Northern Montana College, which had sent a delegation to Helena to fight Melby's plans for administrative unification of the six units, the *Daily News* had this to say: "Give Dr. Ernest O. Melby . . . credit for the old college try, which in his case wasn't good enough. No person is doubting the ability of the good doctor as an educator but as an administrator he didn't pan out. . . .

"The choice of Dr. Melby as chancellor . . . was a wise enough one as far as lining up a man who knows his oats on what should be taught but somehow . . .[he] was not versed in procedures as concerns the educational layout of this state. Instead of trying to feel out and understand methods of administration applicable to Montana's educational problems Dr. Melby took the bull by the horns and attempted to institute ideas based on his own volition. . . ."

Other editors came to his defense. Typical was the *Choteau Acantha*, ". . . Dr. Melby . . . had the fortitude to openly express his views in public before any group. . . . Such candor is refreshing in this age of back-slapping politics." The paper continued by characterizing him as "a captain of an upstream battleship with the courage to lay the right course and to be damned for it, yet be convinced he is doing the right thing by the people of Montana rather than for his own personal gain."

And hundreds of miles away a headline appeared in the *New York Times*, "Melby of Montana Named Dean at NYU." The *Times* article read, " 'The new dean enters his position with the full support of his colleagues at a most significant time,' Chancellor Chase declared, 'and the board of trustees is in accord with me that New York University is extremely fortunate to have an educator and administrator with the wide experience and liberal viewpoint of Dr. Melby.' "

Montana had lost a great educator, and The Montana Study had lost a great defender.

13

Struggle for Survival

With the resignation of Ernest O. Melby, The Montana Study was set adrift—an orphan unable to obtain help from any of the six units of the University.

Designed as it was to deal with the whole range of community problems as they affect day-to-day living, it was considered important for the experiment to be free from external restrictions, yet it was equally important to have the cooperation and the institutional prestige of the University of Montana. It was a delicate balance in which the Study could not survive without the University, yet could not function properly if the six competing units all had a hand in its direction. And without Melby there was no one inside the institution to maintain this balance.

Baker Brownell was at a decided disadvantage, for although director of The Montana Study he was merely serving on a leave of absence from Northwestern University and did not actually belong to the University of Montana. Yet no one felt more than he did the importance of this experiment, and he was determined at all costs to prevent its collapse which now seemed inevitable.

In a letter to David Stevens he wrote, "The fact that Melby is leaving is no less than a disaster for The Montana Study, but at least for the coming year we are planning to hold our own in spite of the fact that Melby will not be here. . . ."

There were any number of problems demanding attention, but as if these weren't enough, the experiment was now facing an imminent financial crisis. Under the original grant which made the Study possible, the Rockefeller Foundation had agreed to bear the entire financial burden the first year, approximately two-thirds the second year, and a little over one-third the third year. The Foundation made two additional grants under which Joseph Kinsey Howard and Paul Meadows were engaged half-time, but the University of Montana was to contribute one-third of the minimum budget in the second year, and about two-thirds in the third. This plan was based on the assumption that as time went on research would gradually give way to action, and the University should be willing to pay for improvements in its own educational services. It embodied something of the old adage, "The Lord helps those who help themselves."

Melby had explained this to the State Board of Education and the six presidents when as chancellor he obtained the Foundation's offer, and on this basis the grant was accepted. When the University's first installment came due, some of Melby's administrative colleagues weren't too sympathetic with the program and others weren't too sure what was going on, but Melby talked to them again and the money was paid.

Meanwhile, the strain of regular activities on University finances continued. There was the fight over University unification, rivalry among the six units was intensified. The Montana Study's position within the university system grew steadily less secure, Melby was suddenly removed from the scene of action. Funds from the Rockefeller Foundation were rapidly diminishing, and there was no indication that the six units were prepared to come through with their next contribution. The special grant for Paul Meadows expired at the end of the first year and he was employed as a full-time instructor by the State University. Had it not been for the services of Bert Hansen, the community dramatist, Meadows' loss would have meant a one-third reduction in the Study's staff.

Hansen, then professor of English at Montana State College, had taken immense personal interest in the experiment from the time he first heard of it, and when Brownell asked for his assistance, he was granted a leave of absence with pay and joined the Study's staff. It was through Hansen's efforts that the highly successful community dramas were organized which became a significant aspect of the experimental program. But his leave of absence, beginning in September, 1945, was good for only a few months.

Until Brownell could be sure of his minimum budget and of adequate staff assistance for at least the three years they had planned, it seemed almost futile to continue, though requests were still coming in for more community study groups and members of the groups already organized were solidly behind the program.

The presidency at Montana State University, left vacant by Ernest O. Melby, was filled in October, 1945, by James A. McCain from the Colorado State College, and Brownell began negotiations with him to bring the financial crisis of The Montana Study to a showdown. In November, McCain presented the Study's financial problems to the Executive Council of six presidents, and in December arrangements were made for Brownell to appear before the Council in person. It had now come to Brownell to deal directly with the six presidents, and there was no Melby to support him.

Brownell found the presidents cordial and ready to listen, but due to financial problems of their own and the combination of misunderstanding and controversy that had arisen, they were as a whole reluctant to provide further assistance. It was a dim moment.

But when it looked as though the Council was ready to back out entirely, the new president, James A. McCain, told them the University of Montana was honor-bound to its agreement with the Rockefeller Foundation, and if they failed to keep the University's end of the bargain it would look as though they were welshing out. McCain told them his unit—the State University—would contribute its share whether the others did or not. Unanimously the six presidents agreed to contribute their share of the Study's minimum budget and to recommend completion of the program's three-year schedule to the State Board of Education, under which The Montana Study had been organized.

Brownell had passed his first major test and was now ready for the next—the State Board of Education.

As a whole, the eleven members of the Board had even less understanding of the Study's program than did the Executive Council. They had approved it in the first place only because Melby told them it was a good thing and had enough power of persuasion to lead them into it. Some, not positively against it, had taken what amounted to a negative view simply because they did not understand the program. Meanwhile, there had arisen the misapprehension that it was designed to promote valley authorities such as M.V.A., and as a result many had accused it of being red. On the Board this kind of thinking was well represented.

Among the eleven Board members was a big, good-natured, and idealistic public servant from Hamilton, Montana, by the name of Guy M. Brandborg, known to friends and enemies alike as just plain Brandy. Supervisor of the Bitter Root National Forest, and a man of genuine liberal ideals, Brandborg had been a faithful advocate of the reforms attempted by Ernest O. Melby. He had been a familiar visitor at the meetings of community study groups in the Bitter Root Valley, and having seen for himself what the program could do for the people, was ready to back it to the limit.

Brandborg probably knew more about The Montana Study than any member of the Board, but there were others who also understood its objectives and who could be counted upon for support; Vic Bottomly, Montana's Attorney General, who has since become a justice of the State Supreme Court; Monseigneur Emmet J. Riley, president of Carroll College, a Catholic institution in Helena; elderly John Q. Zook, who since died in office; and G. A. Bosley, a Great Falls businessman.

On December 14th, the *Great Falls Tribune*, one of the state's leading dailies, came out with an editorial saying The Montana Study "should have the unreserved support of our higher education system."

Four days later the Board assembled to make its decision, and the debate was on. Violent outbursts came from the opposition. They accused the Study of promoting M.V.A., said it had red leanings and perverted the purposes of education in Montana. Instead of continuing the program, they wanted it curbed or stopped entirely. Governor Ford, ex-officio member of the Board, was reported by the *Great Falls Tribune* as admitting previous prejudice against the Study, and saying that he did not believe in " 'turning a lot of foreigners loose with wild ideas.' "

Then, headed by Guy M. Brandborg, the Study's supporters struck back, pointing out that the others had completely misunderstood the program. Speaking as the only Board member who had ever seen a study group in action, Brandborg cited the "remarkable accomplishments in my own Bitter Root Valley," and said, "If a vote were taken among the people who have participated in this fine work, and therefore understand its real objectives, it would be approved by an over-whelming majority."

Of great influence in the debate was the same argument that McCain had used in the meeting of the Executive Council, and after bitter controversy the Board voted to approve continuation of the program. On December 19th, less than one year after Free Halverson and his neighbors in Lonepine had begun the study of their com-munity, headlines in the *Great Falls Tribune* read, "Montana Study Research Survives Board Debate."

It was in the face of this kind of opposition and misunderstanding from the very beginning that The Montana Study, a new experiment in human relations, feeling its way along, had to operate. Had it not been for the people in small communities which were the principal scenes of action, the work would have been impossible. Here, among those who actually participated in the program, there was no such misunderstanding. And when they heard what was being said in official circles many of these people became highly indignant. Angry letters of protest were sent to the Governor and to the editor of the *Tribune*.

One of these letters, signed by Mrs. Lyle C. Marsh, secretary of the Conrad Study Group, and published in the *Tribune* said: "I read with amazement the article on the Montana Study in the Dec. 19 issue of The Tribune. It is obvious from the criticisms made by Governor Ford and other members of the board of education that they are totally unfamiliar with the Montana Study. All of us participating in these study groups are deeply grateful that Mr. Guy Brandborg is a member of the board and was present to give the other members an accurate picture of the work being accomplished.

"Here in Conrad we will soon complete our 10 weeks' study and have found it so illuminating and absorbing that we plan to continue the meetings beyond the 10 outlined in the study guide. If the study of one's community and state, how we can improve and further the both of them and especially make them attractive enough to hold our young people, endeavoring to make a place for returning service men in the community—if these and other subjects similar are, to quote Governor Ford, 'turning a lot of foreigners loose with wild-eyed ideas,' then we suggest giving our beloved Treasure state back to the Indians.

"It is my belief that if this board of education is not more accurately informed on other subjects over which it has control it should be dissolved.

"We urge that the Montana Study continue under the able direction of Dr. Baker Brownell and his assistants."

Gradually the flurry arising from the December meeting of the State Board of Education subsided. Airing of the controversy had to some extent cleared the atmosphere, and better understanding of the Study's actual purposes had been created. The eagerness of people participating in community study groups to defend the program was in itself a graphic demonstration of what the Study had accomplished. Through correspondence and personal talks Brownell won better understanding from the Governor. "I have read twice The Montana Study group guide called *Life in Montana, As Seen in Lonepine*, and I think it excellent," said Governor Ford. Later, while vacationing at Hot Springs, the Governor and his wife were welcome guests at a meeting of the Lonepine Study Group. Although the enemies inherited from battles in which the Study had no part had by no means disappeared, The Montana Study now had many friends and, despite its brief and turbulent history, was beginning to make a lasting impression for human good in the life of Montana.

However, within the university system itself the program was still on a flimsy footing, and Brownell still had the problem of dealing with six autonomous administrations, none of whom fully understood or fully appreciated the philosophy and objectives of his program.

In January, 1946, he wrote to Stevens, "It seems to me that the loan of a man by each of the six units is about the minimum that we can ask and expect to get anything done in extending the work of The Montana Study into more communities in the state and at the same time give it continuity in the higher educational structure. Next year as you know the director will be the only person beside the secretary budgeted for The Montana Study. If the Study is to develop in the state, it will, of course, have to have the cooperation in terms of actual services from the six units. Nevertheless, each unit is so involved in its own staff and classroom problems that I am very doubtful whether they will feel they can lend a man for purposes not specifically in the jurisdiction of that unit. No chancellor has been appointed, and thus the instrument through which The Montana Study normally would work is not available. . . . The next few weeks or months will be critical. . . ."

In February he laid before the Executive Council a comprehensive proposal calling for an expansion of the work into more communities, a plan to make the Study a continuous operation in the university system after the Rockefeller grant expired, and for the loan of six additional workers, two of them for full-time service. No action was taken on this proposal.

Brownell was at this time faced by the loss of Bert Hansen, whose work in community dramatics had now become invaluable as a means of cultural enrichment and community unification, but whose leave of absence from the State College was expiring. And it was just at this time that a seemingly unrelated, though highly important, event took place.

One cold night while Brownell was worrying about the future of the program, Charlie Buck and some other members of the Stevens-ville Study Group were gathering at Al and Bessie Shrock's farm home in the Bitter Root Valley. They had decided to produce a community pageant, and Charlie had the inspiration of asking President Renne of the State College to invite Bert Hansen down there to help them produce "A Tale of the Bitter Root."

On February 20th, Renne came to Missoula with the Stevensville letter in his pocket, and after a conference with Brownell arrangements were made for Hansen to return to the Study's staff if Hansen was willing—and he was willing.

Finally, in April, 1946, the Board appointed a new chancellor for the university system, George A. Selke, an educator of long experience, then president of St. Cloud College in Minnesota, and once a teacher of Ernest O. Melby. The new chancellor arrived in Montana on May 1st, a significant date for The Montana Study, for after long months of being treated like an unwanted orphan it was now to have the haven of anchorage that it needed. Commenting on the months that had passed, Chancellor Selke later remarked, "As far as the University of Montana was concerned, The Montana Study was a floating rib. It is surprising, actually, that the project did not collapse. Much credit should be given to those connected with the Study that it continued to function effectively and to make enduring contributions."

Despite all their troubles Brownell and his associates had continued to pioneer in what they saw as a critically important phase of education designed to meet the needs of this modern day. The success the Study achieved during those trying times can be attributed partly to the perseverance and creative intelligence of the men who guided its destiny, partly to the men and women in small communities whose initiative and determination moulded the study groups into a force for community advancement. But there are many who believe that an even more important reason for its success was an intangible quality of democratic action perhaps imbedded in the program itself which can truly answer human needs as they are found in America's small communities.

It would seem that in all these difficulties there are reflected certain lessons which should serve both to encourage and to caution those in colleges and universities and in other institutions, who may wish to embark upon similar programs.

The Montana Study was lacking in a carefully planned and support-gaining program of publicity and public relations both inside and outside the university system. In order to avoid any suggestion of commercialization or the techniques of ballyhoo, and in an effort to prevent Montanans from gaining the false impression that Brownell and his associates were trying to tell them how to run their state, the Study had deliberately avoided publicity which would have put it in the public eye. The end result was that few people in the state as a whole were given accurate information concerning the program, indeed the majority of Montanans outside educational circles never heard of it. Many faculty members in the university system would have given the Study their support had they known more about it, but the Study's personnel found themselves so busy trying to carry out a program that was already too large for the meager facilities they had that there was no time for intensive work in public relations. As for the red baiting that arose outside the university system many people heard nothing to refute these charges, and the Study's staff simply regarded such accusations as ridiculous and largely ignored them.

Most of the community study groups had been concentrated within half a dozen counties around the Missoula headquarters in western Montana. From Missoula it was more than a hundred miles to the summit of the Continental Divide, and from there Montana stretched across nearly 500 miles to the North Dakota border. In the western one-third of the state were the valleys and high ridges of the Rocky Mountains, and in the eastern two-thirds were the Northern Great Plains. Because of the sharp geographical differences between these two areas people lived differently, they thought differently, and in many respects Montana was split into two distinct regions. Commerce in the mountainous western portion was tied to Spokane and cities along the West Coast, while in the eastern portion it was tied to Minneapolis, Chicago, and cities of the Middle West. East of the Continental Divide lived two-thirds of Montana's population. It was this area that, according to Joseph Kinsey Howard, contained some of the state's most seriously deteriorated communities. Yet only two study groups had been organized east of the Divide, one at Conrad in the extreme western portion of the plains region, and the other at Lewistown, which was actually an urban center.

Thus, while The Montana Study was designed as a state-wide project and had received part of its financial support from the state as a whole, its activities had not begun to cover the entire state, and because of this lack of coverage, together with the lack of adequate publicity, it had no means of gaining support from a majority of the population.

Brownell was well aware of this problem, and was in constant hopes of extending the work more generally into the plains region. Yet keeping up with the work they already had was a rugged job. Fast driving, trips of 500 miles for conferences or lectures were common. Western Montana alone is no small country, and even when staff members traveled out to communities in this area they seldom returned to Missoula before three o'clock in the morning. Drives through the winter months to Lonepine each week meant nearly ninety miles one way over hazardous Evaro Hill and through the mountains, the same distance back was invariably made after midnight—and it never failed to snow on Evaro Hill. There was the drive to Darby, more than sixty miles down the Bitter Root, drives to Hamilton, Victor, Stevensville, and to other points in western Montana—all over mountainous roads, usually three or four such trips a week. There were blowouts, dead fuses, snowstorms, and ten-mile limps late at night into a mountain village for repairs. Still they were trying to reach eastern Montana. It was chiefly for this reason that Brownell wanted more men assigned to the program by the administrations of the six University units.

"But," said Howard, "adequate funds were not budgeted for personnel and travel to cover Montana's vast distances."

Underlying all the Study's troubles were the groping and uncertainty through which all experiments of this kind must pass, for this was essentially an experiment. It was not until after Brownell actually started organizing the program that it began to acquire definite form. Even then mistakes were necessary by which to profit. A plan of operational procedure had to be established, a study guide had to be conceived and written, special projects had to evolve, and meanwhile the whole idea had to be explained to others.

Many of the future difficulties resulted from that same kind of trouble that somehow arises among well-meaning business partners when agreements are not stated definitely and understood thoroughly in advance by the partners involved. Under the circumstances, Montana educational officials were never clear on exactly what they were getting into and simply told Melby in effect, "If you can get the money, go ahead and get it."

Had Melby or Brownell been able to sit down with the Board and the Executive Council and explain in precise terms what services would be expected from each unit of the University, perhaps even drawn up an agreement in writing for each to sign, and had all understood this in advance, then the difficulties that came later would not have been likely to occur. As it was, Melby tried hard to explain in advance, but it was then just a new idea that had yet to be worked out. Here was a great educator with a vision, and while he had advanced a second mile, the others were still making their first. Thus, even before it started, the Study was largely without support from the institution that sponsored it.

14

The Third Year

When George A. Selke became chancellor on May 1, 1946, The Montana Study was assigned to his office, the difficulties it had encountered as an unattached agency began to diminish, and Baker Brownell was free to devote more attention to the experimental aspects of the program.

By the time the Study had reached its two-year mark the organizational methods and techniques for community study groups had been clearly worked out and were no longer experimental, except as new work in any community is experimental. In his second progress report Brownell wrote, "The response from small communities has been highly gratifying. There is no doubt that the study group work is desired and needed. The problem now is to extend it more broadly to all parts of the state."

Despite the hostility and misunderstanding that threatened its operations, The Montana Study had continued to expand. Even while its future looked most uncertain, the people of Lonepine, Darby, Stevensville, Conrad, Lewistown were advancing toward their goals of community enrichment. In the Bitter Root Valley at the county seat of Hamilton, Mayor Joseph Iten had led the organization of another study group, and at Victor, a few miles northward, still another had been started under the leadership of Donald Bunger, their school superintendent, and O. K. Sizer, their chairman. Bert Hansen had developed the community drama into a potent technique for cultural enrichment and community unification and it had been integrated into the study group program. Projects in community recreation and cultural and social development, all designed to make life in small communities more interesting, more significant, had come to fruition. And from all parts of Montana Brownell had received more requests for new study groups than his tiny staff could hope to accommodate.

In the special project phase of their work, Brownell and his associates had published numerous articles in the professional journals describing technical aspects and operating mechanics of the experiment, spreading what they had learned about ways and means of strengthening America's family and community life. Thousands of reprints had been made of these articles and sent to educators, librarians, government bureaus, and community leaders throughout the United States. The Study's staff had given more than 600 lectures and special conferences, and such internationally known authorities on rural life as O. E. Baker from the University of Maryland, and Arthur E. Morgan, former president of Antioch College and founder of Community Service, Inc., of Yellow Springs, Ohio, had been brought into Montana to speak on problems of the family and small community. Howard C. Beresford, U. S. Government recreational specialist from Denver, Colorado, was brought in to advise local groups on problems of community recreation. And from China's Nanking University came Mei-yun Li, young woman doctor and dean, to study the Montana experiment preparatory to starting similar work in the rural districts of her own ancient country.

In nearly every corner of Montana people and organizations were contributing their support to further the work of The Montana Study. Deserving special mention are Montana's Catholic and Protestant churches, particularly Bishops Condon and Gilmore of the Great Falls and Helena Catholic Dioceses; the Reverend Guy L. Barnes, pastor of the University Congregational Church in Missoula; and the Reverend Lauris B. Whitman, town and country representative for the Baptist Church. Giving great assistance to the Study's program were leaders of the Montana Farmers Union, the Grange, members of the State Library Association, the American Association of University Women, the United States Forest Service, the *Great Falls Tribune*, the *Spokesman-Review*, of Spokane, Washington, and several leaders in business and industry such as Branson G. Stevenson, an artist and state manager for a large oil company. Also the Great Falls Chamber of Commerce, which made a cash contribution for a local conference, and many other organizations and individuals having no contact with any of the study groups were helping to promote this effort toward the improvement of community life in Montana.

Many special research projects by the Study's staff and by other agencies cooperating in the work had either been completed or were well under way. From these projects came long reports containing vital information for use in community education. Course outlines were produced for community leadership training, and for elementary school children designed to give young people a greater sense of community appreciation. The research included surveys such as one made chiefly by Edward A. Krug, then professor of education at the State University, to determine how public schools can best contribute toward community enrichment and what qualities should be developed in student teachers for this purpose. A directory of Montana craftsmen to further this creative activity was published under the direction of Ruth Robinson of Conrad. Two major studies by Paul Meadows resulted in detailed and regionally significant reports on Montana's population and the state's regional characteristics.

In response to a need felt by schoolteachers throughout the state, Joseph Kinsey Howard undertook as a Montana Study research project the collection of published prose and verse about Montana for use as a study in regional culture. The collection was to have been made available to local schools in mimeographed form, but Howard did such a thorough job that it resulted in his second book *Montana Margins: A State Anthology*, published in 1946 by Yale University Press. This book was without question one of the outstanding special projects of The Montana Study.

These, and many other research projects each designed to cover a special phase of community life or an aspect of regional culture, were being conducted at the same time study groups were operating in the experimental communities.

"There is no margin to this work," wrote Brownell in a letter to Stevens, "and for every mile that we go ahead we see greatly increased areas of work to do."

But it was inevitable from the beginning that Baker Brownell would sooner or later return to Northwestern University where he had taken leave of absence from his position as professor of philosophy. And late in 1945 while the Study was embroiled in its struggle for survival following Melby's leaving the state, the call came for Brownell's return. He was asked to take the chairmanship of the Department of Philosophy at Northwestern, and although he declined this honor, he felt that the need to return to his work there could no longer be ignored. The Montana experiment had by this time gained wide reputation among American educators and there was a growing demand outside Montana for more information about the program. To help meet this demand Brownell was now asked to establish a five-year project in writing and field work at Northwestern beginning in October, 1946, and financed largely by the Rockefeller Foundation. Through this new program the philosophy and techniques of the Montana Study were to be extended into the rural areas of the Middle West.

At about this same time Joseph Kinsey Howard, whose personal concern for the future of his state and whose extraordinary knowledge of the Montana facts of life had made him a key figure in the program, served notice that because of other commitments in his profession of writing he too would be leaving the Study at the end of its second year. It is doubtful whether without Howard's counseling during its many crises the Study would have developed to the significant extent that it did. And when he left, all the men who founded The Montana Study and launched the program that it followed would be gone.

In order to give the program continuity and to integrate it into the state's educational system, Chancellor Selke asked Brownell to retain the directorship in absentia. The title would be only nominal and would be of no personal advantage to Brownell, but if it would help insure continuity in this important service he was willing. His problem now was to lay plans for the third year and to obtain enough staff members to carry them out.

Plans for the third year called chiefly for a continuation of the work already started: more community study groups and more cultural activities such as arts and crafts, community pageants, and recreational projects in which local townspeople could all participate. The work was also to include more special research projects and the publication of more articles by staff members to further develop The Montana Study philosophy and techniques. Weekend courses were projected for community leaders, to be given in cooperation with liaison committees at each unit of the university system.

Brownell also had other plans for the third year for which there had not been time in the first two years. One such plan provided for county demonstration areas where the Study would cooperate with other agencies—federal, state, and local—in a general program of education in which anyone could participate. It was Brownell's purpose that if all these agencies could coordinate their efforts to do together what they now seek to do separately, the basis for a powerful effort to deal with the problems of community survival and human enrichment would be created. The Study had already provided strong evidence pointing toward the feasibility of such a cooperative venture, and Brownell's first basic principle was that it should be community-centered, not agency-centered or University-centered, and in the long run community-controlled. This plan was strongly supported by Guy M. Brandborg of the State Board of Education, who had helped work it out, and he stood ready to push its organization in the Bitter Root Valley.

Then Brownell had another plan calling for the creation of a "community college," which, in keeping with other phases of The Montana Study, was designed to get the University off the campus to bring its services of education directly to the people in small communities. Actually this was to be a kind of "traveling college" composed of three to six instructors working together who would give organized courses for four to six weeks in different rural communities each year. The courses were to be of practical and cultural interest to the communities concerned, and were to include studies in family problems, regional history, literature, and social and economic development, and would be open to anyone. The experience would give faculty members a first-hand knowledge of the state in which they were employed to train citizens and would provide people in rural districts with an opportunity they do not ordinarily have—one theory being that nobody whether professor or farmer is too old to learn and improve his life.

As for staff members to carry on the work in the third year, it was indeed fortunate that Bert Hansen, who was already familiar with The Montana Study and who had himself developed a significant aspect of its program, was available for another three months in the spring of 1946, and when George Selke became chancellor quick action was taken to have Hansen become a permanent staff member.

From Conrad, Montana, they obtained as another member of the new staff, Miss Ruth Robinson, the young woman whose personal leadership had been a major influence in the success of the Conrad Study Group. Originally from Willow Grove, Pennsylvania, Miss Robinson had come to Montana as a guest on a dude ranch, but after a season's stay she found herself obsessed by the country and became a teacher in the Conrad High School. After two years in Conrad she was writing letters about a kind of beauty that most strangers never see and that even the natives rarely experience. In one of her letters to a friend she wrote, "Conrad folks are the world's nicest people. The prairie is magnificent and the grain elevators along the railroad tracks affect me as cathedrals once did."

Back in Pennsylvania Ruth Robinson belonged to an old newspaper family whose ancestors arrived in America before the Revolution, and which since 1873 had published Montgomery County's leading newspaper, the *Public Spirit*. From her father Miss Robinson learned the newspaper business and later graduated from Vassar with a degree in journalism. Upon her father's death she became president of the family paper and though she still held that office when she moved to Montana shortly afterwards, the West had captured her heart. But still true to her family's traditional interest in civic affairs she had no difficulty fitting into The Montana Study, and from organizer and leader of one of its most successful community study groups, she was now to share in the responsibility of keeping the state-wide program on the track its founders had made for it.

Brownell found his third staff replacement in Frank H. Smith, one of America's foremost educators in the field of community arts, and particularly the country dance. To fill this assignment Smith took leave from the Extension Service of Kentucky where he had been a community recreational specialist, and since recreation is one thing that all communities need whether they are in Kentucky or Montana, Frank Smith was well equipped for this phase of the Study's program, which was later shown through the Lewistown Study Group.

Bert Hansen would devote most of his time to work in the communities of western Montana organizing study groups and developing programs in community dramatics. With the cooperation of Superintendent Manning of Lewistown, Brownell had arranged for Frank Smith to devote his time to community work in eastern Montana, which had hardly been touched; and Ruth Robinson as acting director would manage the Missoula office, carry on liaison with the six University units, and help organize as many other study groups as time permitted. Each staff member was to be largely independent, though all were to cooperate toward the same goal, and The Montana Study as an organization would be directly responsible to the new chancellor, George A. Selke.

After two years of experimenting, much of it by trial and error, during which the whole program was built up from a dream, The Montana Study was getting down to the fine points of a smooth operation. On August 20, 1946, Frank Smith arrived from Kentucky, a week later Ruth Robinson arrived from Conrad, and shortly afterwards Brownell and all three members of the new staff had dinner in Helena with Chancellor Selke to discuss final plans before beginning the third year. Brownell was so pleased by the future outlook that he suggested he drop the directorship entirely, but Chancellor Selke insisted that he retain the title at least in absentia. Thus, although Brownell was actually leaving the scene of action, his name would still be officially attached to the organization. But officially or unofficially, the name of Baker Brownell will always be attached to this experiment, for more than anyone else it was this man who had been the heart and soul of The Montana Study.

And now, having completed his job, the man who had created in Montana a living example of how, by traditional democratic methods, education can be better utilized to improve the life of small communities throughout all America, was prepared to leave.

It was a crisp morning late in September, 1946, a little more than two years since he had arrived to begin the experiment, that alone with his dog Timmy Baker Brownell climbed into his car and drove eastward across the broad Montana plains. On Sunday afternoon he stopped for gas in the historic cow town of Miles City, 467 miles from Missoula, and picked up the local *Daily Star*, the Study's bitterest newspaper enemy. In it an editorial on The Montana Study said, "Certainly we have much better use to put the taxpayers' funds to, in our educational system than pouring it into a lot of socialistic nonsense, by which the pink-eyed boys proposed. . . ."

He tossed the paper in his car. Timmy squirmed and went back to sleep. Brownell drove on, leaving the mountains and plains of Montana behind.

15

Libby

"Libby, Montana," remarked one of its natives, "is like a kid in pigtails, all legs and no solid form."

It's no longer just a country town, yet neither has it reached the status of a grown-up city. And in this awkward stage of life Libby has growing pains, for that's one thing certain—it is growing. But whether it will keep on growing depends on its citizens, of which there are now about 2000, though all told the greater Libby area includes about 3500.

And "growing" doesn't mean simply more people. More important than that is whether the people can consolidate gains already made, give permanence to their local industry, and add the improvements and community services necessary for stability and solid form. Libby has reached a precarious point where permanence, security, and a rich community life will either be assured, or else decay and eventual bankruptcy will carry it down the same path that has led to the end of other fabulous ghost towns now famous in western history.

Thus, Libby was a natural patient for The Montana Study, and it was Libby that early became the center of one of the most intensive research programs undertaken by The Montana Study, and of one of the outstanding community study groups organized during the program's third year of operation.

Set down in a pocket of the mountains on a bend in the Kootenai River, Libby is reached by auto after traveling west over a hundred miles of wilderness highway from Kalispell, winding past deep lakes and high peaks in the extreme northwest corner of Montana. It is the county seat of Lincoln County and the lumber capital of one of the great virgin forests yet remaining in the United States. Approaching along a mountainside from the east, first glimpse of the community reveals piles of freshly cut lumber and the towering smokestacks of J. Neils Lumber Company.

Besides their clean stores and shops, they have a theater where you can take in the same movies New Yorkers see in Radio City, a hotel, a twenty-five-bed hospital, ten churches, and one of the best libraries in Montana. Swinging into the "main drag" you're fairly struck by a big electric sign that says, "Surprise?," hanging over the swankiest restaurant in town, which, for its size, is as good as any between Minneapolis and Seattle.

Most everybody works for a living, and it's a safe bet that anybody you meet first either has worked or still does work for the J. Neils Lumber Company, because that's by all odds the biggest employer in town. More than 600 people earn their living helping to produce the 75,000,000 feet of lumber cut annually in this mill. Another twenty-five to sixty work for the U. S. Forest Service. And around sixty others operate woods outfits of their own; these are the "gyppos," the fellows who practically log with their bare hands, and among them are some of the most colorful people in logging. It is these people who, among other things, have made Lincoln County one of the largest producers of Christmas trees in the whole U.S.A.

A little more than 100 other Libby folks work for the Zonolite Company, mining vermiculite and producing enough home insulation material to fill 600 to 800 railroad cars for shipment every month. Nearly 300 people living right around Libby, or not far away, operate "ranches," as even a garden patch may be called out West, but since this mountainous region grows trees better than anything else, there isn't much land for a real farm. And so the more usual procedure is to operate on the side what agriculturalists call a "subsistence farm," and draw a regular check from J. Neils. The town is on the Great Northern's main line, which everybody considers his private railroad, and about twenty-five or so local residents are railroaders. The Great Northern collects an estimated $6,500 daily from the community in freight revenues, and is the largest single taxpayer in Lincoln County.

From these four industries, forestry and lumbering, mining, farming, and railroading, Libby has had a basic income in recent years of well over $2,000,000 annually, representing about 95 per cent of the original money people have to trade with, and three-fourths of it comes from forestry and lumbering. So when Libby folks say the future of their town depends on what happens to the forest they're talking facts.

Libby is a typical forest community, but of a different variety than the Darby type. Here private timber has not been depleted, the Kootenai National Forest has more commercial timber than the Bitter Root, logs are manufactured locally into the finished product, waste materials are utilized for presto logs and other by-products, and the large operator, J. Neils Lumber Company, is a local concern with unusual community interest. Here there is an opportunity for proper action before natural resources are exhausted. Thus, the problem facing Libby is one of prevention rather than cure. It involves a problem that is today one of the most difficult in America—joint planning by the public, labor, management, and government. And since most of the timber produced in America comes from private land, much of which is being rapidly depleted, Libby's problem is one of broad significance to every American in these United States.

Lincoln County was settled first by gold prospectors who soon cleaned up and got out. Substantial logging activities began in 1906 when the county's first large sawmill was built at Libby by the Dawson Lumber Company. Later that same year a second large saw-mill was constructed at Eureka in the northern part of the county, a third was built in 1907 at Warland, some miles northeast of Libby, followed in 1911 by still another at Fortine, southeast of Eureka, and a fifth at Troy, a few miles west of Libby. By 1916 the lumber output in Lincoln County had reached an estimated 170 million board feet annually. Libby was rapidly increasing in size, Eureka was booming, Troy had become a railroad division, Warland and Fortine were rocking from prosperity. Everybody had money to spend, and they spent it. But Lincoln County could not hold its gains, and the boom was soon over.

By the mid 'twenties Eureka's mill was silenced forever, the mills at Warland, Fortine, and Troy were abandoned. Lincoln County's lumber output had fallen to a tiny fraction of the boom production, fortunes had disappeared, people packed up and left, and those who stayed found themselves struggling for a living. Troy was abandoned as a railroad division point, more businesses closed, Warland and

Fortine became virtual ghost towns. Eureka, perhaps the hottest town in Lincoln County during boom days, was nearly done for. Yet throughout this entire decline the mill at Libby, purchased in 1919 by the Neils brothers, kept operating, and Libby, which had seen ruin on every side, managed to escape the disaster.

But unless preventive action is taken, the same thing could yet happen to the one mill still remaining in Libby, and the people who live there would witness the decay of their community.

The sawmills that made boom towns of Libby's neighbors and then left them in poverty did not fail because the forest had been cut clean as has so often happened in the lumber industry. Billions of board feet still remained. But the early sawmills were located adjacent to heavy timber stands in river bottoms and flats, and logging was concentrated on these tracts that could be easily reached. As this easily accessible timber containing species of high value was cut, it became necessary to move logging operations back into the high country which, even in summer, could not be reached without immense capital investments. And by cutting year round in the valleys there was eventually nothing left for the winter months when snow and ice made operations in the high mountains virtually impossible at any price. Thus, while great mountainsides of timber were still within sight, it was the incontrovertible laws of nature and forest economics that broke these early mills, and it was the people in their communities who suffered.

The threat of timberlands logged out entirely, depleted of their valuable species, or cut back to the point of diminishing returns, has been the eternal menace to forest communities. From Maine to Washington State hundreds of deserted towns bear witness to this menace, and as America's timber resources continue to decline, hundreds of forest communities still thriving face the same inevitable threat.

To spare Libby from this disaster, and perhaps establish an example that could also save hundreds of other forest communities, technicians of the U. S. Forest Service went to work with their maps and surveys, and after years of intensive research found that the only solution was to set aside enough timber for what they call "sustained yield management," so that the mill upon which this town depends for 600 jobs and a major share of its trade could keep operating for all time. But there was one catch. The major part of Libby's forest area was divided in ownership between the United States Government and the J. Neils Lumber Company, and neither owner had enough timber of the right species in the right location to do this alone. And without an act of Congress there was no means by which the two owners could legally get together and pool their resources.

In March, 1944, Congress recognized the national significance of forest problems such as those facing Libby, and enacted Public Law 273, known as the "Sustained Yield Unit Act," under which the Forest Service was empowered to negotiate cooperative agreements with private owners, "in order to promote the stability of forest industries, of employment, of communities, and of taxable wealth, through . . . a continuous and ample supply of forest products. . . ."

Then, armed with this new legal power, the Forest Service technicians again went to work and after more surveys and more study, came up with a proposed cooperative agreement with J. Neils whereby the Neils' timberlands and a large part of the Kootenai National Forest would be combined into one natural unit to be logged under a plan of unified management which would make the forest inexhaustible. It was a new innovation in American forestry designed to preserve the life of a forest community, and although Neils was willing to sign, there was still one catch.

As soon as the plan was announced sharp opposition arose in Lincoln County over the contention that if the proposal were put into effect it would create a monopoly on the National Forest, give Neils inordinate privilege in local industry, put labor at an unfair disadvantage, squeeze out the small operators, and deprive the people free use of the National Forest for hunting, fishing, and other forms of outdoor recreation. Libby was split wide open, each faction shouting bitter allegations at the other. In Troy, with a remaining population of about 800 and located only eighteen miles west of Libby, people charged discrimination against their community, saying that Libby was to be stabilized at the expense of Troy.

The Forest Service planners now found themselves knee-deep in human relations, and they knew that until more facts were at hand as to the social implications of their proposed cooperative agreement it would be unwise to make any final decision. And it was at this point that Baker Brownell suggested an independent survey by The Montana Study to search out the facts concerning the human aspects of the problem and to help determine the social policies that would best contribute to a rich and stable community life in the area concerned. Thus it was early in 1945 that negotiations began which were to lead to one of the major special projects of The Montana Study.

The Forest Service was interested in Brownell's proposal because the primary objective of the sustained-yield program was not only to promote better forestry, but to insure the human welfare of a community. Brownell was interested because to him the problem involved was a significant example of rural and community decay in America and of proposed ways to correct it. It was not his purpose to support either side in the controversy. In this The Montana Study was neutral. But in the Forest Service Brownell had found a government agency interested in the same problem of community survival for which his program was designed, and for this reason the two agencies now joined forces.

To accomplish their joint undertaking they agreed to employ a trained sociologist who would study the human problems in Lincoln County and submit his findings in the form of an advisory report to be used in planning the forest management. The Forest Service would provide funds to finance the project, but to insure a free expression of views, it was to be independently directed by The Montana Study without influence by foresters regardless of how much the resulting report might criticize Forest Service procedures. It was, as Brownell put it, "A thrilling example of how by working together government and education can use the democratic process to learn how to solve a major problem in our democracy."

The Montana Study brought in from the University of Missouri young Harold F. Kaufman and his wife Lois, both with doctorates in rural sociology from Cornell. With instructions to get the facts regarding the human problems of Lincoln County, and to make recommendations as to what social policies would best serve the people, this husband and wife team went off to live in Libby for fourteen weeks during the summer and fall of 1945.

It was an immense undertaking but the Kaufmans soon found themselves engaged in so many community activities they felt like permanent residents. The Lincoln County Free Library loaned them an office and provided a million leads to information. Brothers Walter and George Neils and their fellow officers in the Libby Mill contributed information from the standpoint of industry. Laboring men and local union representatives had their say pro and con, the small woods operators, the gyppos, who by nature had no more use for Neils than any other big outfit, said how they felt and supplied more information. Main Street merchants, school people, churchmen, housewives, all contributed their thinking. And in this way the Kaufmans learned first hand about life in this community and how people felt about the way their forests should be managed. They held personal interviews on specific questions with nearly 100 people, and at group assemblies they met and talked with over 400 others. They prepared questionnaires on the forest program which were filled out by nearly 450 people, and made a personal investigation of community organizations, social life, public services, and local industrial possibilities.

Before they had finished, Harold and Lois Kaufman found that although people in Libby and Troy were in favor of a program to make their forest permanently productive, they were equally concerned with the manner in which it was to be done. They wanted above all to have a voice in the policy that was to determine forest management, for the forest was a natural resource from which two-thirds of their basic income was derived. And the greatest part of that resource was publicly owned, administered by the Forest Service which represented them, the people. Hence they had every right to feel that it was literally "their forest," realizing all the while that it also belonged to every other American whether he lived in Libby or Bangor, Maine.

From the Kaufmans' study came a 95-page report entitled, *Toward the Stabilization and Enrichment of a Forest Community,* giving in detail their findings, conclusions, and recommendations. In it they analyzed the community in general, its problems and possibilities, and suggested several courses of action for improvement. It presented the advantages of the proposed sustained-yield program, and also stated in pointed language local criticisms of the Forest Service and the objections expressed to the proposed agreement with Neils. But the Forest Service printed the report without editing and distributed it to the public. If there were any shades of local opposition not expressed before, that was all changed now. Even petty complaints were brought out openly, and the controversy was stirred anew. Actually nothing had been solved, but the report had brought local interest in community stability up to a level it had never reached before, and had made it clear that if forest production were to be perpetuated concessions would have to be made by all interested parties—the Forest Service, Neils, and the local public. And it was far better to have controversy then than to have it later. For forest planning must of necessity be a long-time proposition. Thirty-five U. S. presidents may be elected within the life of a tree and unless forest policy is accepted by the people there can be no sound forest policy.

Under Public Law 273 the Forest Service could, after thirty days notice, hold a public hearing on the proposed cooperative agreement, and since Neils was already willing to sign could then put the plan into effect whether local residents liked it or not. But the Forest Service had no desire to assert its authority in this manner, and with the Kaufmans' report and the public discussion it provoked, now began to reconsider its proposal and to consider changes which would provide added safeguards for the public interests and insure a greater degree of stability for Troy.

Having completed their survey, Harold and Lois Kaufman returned to Missouri, and for more than a year the controversy in Libby continued unabated. Although public discussion was desirable, it was all too evident that as long as people's thinking was ruled by emotions, as long as bitterness, controversy, and misunderstanding prevailed, community betterment, permanent productive forests, and economic and cultural stability could be nothing more than idle dreams.

But there was in this forest community a young energetic brunette named Inez Ratekin who had lived in Libby most of her life. Inez was the county librarian, and a woman with intense interest in the welfare of her community. While the Kaufmans were living in Libby, Inez helped organize a public forum to discuss the proposed sustained-yield program, and for several months after the Kaufmans had gone these meetings continued in the Lincoln County Free Library. But eventually it came to the point where they were just hashing over the same old arguments, and Inez decided that what Libby really needed was a regular Montana Study Group.

This would give them a definite outline to follow instead of just arguing over opinions, and would enable them to approach local problems through objective study by the people themselves. In this kind of a group sustained yield would be only one of many questions to study. It could be considered in proper relation to all other local problems, and by creating an objective attitude toward community problems in general the controversy might well give way to research and understanding through which the people could make their own intelligent decision, and could perhaps find a solution for many other important community problems.

Inez Ratekin had already discussed the idea with Brownell, and in the fall of 1946 she began talking it over with the town's community leaders. After many personal contacts to make sure all shades of opinion and all levels of local society would be well represented, she issued a notice in the *Libby Western News* that the library was sponsoring the organization of a Montana Study Group, open to anyone interested.

On January 7, 1947, nearly four months after Baker Brownell had left Montana, the members of the Libby Study Group assembled around a large table in the Lincoln County Free Library and began the systematic analysis of life in their community. Ruth Robinson, then acting director of The Montana Study, was there for this first meeting, but after that the group proceeded on through the study guide with no outside assistance.

Inez Ratekin was chosen as the group chairman, Mrs. H. W. Redfield was made secretary, and it was decided to rotate leaders for each meeting. Weekly question committees and research committees were selected well in advance, and standing committees were appointed on business, community history, and recreation. The group included representatives of the local loggers' union, officials and employees of J. Neils Lumber Company, officials and employees of the Forest Service, school people, town officials, housewives, farmers, clergymen, businessmen, and the Zonolite Company's Libby division manager. Thus, the first requirement for a successful study group, a diversified membership representative of the entire community had been met.

And nobody hesitated to say what he thought no matter how contrary it might be to the opinion of others present. Neither were there any hurt feelings. It was the first time in the history of Libby that all the individuals in this group had ever sat down together at a conference table to discuss the common problems of their community, though most of them had lived in Libby for many years.

Proceeding section by section through the objective guide to community analysis provided by The Montana Study, ferreting out each

problem of community life and examining it as they went along, they
came eventually to the proposed cooperative agreement between Neils
and the Forest Service—the most controversial issue in Libby. This
was the supreme test. It was no special accomplishment to keep discussions candid, objective, and friendly on lesser issues, but now the
Libby Study Group was encountering a question that vitally affected
the personal rights and incomes of them all. Here there was intense
natural conflict, prejudice, and emotion on both sides. How could any
group in Libby discuss this question and remain objective? They
could do it because their study was just that—a study, not a debate.

In seeking information for study, they had the Kaufman report,
they had printed matter issued by the Forest Service, they had Neils'
side of the story, and they had the arguments of labor and of the small
woods operators who had been most vocal against the proposed agreement. But they also had their own research committees to write histories of the community from the raw facts they collected themselves,
and to gather information for analyzing the economic basis of their
town.

"I've been in this town for twenty years," said one Study Group
member, "and from the day I arrived I've heard Libby was about to
be abandoned because the logging was drying up. And I know that's
not idle talk. I've lived to see it happen to at least six other towns
right around us."

"What we're interested in," said another, "is not what will be here
next week, but sixty years from now, a hundred years from now."

"That's right—we won't be here then," another spoke up, "but if we
know the town will be here, people will feel a lot more like building
on a permanent basis now. It's all this talk about the town folding up
that has caused so many people to build temporary homes here and
make temporary investments. Until we can lick that feeling of being
temporary, what kind of a community can we expect?"

But if through the proposed sustained-yield agreement permanence
was assured in this forest community, what about the evils of private
monopoly that for months had been the cause of heated controversy?
Every question involved in this controversy had to be carefully examined before the Study Group could arrive at an intelligent understanding of this vital community problem. Just what did the agreement
provide anyway?

When members of the Study Group finished their investigation they found that instead of creating an unregulated monopoly, the cooperative sustained-yield agreement actually constituted a government lien on the J. Neils Lumber Company.

Under the terms of this agreement Neils would voluntarily relinquish many of the most vital property rights that are guaranteed to all Americans. Once this agreement went into effect Neils would place all of its vast timber holdings in Lincoln County under complete supervision of the United States Forest Service. The company could not cut a tree on its own property or build a road, or sell an acre of land without permission from the federal government.

The company would be required to manage its own lands, erect conservation improvements, maintain forestry practices, build roads, and develop its manufacturing facilities in accordance with minimum standards dictated by the Forest Service. It would be required at its own expense to build and maintain roads into the National Forest which would then become government roads controlled by the Forest Service. The agreement contained specific provisions safeguarding the public use of all roads in the National Forest, and protecting the rights of the people to use the forest for grazing, berry picking, hunting, fishing, and other forms of outdoor recreation. And in addition, these public rights were to be extended to Neils' own lands, the only restrictions being with regard to safety measures on forest roads where logging operations were in progress, and these restrictions were already in effect. In the event of disagreement the Forest Service would have final authority enforceable through the federal courts. Compliance with the terms of this agreement would involve an immediate expenditure of several million dollars by the Neils Company, and that was only the beginning of cash outlays it would have to make. To voluntarily subject itself to such government control as this, to so encumber its holdings for sixty years, the life of the agreement, and to relinquish its right to sell out either in whole or in part, without government approval, would be unthinkable for most private companies. Yet Neils was favorable to this plan. And this, the Study Group concluded, was in itself evidence of Neils' sincerity in wanting to assure the stability of their community. It was a master plan for welding together one great forest into a single coordinated unit, irrespective of ownership, and was an example of maximum cooperation between government and industry for the public welfare.

In return, Neils was guaranteed enough timber to keep its mill

operating at its current level for a period of sixty years, the life of the
proposed agreement, thus guaranteeing the community approximately
600 steady jobs. After sixty years, new growth and oncoming young
stands would, according to Forest Service calculations, actually increase
the volume of timber. Thus, if proper management is practiced in the
future, this agreement would in effect assure the community of adequate timber supplies indefinitely.

"The fact that Neils happens to own this mill is beside the point," a
member of the Study Group remarked. "The thing we're interested in
is that mill and how to keep it running."

To accomplish this objective Neils was given the right to buy without competition, though at fair market value subject to public scrutiny,
an average of 50 million board feet annually from the National Forest,
12 million of which would be white and ponderosa pine, the species of
highest value in this area. To this amount Neils would add another
18 to 20 million board feet annually from its own lands, of which
8 to 11 million would consist of the valuable pines. And, as further
protection to the community, the agreement contained specific provisions requiring local manufacturing and employment of local workers.

As their analysis continued the Study Group concluded that those
who said this agreement would create an unregulated monopoly were
either prejudiced against big companies simply because they were big,
or else had not bothered to read Public Law 273 and to determine what
provisions the agreement itself contained. Certainly this agreement had
none of the features of exploitation traditionally associated with
monopoly.

Still searching for answers to questions that had been a major source
of controversy, the Study Group found also that instead of robbing
Troy of its industry in order to stabilize Libby, the agreement provided for Neils to construct and operate at Troy a modern band mill
producing 10 million board feet annually—a major new industry large
enough to allow for substantial expansion of population in this community. And in order to protect the small operators, nearly half the
annual volume of wood products from the Kootenai National Forest
was omitted entirely from the proposed agreement with Neils. In addition to a vast area known as the Tobacco River Drainage in the
northeastern part of the county to be logged by small and medium-
sized operators for the benefit of people and communities in that area,

this included an annual 6 million board feet of saw timber for the exclusive use of small operators within the Kootenai Management Unit, nearly 2 million feet more than they had ever cut from the National Forest even in their best year of production.

Excluded also from the proposed agreement with Neils were 27 million board feet annually for poles, posts, ties, and similar items which had always been the chief products of the small operators. Excluded from the agreement were all Christmas trees cut in the National Forest, another major product of the small operators. And to prevent draining timber supplies from nearby communities outside the proposed sustained-yield unit, the Neils Company was prohibited from buying National Forest timber elsewhere and shipping it into Libby or Troy for manufacture. But the thing the Study Group found most impressive was that under this agreement a great forest resource—both private and public—would be made to last indefinitely and through scientific management its volume of growing timber would actually be increased.

Thus, without emotional conflict, but through objective study, a group of Libby citizens representing all shades of local opinion had arrived at an intelligent understanding of the most controversial issue in their community. And this was a major achievement.

At the tenth meeting they were still working on the eighth section in the study guide, "The Future of Our Town in Relation to its People."

"We just got started and couldn't stop," said Louise LeDuc, a Libby housewife.

"And with all the opinions we had represented," said Art Shelden, their Grange master, "everybody had a different light to throw on the discussion and that took a lot of time."

But gradually every member of the group found his opinions changing, new thoughts developing, old ideas being tempered. Individual opinions were coming into common focus, and a new kind of thinking —group thinking—was emerging.

Then someone suggested, "There's no use making all this study unless we do something about it."

The suggestion was approved unanimously.

Each member went home and began writing down recommendations to bring in for discussion at the next meeting.

"From the number who came back with the same recommendations," said Inez Ratekin, "you would have suspected collusion had you not known better."

One recommendation was submitted by every member of the group —to actively support consummation of the proposed cooperative agreement between J. Neils and the U. S. Forest Service, which they said, ". . . in the opinion of this group would have the desired effect of stabilizing income and values to the residents of this entire area and would result in long range planning by all."

Even previous dissenters now approved, and by the thirteenth meeting the whole group had discussed every recommendation brought in, changed some, omitted others, until none of them was the product of any one individual—but a part of everybody.

They had now completed their course of study and the call to action had been sounded.

Reminiscent of the spirit that swept Conrad only a year before, the group began its campaign for a greater Libby. A proposed constitution was drawn up for a permanent organization to be known as the Greater Libby Association, and on April 7, 1947, through a full-page advertisement in the *Western News,* they placed their recommendations for community improvement before the town. A mass meeting was called for May 8th. Letters were mailed to every organization in town urging them to send delegates, and on the day scheduled for the meeting circulars were distributed by school children. That night 157 citizens assembled in the Junior High auditorium. Copies of the proposed constitution were handed out as people came in, and after a verbal challenge from members of the Study Group, the community launched its Greater Libby Association.

Consisting of delegates from more than fifty local organizations, and headed by an executive committee of twelve elected members, ten of whom had been members of the Study Group, the new Association was designed to promote a program "for the improvement of our living in this area." The executive committee elected as its first chairman Allo Agather of J. Neils Lumber Company. O. L. Gillespie, their school superintendent, was elected vice-chairman, and Inez Ratekin secretary-treasurer. At the suggestion of Ed Dutton, leader of the Loggers Union, also elected to the executive committee, the Association chose for its slogan, "An organization of organizations for the betterment of our community." And to make this slogan known it was printed on official letterheads.

In its form of organization, the new group was patterned after the Conrad Education and Recreation Association, but it differed in mode of operation. Actually, the Libby organization was not a direct action group, yet action was the very thing it accomplished.

This is how it worked. A public issue would come up for consideration by the executive committee which made a thorough study and reported to the Association. If the Association decided to support the issue, a member organization, such as the Chamber of Commerce, was asked to take action and all other organizations got behind that group. In most cases the executive committee could decide whether to lend support from the Association, thus making for greater flexibility and avoiding the necessity of regular community-wide meetings.

Under this system the Greater Libby Association coordinated all community organizations toward common goals and eliminated duplication of effort and competition for credit among local factions. It made suggestions and recommendations, it gave moral support, it marshaled public opinion, but it did not seek credit for itself. As a practical matter, however, members of the executive committee did plenty of work themselves to push the action, but they acted always in the capacity of a supporting agency. Yet despite its modesty—or perhaps, because of it—the Greater Libby Association carried tremendous weight, for through its member organizations it represented the entire community.

One of the first moves was to begin a drive for the proposed sustained-yield agreement. Members talked it up everywhere they went. Public meetings were held. Member organizations studied it at their own meetings. Printed leaflets bearing the name of the Greater Libby Association and presenting terse statements about the proposal were mailed to every box-holder. From drawings made by Dick Hennessy, a Libby artist, these leaflets pictured the alternatives between accepting or rejecting the agreement—a ghost town with its abandoned streets and decaying buildings, or a prosperous and permanent community with modern public schools, flourishing industries, and landscaped streets. Letters from the Greater Libby Association were sent to public administrators from the Secretary of Agriculture on down, and to all senators and representatives from Montana, Idaho, and Washington.

Then a town meeting was held with Axel Lindh, assistant regional forester from Missoula, as guest speaker, and that night Mr. Gillespie called for a vote to test public sentiment. The response was overwhelmingly favorable. Their program of education was beginning to tell. And then came their next big move.

The Chamber of Commerce suggested sending a delegation of labor representatives out to the West Coast lumber town of Shelton, Washington, where the Forest Service and the Simpson Logging Company had already signed the first cooperative sustained-yield agreement in the United States. There they could observe for themselves how the program worked in actual operation. In Shelton where the Simpson Logging Company occupied the same position as Neils did in Libby, the same arguments had been used against the agreement as were now being used in Lincoln County, and in both cases the greatest hostility came from labor and small operators.

The Greater Libby Association immediately pledged its support to this plan, and offered to help with expenses. With this backing the Chamber of Commerce rounded up six labor representatives and three small businessmen to act as delegates. All traveling expenses were paid from contributions, and Neils paid full wages to the labor representatives from its mill making the trip. And when the expedition returned there were a lot of surprised people in Lincoln County.

"We stayed out there a whole week," said a labor official, "and we really sampled the town. Merchants, ministers, company officials, Forest Service men, union leaders, and dozens of gyppos. We went through the Simpson mill from top to bottom. Must have talked to 500 workers. And by gosh, we couldn't find anybody with anything against it."

"That's right," said another. "The cooperative agreement has sure worked out okey for Shelton."

"And they let us go wherever we wanted, talk to anybody we pleased, and without company agents or Forest Service men to interfere."

Somehow the terrible monopoly predicted for Shelton once the agreement was signed had failed to develop, and opposition had melted away. As a means of self-education for the delegation from Libby nothing could have been more successful.

Libby began to witness a change in the attitude of her union locals. People who formerly fought any such program were out making speeches for the other side, and while there were still a few changes they would like to see made before the Libby agreement was signed, the unions were now firmly convinced that a cooperative sustained-yield program should be carried out in Lincoln County.

Meanwhile, the "organization of organizations for the betterment of our community" was hard at work on other long-range recommendations: a new hospital, municipal ownership of Libby's water system, improved sewer facilities, revamping of outdated tax appraisals, town beautification, expanded tourist facilities, the publishing of factual information on local mineral deposits, wider interest in public affairs.

Engineers were brought in by the City Council to make cost surveys. A special committee headed by Paul Church, city clerk and one of Libby's most community-minded citizens, was appointed to work with the City Council on street improvements. As a result of these combined efforts, Libby has been oiling streets, building new blocks of sidewalks, and brightening up the business section with new street lights.

Through the Association's executive committee the Libby Garden Club got community backing for the landscaping of a large weed patch that had for years been a disgrace to Libby's east side. Neils brought in ten truck loads of top soil, the Zonolite Company donated fertilizer, and women did the planting. Now there is no more weed patch, and on another piece of city property the Garden Club is planning a new park.

The community had long suffered a major financial handicap because many of her people enjoying tax benefits lived outside the legal boundaries and were thus exempt from paying their share. Two years earlier an effort to extend the limits had failed because outlying citizens objected to what they called highhanded tactics. But now with the new spirit of getting things done that was all changed, and Libby has been adding new citizens by pushing out her boundaries.

"I led a campaign against going into the city when they tried it before," said one of the new citizens, "but this time nobody tried to bully us, so I got out with a petition and signed up all but three property owners."

Then there was a problem of what to do about the young people on Halloween. For two years William C. Stearns, pastor of the Methodist Church, and two women had carried the responsibility of putting on parties to keep the children out of trouble. But to be done right the affair needed stronger support. So Mr. Stearns went to the Greater Libby Association, and got support from the whole community. The P.T.A., one of the Association's affiliated organizations, agreed to assume responsibility for direct action.

As it happened, Mr. Stearns found himself back on the Halloween committee, but this time with plenty of support, and the result is that Libby now has an annual Halloween celebration for every child in town from toddlers to high school young people. And it's really an elaborate event. It begins about six o'clock in the evening with bands playing, children of all ages parading through town in Halloween costumes, and the streets lined with adult spectators. Businessmen award prizes for the youngest child, the smallest, the fattest, the costume judged most original, the most gruesome, the funniest, and for about anything else they happen to think of. The affair ends with gay parties and folk dancing in the school buildings, and after it's all over every garbage can in town is still standing upright.

In 1948 the School Board found itself faced with the need of raising $165,000 for additions to the grade building, and $95,000 for construction on the Central gymnasium-auditorium. Two bond elections were scheduled for the 2nd of October, and Superintendent Gillespie took his problem to the Greater Libby Association. The executive committee considered the issue and got busy with its network of organizations. About eighty per cent of the cost would be borne by Libby's big taxpayers, J. Neils, the Zonolite Company, and the Great Northern Railway, while the annual cost to average taxpayers came to only $4.81. Carlton Joughin, manager for the Zonolite Company, and Allo Agather, stockholder and official in the Neils Company, were both leading members of the Association's executive committee, and they worked just as hard as any other member to make the bond election a success. Advertisements were carried in the newspaper and flashed on the screen of Libby's movie house. Cards giving pertinent information were mailed to every eligible voter. Executive committee members went out and personally interviewed hundreds of people. When election day arrived they had cars out to bring the voters in. And the bonds passed by a great majority. Through her "organization of organizations" Libby had won another victory.

"We're all in this community together," said Carlton Joughin. And the fact is that everybody else—mill workers, foresters, housewives, merchants—they're all saying the same thing, for Libby is today a community of united people who intend to keep on living there and make a permanent home for their children.

Shortly before the Old Year of 1948 ended, the executive committee met in the Lincoln County Free Library for one of its most significant sessions. The U. S. Army Engineers had announced plans to build a large dam on the Kootenai River just above Libby. Many of the town-folks were against it, but, said the committee, "The dam will probably come whether we want it or not. And instead of complaining we should do a lot of preliminary planning to get the most good out of whatever comes."

They had only to look at other large dam sites to envision what could happen to their community—a sudden influx of workers, a squalor of trailer camps, shacks, and cheap dives, and the unwholesome, unsanitary, and immoral conditions that inevitably spring up with large construction projects when a community lacks the foresight, or is too preoccupied with thoughts of sudden profits to make advance planning for these social problems. But when and if dam construction begins at Libby, the Greater Libby Association will be prepared. Streets, police protection, new ordinances and regulations, zoning, sanitation, expanded school facilities, recreational centers—these are the problems the Association was now preparing to meet. Rarely do small towns have such foresight, or the will to be bothered so far in advance—but neither do most small towns have an "organization of organizations" with the enlightened attitude that has developed in Libby.

More than three years had passed since Harold and Lois Kaufman brought The Montana Study to Libby and began their special project, "Toward the Stabilization and Enrichment of a Forest Community." The findings of that research and the public discussion it evoked had helped the U. S. Forest Service in its plans to perpetuate a great natural resource for the people's benefit. And in the people of Libby there had been inspired an intensive study of community life. During the thirteen weeks of this study people learned that by honest objective means men and women of widely divergent views, representing all levels of social and economic position, can forget personal differences and work together for the common good. It had given them a new appreciation of the natural resources upon which their community depended, and a broad understanding of local problems. People had awakened to the advantages of long-range planning over the frontier philosophy of freedom to exploit without regard for the welfare of others and "letting tomorrow take care of itself."

"Our Study Group," said Bill Guernsey, their National Forest supervisor, "was like a town meeting, only better, because we had a systematic outline of community analysis to follow which kept us from being helter-skelter, and turned discussion into constructive channels. And it has been a great lesson in discussion procedure for other community groups, and in this way has helped them to get more things done."

"The Study Group," said the Reverend Mr. Stearns, "has stimulated new interest in the church, and the thing that impressed me most was the people's willingness to take action once they had completed the course."

Their biggest project, consummation of the proposed cooperative sustained-yield agreement, had yet to be completed. But the intensive study that had been made, and the drive to teach people the facts, had transformed local opposition into real support. Among the residents of Libby, the people who would be most vitally affected, there were only a few who still remained hostile. Yet outside Libby where there had been no study group the controversy over charges of monopoly, favoritism, and special privilege still went on. And it was this controversy that had been chiefly responsible for preventing the agreement from being signed. But sooner or later the Forest Service would call an official public hearing, and when it did the majority of people in Libby would be ready with a solid front. At this writing they have been at work for two years since launching their "organization of organizations," and they will keep on working until, as they say in Libby, "We will eventually have our cooperative agreement."

Ed Dutton of the Loggers Union put it this way: "It's not the union we're working for, and we're not interested in helping J. Neils—it's our community that we care about because that includes all of us."

"Yes," said Carlton Joughin, "we have all the opportunities you could ask for, in as beautiful a setting as America can offer—if we can only make people think."

16

Indian Pioneers

Not long ago a detective in Cincinnati, Ohio, picked up a man suspected of illegal entry into the United States.

"How did you get into this country?" asked the detective.

"I'm a full-blood Sioux Indian," replied the man. "I was born here. How did you get in?"

Picture, if you will, a time when this continent was inhabited only by Indians and there was no Cincinnati detective—in fact, no Cincinnati.

Then some Europeans discovered America. Later more Europeans moved in and claimed possession. America became the United States and its former owners were told to move. Their wishes were unimportant for they were "savages," and they had more space than they needed anyway. Then the newcomers moved westward. By the Louisiana Purchase they bought most of the country from France, though neither France nor Napoleon, who authorized the sale, owned a foot of it except through "claim." The actual owners had no more voice in the sale than they did in the original claim. Eventually the newcomers took possession of all the land and the former residents (who had never been recognized as owners) were crowded into areas called "Indian country"—not because these areas belonged to the Indians, but because there hadn't been time for the newcomers to move in. Finally, the newcomers did move in, and after getting nicely settled they suddenly realized that the Indians had been robbed. So they gave the Indians back a few pieces of land in the form of reservations and told them to live there.

Such generosity didn't last long, however, and gradually they took back most of the reservations. They told the Indians this was unfortunate but civilization had to progress. The Indians were advised to forget it and adapt themselves to the newcomers' ways. Some Indians took this advice. Others didn't, though they might have been better off if they had.

The result is that the newcomers have made America the world's greatest country, but it has been done with the Indians' land, without their consent. And it has left both whites and Indians with unsolved problems, which perhaps reflect a white virtue. For if the whites had no conscience they would have simply liquidated all Indians and there would be no problems. Americans today have a sense of moral honor that tells them the Indians have been wronged, yet that feeling is not strong enough for a restitution satisfactory to the Indians. In fact, the Indians are seldom consulted as to how these problems might be solved, and until this is done more often, the problems will be solved only when the blood is so thinned by intermarriage that no real Indians remain.

It was an attempt to help understand some of these problems that gave The Montana Study one of its most unusual projects. It started from a new study group organized by Bert Hansen in the little town of Dixon shortly after Baker Brownell had returned to Northwestern.

Dixon is one of fifteen communities in western Montana founded in violation of a treaty between the United States Government and the Confederated Tribes of the Flathead, Kootenai, and upper Pend d'Oreille Indians. Under the terms of this pact, known as the Hell Gate Treaty of July 16, 1855, and ratified by Congress in 1859, the Indians relinquished about 16,000,000 acres including most of the Bitter Root Valley where their ancestors had lived for many moons, and were granted in return an area of less fertile land sixty-five miles long and thirty-five miles wide in the Jocko and Flathead Valleys, to be known as the Flathead Indian Reservation. This reservation was given to the Indians for their *"exclusive use and occupancy,"* for, as the tribesmen say the white men told them, as long as the grass grew and the water ran. Part of the Indians moved to their new home, others remained in the Bitter Root on land they still held.

Then in 1872 another agreement was drawn up by General James A. Garfield, later President of the United States, which took from the Flatheads all of the lands they had left in the Bitter Root Valley and paved the way for the forceable removal of all the Indians to the reservation. Old Chief Charlot refused to sign this latter agreement, but his mark was conveniently forged to the document, and in 1891 he and his followers were driven from their ancestral home. The story of this historic event was re-enacted by the people of Stevensville in their pageant-drama, "A Tale of the Bitter Root," with the tribe's hereditary chief, Paul Charlot, coming back from the reservation to play the role of his grandfather.

Even before the old Chief and his band of Indians had left Stevensville in 1891, Congress had enacted laws permitting large parts of their new "permanent" home to be sold by the government. Then a few years later Congress threw open the entire reservation. And though the grass was still growing and the water was still running, thousands of homesteaders came to establish white communities, while the Indians watched with their piece of paper. Dixon was one of these communities.

To most white people these early events have been lost in history, though the Indians have never forgotten. With the passing of time most of the reservation has come into white ownership, and now only about 300 full-blood Indians remain. Today these native Americans are a minority of a minority, for there are about 3500 others whose blood varies from a half to a 32nd-degree Indian. Younger, usually more educated, and far more aggressive than the full bloods, these part Indians now dominate the tribe and have little patience with the old full bloods. Yet the cleavage that exists between full bloods and mixed bloods is no deeper than that which exists between 100 per cent whites and almost anyone who has a drop of Indian blood in his veins. And though the three groups now live side by side and daily pass on common streets, they are separated in their thinking by a universe of space, each group having its own opinion of the others.

Located only two miles from the Flathead Indian Agency, Dixon has become a center of life on the reservation. Its main street stretches along the foot of the mountains that form a boundary of the Indian nations. Red men are as common on this street as white men.

When Bert Hansen came to organize the Dixon Study Group he met a mixed gathering of part Indians, perfumed paleface ladies, white townsmen, and officials of the U. S. Bureau of Indian Affairs. On the surface, at least, these people had little in common and Hansen found himself in the position of a lecturer whose response from the audience was little more than dead silence broken occasionally by someone clearing his throat. The meeting was supposed to start an informal discussion, but there they sat, stolid as stones.

Hansen repeated his explanation of The Montana Study. He elaborated on the purpose of the study group. He passed out copies of the printed study guide and read a few pages aloud. He re-emphasized the idea that this was to be their discussion, that he was only there to help them get started. He ad libbed some more, and still no signs of discussion. Then he suggested they choose their chairman and secretary. Gradually the meeting loosened up and by closing time they were acting like friends. The defrosting of Dixon had begun. And before they had finished their ten weeks study a member had to be fast if he wanted to say anything. White women and mixed-blood Indians sat next to each other exchanging ideas with little thought of social differences. Once more The Montana Study had proved its democratic effect, and class barriers had been broken on the round table of discussion.

It had not been unusual for Montana Study groups to discuss the effect of Indian life on their communities' histories, but here there were Indians present to speak for themselves. And a new field of operations was being opened to the experimental program of The Montana Study.

If this kind of self-analysis could help an ordinary American community to understand its own problems and thereby promote a richer community life, why couldn't it also be used to understand problems that were exclusively Indian? And if it could, perhaps the same technique might be of value in dealing with the problems of all racial minorities. The study guide might need changing a bit, but the principle followed would be identical—systematic self-analysis, open and friendly discussion by the group.

Among the members of Dixon's Study Group was a man whose understanding of the Indians is indeed rare among white people. A man of heavy frame, he speaks in soft tones, his features are sharp and clear, his eyes penetrating, his smile genuine. He is usually seen wearing a tailored gabardine shirt, a neatly knotted necktie, and a well-kept hat of distinctly western style. Coulson C. Wright, superintendent of the Flathead Indian Agency, known to the full bloods simply as "Wright," is one of those people who works by painstaking methods which he has used diligently in his years among the Indians.

After seeing what The Montana Study had accomplished in Dixon and the educational possibilities it offered, Wright became interested with Bert Hansen in forming a special study group to consist entirely of full-blood Indians.

The Flathead Indians, whose heads are not flat, are the native Salish and other tribesmen who were forced out of the Bitter Root Valley. Many of their present-day problems are an outgrowth of the unhonored treaties and broken promises that preceded and followed that tragic event. Most of the full bloods are old men and women living under conditions of extreme poverty. Farm work is the principal source of their meager incomes, though some have attempted stock ranching for themselves. Others receive small rentals for land leased to the whites. They hunt, fish, trap, and a few sell the products of their native handicraft. As long as they stay on the reservation, which they are free to leave if they so choose, they are wards of the United States, though they receive no pension or dole from the government.

Many of their ancient customs are practiced today in the same manner as they were practiced by their tribal ancestors before the coming of white men. Medicine men still engage in their arts, and each January the full bloods hold their annual medicine dance, take the sweat cure for diseases, and live together in their tepees for the week-long ceremony. During this ceremony the Indians may still be seen running out naked from their low mound-shaped sweat huts to dive into an icy stream. This is followed by an evening of feasting and dancing to ancient rhythms presided over by the medicine men. By this process the Indians are treated for colds, rheumatism, and other diseases. Many of the old men still wear their black hair in braids that hang over their shoulders, and the women are usually seen in their full bright-colored skirts.

Several families often live together in a single one-room cabin which has few of the modern conveniences, but which has all the hospitality of a white man's mansion. There is usually an old-fashioned wood range for cooking, a round oak table for eating, a wooden bench near the door for pails of water that are carried in from outside, and a few battered aluminum basins for washing and bathing. A great heating stove stands near the center of the room, beds often consisting of blanket pallets laid on the wooden floor are crowded against the chinked log walls, and on nails driven into the log siding hang piles

of personal belongings. Despite their miserable surroundings, the full
bloods' ancient dignity has not diminished, and they envision a day
when the federal government will settle their claims arising from
broken treaties and thereby help to relieve them of their poverty.

It was a warm evening in April, 1947. Outside the old Catholic
Church in the little town of Arlee, Montana, the sun had faded over
a red horizon, its long rays still lighting the craggy peaks of the Mission
Range on the far eastern side of the valley. Inside the church twenty-
four native Americans had gathered for the first meeting of the Full
Blood Indian Montana Study Group.

Pierre Pichette, the interpreter who had helped bring this group
together, was an old leader of the Flathead Tribe who well remembers
when the first homesteaders staked claims in the reservation. For more
than fifty years Pierre has been blind, but his keen intelligence has
enabled him to see many things that other men could not appreciate.
Long ago he learned to read and write the English language in Braille,
and now, alone in his world of darkness, he records the legends of
his tribe, interpreting his race to the white men. He is alert, friendly,
and desperately anxious for people to know that Indians are as human
as whites. Yet he can still smile when he tells how white children run
to their mothers as he walks down the street in Missoula.

Seated near Pierre was old Paul Charlot, their hereditary chief who
came with his parents from the Bitter Root in 1891. Charlot has never
recovered from that indignity, and by virtue of an act of Congress he
is now forced to live out his remaining years as the dethroned ruler of
a vanquished people.

Across from Charlot sat Eneas Conko, now past seventy-five, his
long braids tied neatly over his chest. Conko is a stalwart and dignified
old Indian who believes that it was in accordance with God's plan to
make the world all one that Columbus came to this "island" in 1492.

"God's plan is good," said Conko. "But white men have not respected
Indian's rights."

There was Pete Pierre, in whose cabin they met for most of their
later meetings because they could not smoke in the church, and his
wife and family who help him run his stock ranch. There was Louie
Ninepipe, a medicine man known as "Happy" for his seemingly perpetual smile; Baptiste Finley, an old patriarch; Pete Vandeburg,
another of the tribal interpreters; Joe Big Sam Woodcock, youthful

full-blood veteran of World War II; and Sophie Moiese, a buckskin and bead artisan nearing eighty. It was Sophie who once said, when asked if she wanted to go on an old-age pension, "I have never accepted charity and I am too old to start now. I will make my gloves and moccasins and get along all right."

These were the kinds of people who were to form the new Study Group. Many of them spoke little English, others none at all. They were the last remnants of a defeated nation, and though they had many reasons for bitterness there was no bitterness in their hearts. Yet they were proud, as Pete Beaverhead said, that as Indians living on the reservation they did not have to pay taxes, for to them taxes would be a tribute exacted by the conqueror from the vanquished.

The tribesmen were intent, skeptical, yet drawn by their red curiosity to learn the real purpose behind this Montana Study. Was it really for the Indians' good as it had been told to Pierre, or was it another of the white man's tricks?

With them in the church was their friend Wright with his wife Geneva, and Bert Hansen whom Wright had brought to lead this new kind of council meeting. Hansen was not entirely new to the full bloods, for some of them had met him when they were invited to Stevensville to play the role of their red ancestors in "A Tale of the Bitter Root." Yet they did not know him as they did Wright. And from long experience the old full bloods have learned to be wary of white men with propositions until their motives have been proved.

Charlot spoke what the full bloods were thinking, "Whites have deceived Indians many times. Sometimes innocent and respectable meetings have been turned against us."

Then the red men looked at Wright as he stood to speak.

"This," he said, "might be a different kind of meeting than you have ever held before, or at least for many, many years. This is the first time that a white man not in the Indian Service has been interested enough to come here and hold meetings with the Indians."

He told them about Hansen, his connection with The Montana Study, and reminded them of the pageant in Stevensville.

"Bert Hansen has made a study all winter with some people down at Dixon, a sort of school," Wright explained. "And we thought maybe you full-blood Indians would be interested in the same kind of meetings this spring."

The Indians kept listening.

"I believe white people have never understood the Indians very well. Bert Hansen thinks the same way. He thought if we could have some meetings here and you people would talk over your problems with us and we could take them down on paper it would help improve our understanding between ourselves and with the white people."

Wright introduced his "squaw," who he said would take the notes, said she was no good at home, cooking and keeping house, "So I brought her here where she could be useful."

The Indians smiled and kept listening.

"I assure you we have no secrets," Wright continued, "and we have no motives you would not like. Most of the written material that goes into Washington or to the newspapers comes from what the mixed bloods say. Back in Washington they say, 'Here is what the Indians think,' but it is not the full-blood people at all, it is some mixed-blood person that speaks instead. So we thought meetings like this would be educational to us and educational to you."

The white man sat down and Charlot rose to speak.

"There are rumors," said the old Chief, "there is to be no more Indian Service, and Indians will be turned loose. Indians do not like this. Rumors say these meetings for that purpose. We do not wish to betray our people in this way. That is all I have to say."

"No," said Hansen, "that rumor is not true. There is no connection between these meetings and this talk of turning the Indians loose."

He told them about the meetings in Dixon, Stevensville, Lonepine, Darby, said these meetings were to be like that. Wright told them Hansen spoke the truth.

There was a mumbling in Salish and a long session of hand waving with the Indians all talking at once. Then silence, and again Charlot rose to speak.

"I am thankful for this understanding," he said, and sat down.

The Indians felt better now. They liked this kind of meeting and they wanted to believe there was no secret motive behind it. But it is not easy for people to be trusting after they have been deceived for three generations.

If this Study Group did nothing more than give the old full bloods faith in the white men's sincerity it could be considered a success in education. But Bert Hansen and Coulson C. Wright expected to achieve more than that; to them it offered a new hope of friendship and understanding for the tribesmen. To give the study direction the two white men had prepared an outline for discussion based on the community study guide followed by other groups, though adapted more specifically to Indian problems. The outline began with a discussion of tribal history and customs, it called for a consideration of government relations, the changes in Indian life, Indian culture, legends and beliefs, the Indians' position in Montana, their economy, education, and the future of the Indian community.

After long and tedious explanations about the purpose of the study, and repeated reassurance that it had no connection with rumors of "turning the Indians loose," the meeting finally got under way with a discussion of what territory the Flathead Indians inhabited before white men came, and the origin of tribal names.

The discussion was just getting started when it became obvious that instead of following what was being said, all eyes were on Geneva Wright, happily unaware that she was being watched, and busily taking notes. Several old full bloods clustered around Charlot were motioning toward the white woman and whispering to each other.

Wright, sensing the trouble, interrupted the meeting to explain again the importance of taking minutes so that people could know exactly what the Indians thought.

"We want to send these notes to the congressmen who help make laws regarding you people," said Bert Hansen. "It might help you to have them know what you say about these things."

With this extra reassurance the Indians seemed satisfied once more, but the discussion no more than started again than they were back on the original question of "turning the Indians loose."

Old Conko stood erect.

"Full bloods cannot take care of themselves now as they used to," he said. "We would starve in our own country if whites taken away. We do not know how to farm by white man's method well enough, we do not remember ways our fathers made a living."

Then he began to explain how their fathers had lived. "Four kinds of food taken from pine tree. They used inner bark, nuts from cone, the gum, and black moss."

He described an economy in which roots such as wild carrots and parsnips, fruits and meats, were gathered and stored—often for two years in advance. The bitter root, the camas, the chokecherries, huckle-berries, and all other native berries were gathered in season and pre-pared for winter.

"As today," said Conko, "some were better rustlers than others and provided well against day of want; and some, lazy, depended on work of others. Meat was provided mainly on big buffalo hunts in late fall and winter. This too dried and stored. If any families run out of food or clothing their relatives supposed to help them. If relatives could not do this, chief announced to whole village need for contributions. Then everybody brought some of own supply until there was enough and more for those needing help. Always plenty on hand, sometimes so much that after couple of years worms began eating food and it had to be thrown away."

"One reason this history is important," said Wright, "is that some people say the Indians are better off now than they were before white people came. Conko says they used to have food ahead for two years."

"It is so that Indians used to be better off a long time ago when everything was open," said Pullassie. "They got everything they needed and now we get eighty acres and can't make a living on it."

Hansen asked if the Indians would be happier if white men had never entered their territory. His answer was a unanimous "yes." If white men had never come, they said, they wouldn't have to bother about hunting licenses, marriage licenses, or any kind of licenses.

"We would be free like we used to be."

"But haven't you gained some advantages since the white men came?" asked Hansen.

Pullassie: "Maybe there are some advantages. I try to be like white man by getting a bald head. I am only Indian I know who is bald. Maybe this is an advantage."

"But what about automobiles, trains, electric lights, and other mod-ern improvements?" Hansen wanted to know.

"For those that have money it is good," said Conko, "but for those who have not, it is no good. We cannot get along without these things the way country is now. If we could go back into those days long ago, maybe we could."

It was also unanimous that since white people have taken a whole continent from the Indians and now enjoy its luxuries, the Indians should be helped enough so they too can enjoy the benefits of modern inventions. This, they said, would be a small price for getting a whole country.

"My old folks said it was better to stay in Bitter Root," said Charlot. "White men promised if we come to reservation it would always be ours, and our customs would be our customs. White men also promised stock horses, and cattle, and said they would build houses for us, and we could pick out what kind we wanted when tribe passed through Missoula. White men did not do these things. They did build some houses, but they not cost over $100. White men lied to Indians."

"Charlot is right," said Pierre. "Nothing came of white man's promises. Government promised $120,000, spread over twenty years, to buy clothes, food, supplies, and this and that. I do not think any of tribe got any help at all. I do not think twenty houses were built."

"Forty years ago before reservation was opened to whites it easy to get rich," said Sophie Moeise. "Pasture not fenced then and lots cattle and horses. When white man come this cannot be. White man has spoiled Indians' ambition, crops die, and we give up. For awhile on reservation we have own irrigation ditches, use water whenever needed. Now ditches locked up and when our gardens need water we cannot irrigate. That is difference now and forty years ago."

"I witnessed some of that when I came from Bitter Root Valley," said Charlot. "I could go anywhere, see cattle and horses all over reservation. Wherever Indians lived it was the same. And there were buffaloes, Indians' buffaloes. Ever since reservation opened to white man we all go broke and stock disappear. No Indian in tribe was poor like now. We had too much stock for little land whites leave us, so Indian give up ambition, sell stock, and get poor. That is what I have seen and witnessed."

Hansen asked Charlot if the Flathead Reservation differed from others.

"I do not really know what to say," the old Chief replied. "I have a little blood from Nez Perce and used to go over there quite awhile ago. The difference is, their land lots better than ours. I have never remembered when they had crops fail. Even in hills they plow and plant and get same results, and every fall they get big crops. I worked for a full blood there one summer and about ten days after Christmas I went back and worked till spring. Our downfall here is water. It is like Sophie says, I cannot get water when I want it. When we had own water rights many Indians had good crops. Since Reclamation Service come, I put in my crops and when I am ready to irrigate when it is hot and dry they tell me they will turn on water such and such day and we wait and wait until it is too late. That is why Indian's ambition disappears."

"In my early days when I married," said Ellen Big Sam, "I was nineteen years old. My father-in-law, Big Sam, was raising gardens of all kinds—watermelons, spuds, and everything that grows. We had water right that came out of LaMousse Canyon. For many years we know that each season we would have plenty, until Reclamation came and took our water right. For few years after that Big Sam tried to raise garden like before and each year failed—not enough water. Finally he got too old and quit altogether. Then we moved where we live now. Since I been up here, south side ditch come through and I try to stop it, and didn't want to sign for ditch to come through my place. They surveyed and thought I would pull out stakes but my husband stopped me. He said maybe we get water now. So ditch go through. I waited and put in garden but only got water once that year. Last year my aunt put out little war garden. I asked for water and couldn't get, so my old aunt carried water to take care of garden but she too old and couldn't carry enough, so garden burn up. Now I have letter from Agency asking me to put in garden this year on account of food shortage but I am afraid if I do it will fail again."

Hansen looked at Wright. "Can you answer that question?"

But Wright was only a government official. He could only do what the law provided. "I do not have an answer," he said quietly. "Except that I know what she says must be true and I do not yet know how to cure the problem."

There was a feeling of helplessness in the Indians' story. They were not like white communities that, having once become aware of their problems, are inspired to action. These people were resigned to their fate. For them, it seemed that help could come only from a benevolent government and, until then, they would live on in their poverty. Yet somehow their morale seemed refreshed by just being able to tell the white men their story. For even this was a rare opportunity.

"We might as well say we are just moving rapidly on," said Conko. "It won't take very long. All of Indian customs in not many years will melt away. Very few of us still have our braids and whenever that custom passes away old Indians will be gone."

"You can't expect to get help if you don't try," said Hansen. "The full bloods must not give up but must assert themselves and not stay in the background."

The discussion moved now to religion as it affects the Indians. They talked about education, an advantage that appeals to the mixed bloods and young full bloods, and is gradually assimilating them into the American society. But for the old full bloods, schools and colleges held little interest. For them the Study Group was the best that education could offer. It could not solve their basic problems. That was a job for the government. But if it could give them a feeling of greater significance, if it could bolster their self-confidence, if it could only provide them with an enjoyable activity, their lives would be richer than before. Hansen and Wright kept thinking along these lines, and meanwhile the meeting continued.

The red men have long considered it an insult to their race that federal laws prohibit the sale of liquor to an Indian, or its possession by an Indian, on the reservation. Yet in towns that have grown up in the Flathead Reservation area are dozens of bars and saloons ranging down to cheap dives where members of any other race, white, black, yellow, or brown, can drink as long as they can stay conscious. State liquor stores in these towns sell large quantities of bottled goods to anything that can stand upright except animals and Indians. To the Indians, this prohibition in what they feel is their own country is merely another example of white discrimination that has been imposed upon them since the days of covered wagons. And the Indians' resentment is not merely a question of being thirsty. It is only a part of their desire to be treated with the same respect that is accorded white men. If there is to be prohibition, say the Indians, let it apply to all men alike.

The effect of this prohibition-by-race has been to make the Indians ripe subjects for an illicit liquor traffic. Excitement is sought out by the Indian youth in road houses where bootlegging is in vogue, and the problems of red delinquency have been only intensified.

Thus it was not without reason that the question of liquor control should come in for discussion by the Full Blood Indian Study Group.

"It seems like this intoxication is not right," said Conko. "Often the married couples break up and leave, often the children are separated. Indians are doing that and also the whites. There is nobody can tell me it is good for one to be drunk."

"There is a general belief," said Hansen, "that liquor is worse for the Indians than for the whites. Is that so?"

"That is not so," said Pete Pierre.

"The reason liquor seems worse for Indians," said Big Sam, "is that Indian has to buy bootleg liquor which he drinks fast in bus station toilet or someplace before he gets caught. It wouldn't be so bad if he could buy regular liquor and drink it like white men do."

"What is the reason that Indians cannot buy liquor like white men?" asked Conko.

"In the early days," said Wright, "the Indians were called savages. People said if an Indian got a drink under his belt he would kill his wife, become very fierce and dangerous, kill everybody. Liquor was supposed to make an Indian very savage, so Congress passed the Indian liquor laws."

"Doesn't liquor act the same on white men?" asked an Indian.

"Oh no!" Wright exclaimed. "White men are very tame and gentle when they get drunk. They never get mean. They are always kind."

The Indians all had a good laugh. Then after they had discussed the problem at length, Hansen wanted to know if the Indians felt there would be less trouble from liquor if the prohibition were removed.

To an Indian the answer was "yes."

"For awhile," they agreed, "we would be kind of bad, but in the long run we would be better off."

"Of course," said Conko, "some will always be bad, just as with whites."

"I might say," Hansen added, "that when you came to Stevensville for the pageant, one thing that greatly surprised the white people was that the Indians did not drink."

Louie Combs said he thought the whites and Indians wanted to be friendly with each other, it was just a matter of understanding.

By this time they had talked far into the night. The meeting ended with the full bloods all anxious for more. Next time they would get down to assigning questions and begin their study in earnest. But the first meeting of the Full Blood Indian Study Group had shown the old Indians that a university professor, a white man, was interested in them—not as a curiosity, or as mere subjects for an academic study, but as a group of live American people who have very real problems that should be recognized and dealt with intelligently if they are to enjoy the maximum benefits of living in their own country.

During the weeks that followed, the Study Group grew to forty Indians, and at each meeting they probed deeper into the life of their tribe, its history, its current problems, and the causes behind them. Methodically and with an eye toward improvement, they discussed Indian family life—past and present—the impact of white beliefs on Indian culture, how they had been affected by laws and politics, the tribal economy—its dependence on hunting and what goods and services could be produced to replace this dependence on wildlife. They talked about Indian social life, what the tribe did for a good time—celebrations, stick games, shinny games, and dances. Considerable time was given to a study of Indian feasts and wakes, Indian legends, stories, and traditions such as the mysteries of the medicine men that hold profound meaning to the tribe. Many of the legends that had been known only to Indians through generations of campfires were now recorded on paper. Included was an account of the Indians' meeting with Lewis and Clark, the first white men their tribe had ever seen. History books are filled with such stories as told by the members of this early exploration party and recorded in their famous journals, but here they were told as they had been passed down by old Indian warriors through many moons of their unwritten language.

After weeks of discussion the Indians came to some new and important conclusions. The white men had brought many changes the Indians did not like. But these changes could not be undone. Instead of wishing for a past that could never return, they concluded, the Indians must recognize life as it is and adjust themselves accordingly. For only by this attitude can the red man improve his lot in modern society. To white men this conclusion might seem obvious, but for a group of old full-blood Indians who have been tricked and cheated since the day they were born by a race that considered itself superior, who have been frustrated and demoralized by a government that drove them from their ancestral homes, and then reduced them to poverty—for these people this conclusion was neither easy nor obvious. For them it was a conclusion that could be reached only after resolute study and through a kind of courage that gives the old full blood his simple dignity.

"We should not find fault with what the white people do," said

Pete Pierre. "Instead we should try to make an understanding between Indian and white man so they will get along."

For the white man's schools and colleges, many of the Indians had shown little respect. But at their eighth meeting on May 21st, Octave Morigeau expressed another attitude that brought group approval.

"Last night," said the old Indian, "we had a graduating class in Arlee. I noticed that in a bunch of young students there were three Indians. That looked pretty nice to me. We should all try for a better education. Of course if we had a strictly Indian school close by, that would be pretty good, but I think our public schools all over the country are pretty nice too. It carries them pretty well forward, mingling with white children. An education once acquired can never be taken away from us. It is ours to keep. We have all heard a lot about these Indians from the Middle West and eastern part of the United States. They have good education, some of them are doctors and lawyers and statesmen and politicians. I think it would be good thing if we would take it up. That is all I have to say."

At the last meeting their interpreter, Pierre Pichette, stated in simple terms the group's enlightened attitude.

Standing with his cane, his black hair braided against the sides of his dark-skinned wrinkled face, his eyes seeming radiant though they had not seen light for fifty years, he spoke slowly and in resonant tones.

"As we have found understanding through The Montana Study which may bring whites and Indians more closely together with understandings, acquaintances, and friendship, why not stand together to work and face problems and bring them to a proper accomplishment which will be for the welfare and prosperity of the state and Indians of the State of Montana."

But the Full Blood Study Group did not end with discussion alone. Bert Hansen, with his yen for community pageantry and his belief in the idea that culture should be engaged in instead of talked about, had sensed the possibility of a great Indian pageant which would present to local whites a graphic account of their past relations with the red man. It would give the Indians a vivid demonstration of their own significance, and thus become a spiritual therapy for their drooping morale.

Since the historical events of the Flathead country had been a story of both Indians and whites, here at last was an opportunity to bring the two races together in a cultural project which could emerge from their now common community. The drama could be written from the actual life in which both had played living parts, and could be a means of reidentifying the two peoples with themselves and with each other.

To accomplish such unification, Hansen put the idea up to both the Full Blood Indian Study Group and the Dixon Study Group, and with high enthusiasm the two groups began work on their joint undertaking.

In 1847 a Scotsman named Angus McDonald was sent by the Hudson Bay Company to head a trading post in the Flathead country. The old Scotsman married a full-blood Nez Perce and became widely known for his fair dealings with the Indians. In the Flathead country today there are mountains, lakes, and streams bearing his name, and part of the trading post he named Fort Connah is still standing near Post Creek, Montana. At the suggestion of Ed McDonald of the Dixon Study Group and grandson of the famous Scotsman and his Nez Perce wife, it was decided to hold the pageant in conjunction with the centennial celebration of Angus McDonald's arrival at Fort Connah.

A writing committee, headed by Geneva Wright and assisted by members of both Study Groups, was appointed to work with Bert Hansen in preparing the script. From libraries, early records, newspapers, and interviews with dozens of old-timers—Indians and whites— historical material was gathered for the story. Pages of script were rejected or approved by the Study Groups, torn up and then rewritten until they had the approval of both races. For weeks special committees of Indians and whites met separately and then together. Truck loads of properties, Indian travois, tepees, cradle boards, public address system, outdoor lighting facilities, bleachers, and hundreds of other items were hauled onto the grounds of the old fort at Post Creek. Bulldozers and grading machinery had to be brought in to level the arena, and hand labor was volunteered by hundreds of people.

As the planning gained momentum it was extended to include people from all sections of the reservation until eventually the project embraced the townspeople of four communities: Dixon, Polson, Ronan, and St. Ignatius, but with the Indians still holding the spotlight. A museum of Indian arts and crafts was arranged in one of the old Fort Connah buildings. And, after months of preparation, "A

Tale of the Shining Mountains," the most extravagant dramatic project of The Montana Study, was ready for production.

In a grassy meadow where roving tribesmen made camp in centuries gone by stand the log ruins of old Fort Connah. Reaching back in semicircular patterns from the winding creek that flows between rows of trees at the meadow's edge rise the earthen banks cut by a thousand floods in the form of ascending stairs. Here in this natural amphitheater, under outdoor floodlights, was produced the pageant-drama, "A Tale of the Shining Mountains." Behind stretched the broad valley of the Flathead with its rolling fields, its herds of cattle, and the spires of its towns and hamlets. And beyond, to the east, rose the shining mountains of the Mission Range. Nearly a hundred tepees rimmed the verdant meadow and smoke curled into the evening sky. Dogs lay near the campfires, ponies grazed in the meadow. Rhythmic sounds of beating drums filled the fragrant atmosphere, and Indians in the native costumes of their ancestors moved quietly about.

Around this theater of action were the thousands who had come to watch, overflowing temporary bleachers on the banks of the creeks and crowding into nearby trees. It was the evening of the Fourth of July, 1947. Suddenly the drums became louder. An Indian mounted on his pinto pony rode into camp and handed a message to the chief. And from this dramatic opening the pageant-drama, presented by Indians of the Flathead Reservation and the white townspeople of four communities, related the true story of a hundred years of white and Indian relations in this western country.

As in the pageant at Stevensville, the dialogue, in specially selected dialects—Scotch, French, Irish, Indian—was read over a loud-speaker system, while actors in the outdoor arena synchronized their movements with the narrators' voices. It was a pure dramatic expression of the people of two races, an artistic synthesis of their own lives and culture, an achievement that Broadway with its commercialized executions could never equal.

On July 10, 1947, the weekly *St. Ignatius Post* had this to say: "The 8,000 people who witnessed the production on Friday and Saturday nights of 'A Tale of the Shining Mountains' were conscious of the fact that they were seeing something out of the ordinary.

"And it was."

The Full Blood Indian Study Group did not produce action such as that taken by the people of Libby and other places, but it was an achievement in education.

Said the *St. Ignatius Post*: "Many heard for the first time the story of the land in which they live. . . ."

There was a time not so long ago when the Flathead Indians had faith in the white man. They welcomed him to their native land, fed him when he was hungry, clothed him when he was cold, and defended him against hostile tribes. In that day the Indians were supreme and the newcomers were a minority. Then this state of affairs was reversed and the white man became dominant. He called the Indian a savage and destroyed his faith. What happened in the process is history. But through the Full Blood Indian Montana Study Group a new start was made toward the restoration of that faith. When the Indian and the white man, with his inventions, his educational resources, and his wealth that has been gained from Indian lands, are ready to begin together where the Indian Study Group left off, a richer and fuller life will be created for both races.

And it will not be a one-way proposition—for neither race will find the other lacking in culture or intelligence.

17

A Challenge to America

January, 1947, had come to Helena, Montana.

The lobby of the Placer Hotel was jammed with humanity, the air filled with a din of jumbled voices, the overhead lights blurred by a haze of tobacco smoke. Bellhops loaded with baggage rushed in from the streets, collected their tips, and ran back for more. Men with cigars stood in groups, their mouths working like perpetual motion. Here and there a stranger stood bewildered by the commotion. Crowds of excited men shoved toward the front desk and clamored for rooms. Ice tinkled in pitchers as room-service moved trays of refreshments toward the elevator. From the hotel bar a blare of noise welled forth to mix with the lobby clatter, and in rooms upstairs politicians, red-eyed from burning cigars, talked strategy over glasses of liquor. The Thirtieth Montana State Legislature was about to convene, and somewhere in this maze of political machinery lay the future of The Montana Study.

Back in 1943 when Ernest Melby made his appeal for assistance from the Rockefeller Foundation he had assumed that as The Montana Study passed beyond the realm of research and developed into a workable plan of education for enriching the life of small communities, it would be established as a permanent function of Montana's university system, supported and directed by the state for the welfare of its people.

Now, after nearly three years, the operation was nearing the end of its experimental schedule. The Rockefeller grant was expiring. If The Montana Study were to continue on a permanent basis as Melby had envisioned and as hundreds of Montanans who understood its program now hoped, it would need an appropriation from the state legislature. In addition to the budgets submitted by the six University presidents for operation of their units, George A. Selke, the new chancellor, had inserted a special item calling for $50,000 to support The Montana Study for the next two years.

Melby was gone, Brownell was gone, and Howard was no longer connected with the project. The six presidents, all backed by delegates from their own sections, would make their customary trek to Helena to argue for their individual units. But, except for Selke himself, there would be no one in official standing to argue for The Montana Study. It was a slim hope, but as chancellor, it was Selke's job to make education serve all the people throughout the state, and as an educator he was convinced that $50,000 was a cheap price for the value to be received from this program.

From the party caucuses and hotel political meetings, where the lobbyists played their usually prominent roles, there emerged in the House Appropriations Committee a four-man subcommittee on University appropriations to which Chancellor Selke was to make his request for The Montana Study. The four men had varied backgrounds, but one thing they all had in common—they had no conception of what The Montana Study was all about, three of them having never heard of it before their arrival in Helena.

Despite the success of its community study groups and the invaluable research conducted through its special projects, the political impact of The Montana Study upon the state as a whole had been small indeed. A shortage of staff personnel combined with tremendous Montana distances had left vast areas of the state virtually untouched. Publicity of the kind that would create widespread understanding and appreciation of the Study's objectives and achievements had been practically nil. There had been mistakes in early planning, detectable now, though inevitable in any program never before attempted. But the principal source of its political weakness was essentially a combination of the project's inheritance and the fact that not enough people understood its purpose.

It had been alienated from the six units of its institutional sponsor, the University of Montana. It had inherited the scars of battle over University reorganization. It had inherited powerful political enemies, and eventually it had fallen into the ridiculous position of being called "communist inspired." Whatever else The Montana Study may have been it was certainly not communist, for its program was a direct antithesis of anything resembling the Marxist or Soviet doctrines. Indeed it would be difficult to devise a more effective method to combat the evils of communism.

But with at least two-thirds of the state ignorant of the project's existence, and with a small though powerful group of inherited enemies eager to dispose of it, these misconceptions of the Study's objectives did not lend political strength when it came time to enter the legislative arena for total financial support. Indeed it is surprising, in light of these circumstances, that the program had been able to function at all, to say nothing of its achievements.

Many allegations of backstage lobbying have been made as to what happened to determine the legislative destiny of The Montana Study. And though there is partial evidence to support some of these charges, the complete story will remain forever conjecture. Yet one thing is certain. When Chancellor Selke appeared before the four-man subcommittee he found that nothing he could say was sufficient to justify the Study's continuation to this committee. Each of the six University presidents appeared in person on behalf of his individual unit and there was little argument concerning their requests. But when the subcommittee's report went out to the House Appropriations Committee there was no mention of The Montana Study.

There were but a few legislators in the entire assembly, such as LeRoy Anderson of the Conrad Study Group, who knew what the Study really meant. Anderson and the representatives who supported him would have made an open fight for the program, but they never had a chance. Selke's request never reached the floor of the House. It failed even to come up for discussion in a full committee—it was killed by a four-man subcommittee, none of whom had any conception of what the program had done or what it really stood for. And even those who would have fought for it unwittingly voted against it. For when they voted "Aye" on the University appropriation, they automatically voted "Nay" on The Montana Study—not knowing that its omission from the committee's report had denied them the opportunity for a separate vote.

And so, a dream to lift the level of living in small communities throughout the State of Montana had been shelved in the files of memory. On July 19, 1947, three years after Baker Brownell had launched the experiment, The Montana Study closed its office on the campus of the State University. The Study's third progress report states tersely, "A request for $50,000 to finance the work of the Montana Study for the next biennium was not granted by the 1947 Montana State Legislature."

The same kind of politics that had driven Ernest O. Melby from Montana had now killed the program nearest his heart. But in the history of this western state it was merely the ending of another episode. From the days when Bannack was a roaring gold camp and the plains were an open range there has been a philosophy in Montana which has left little room for community planning. It has been the philosophy of reckless exploitation of natural resources, of men driven by the motive of individual achievement with little regard for social welfare, a philosophy that has left Montana and vast sections of all America dotted with ghost towns and decaying communities. This has been the pattern of development in Montana, and, in miniature, a replica of western America. Historically, Montana is only an infant. Culturally and socially the frontier yet remains. Scores of thousands are still living in culturally impoverished towns—barren, monotonous, with little economic opportunity, and their minds unaware of the rich and fruitful community life that could be theirs. Then, through The Montana Study, there had been new hope. Now that was gone. But no four-man subcommittee, no assemblage of politicians, could kill the imprint of human advancement that had been left in the minds of those who, through their own study groups, had made their communities better places in which to live. For these people the concept of The Montana Study will never die.

During three years of operation, community study groups had been organized in fourteen Montana communities, and more than fifty related projects had been carried to completion. From the stimulus to establish home industries local incomes had been raised by hundreds of thousands of dollars, and from scores of community projects, both cultural and physical, local citizens had found the meaning of creative living. Adult men and women had gained a deeper feeling for American democracy and had become alert to the needs of their local society. Through their influence this kind of community planning will go on and on until the original stimulus has been lost in time. And perhaps it is this kind of planning that will help rural Montana to emerge from her cultural frontier.

Despite its lack of coordination with the six units of the University, The Montana Study had made a profound impression on the thinking of many instructors. Almost without notice there had developed a new consciousness of the gap between formal classroom instruction and the daily problems of people in their communities. Out of this realization is growing a new philosophy in the University of Montana which recognizes a responsibility of service beyond the narrow limits of the campus. Professors are beginning to realize that in this experimental program Montana had taken the lead in a new approach to the study of the American community. And now, two years after The Montana Study officially ceased operations, its effects on the University are showing up.

In a letter to Chancellor Selke on March 2, 1948, Andrew C. Cogswell, director of a newly established Public Service Division at the State University wrote, "I have given credit, rightly or wrongly, to The Montana Study for opening for us here at the University a type of off-campus education that gets off its academic pedestal and applies itself to the problems of the community, as seen by the residents themselves. . . .

"Closely related to the above is my belief that The Montana Study created among many people it contacted an understanding that the University campus is not something separate and apart from them; that education is a logical approach to their personal and group problems. There can be no doubt that in many of the communities in which study groups were organized leaders were developed and techniques evolved whereby small communities could meet and solve many of their own problems; I am working with many of those leaders today. It left many of us with a finer appreciation and understanding of our state and our respective communities. In the latter respect, the publications by the Study's staff are invaluable.

"We are richer, too, in the field of education in Montana for the techniques the Study evolved in the handling of adult groups. Those instructors who worked with the Study are the ones we prefer on our current extension efforts. . . ."

In his social work laboratory Harold Tascher, professor of social administration, has incorporated many of the Study's principles, and is instilling in the young people with whom he works a greater sense of responsibility toward their communities.

In the fall of 1948 the State University gave Bert Hansen the job of initiating a new program patterned after The Montana Study, and once more Hansen is busy organizing community study groups, helping to develop community dramas, and taking the University off the campus.

But there are in Montana today men like Guy M. Brandborg of the State Board of Education who will never rest until the Study itself is re-established. Many people, now conscious of their loss, are wanting to know why it was discontinued, and are asking for its revival. Members of the Board who previously opposed the program have reversed their positions. In July, 1948, the Second Annual University Institute for Social Welfare, attended by approximately 200 delegates from both public and private agencies, went on record as recommending, "That the methods and objectives used by The Montana Study be recognized as productive of community welfare and that the Greater University of Montana reestablish a similar program as soon as possible."

Chancellor Selke, backed by the State Board of Education, with full approval of the Executive Council of six presidents, and with the personal assistance of Guy M. Brandborg and Joseph Kinsey Howard, is at this writing working toward a full-scale revival.

When Baker Brownell went west in 1944 his mission was to "find ways to improve the quality of living in Montana." That mission was accomplished. But the principles and techniques that were developed and demonstrated are not limited to Montana. Their significance is universal. Though Montana had been the testing ground, the experiment was launched with the express purpose of developing techniques that could be used to strengthen, improve, and enrich human life in small communities and rural areas anywhere in America. And just as its founders had hoped, the work has now spread beyond the borders of Montana.

In twelve other states of the Union from New York to Kentucky, to Wisconsin, to Texas, to California, and in five foreign countries, educators are using the literature of The Montana Study in similar programs of their own. At Northwestern University Baker Brownell is engaged in his new five-year project to further such work in the

Middle West. Never a week passes that he does not receive requests from all parts of the country for information about the study in Montana. Typical of these requests was that from Hilden Gibson, associate professor of political science and sociology at the University of Kansas, who wanted to "do a Darby" in a small Kansas coal town where the coal mines had become unprofitable.

It has attracted the attention of such distinguished citizens as Owen D. Young, chairman of the board for General Electric, who, as a leading American, has been concerned by the drainage of people from the country villages of upstate New York, and their subsequent concentration in industrial centers. For, as Mr. Young succinctly observed, such movements as this can only "intensify the breeding places for the worst of the social problems with which our democracy is faced." And here is the fundamental reason why The Montana Study deserves consideration from every educator in America. For although American colleges and universities have been highly successful in many ways, they have often intensified the desire of young people to escape from the nation's small communities and rural areas, and there is thus a loss to these areas in wealth, education, and productive power that may well be irreplaceable. Nowhere in the university system is there any appreciable emphasis on a way of life where individual welfare is achieved through enrichment and stabilization of small community and family life.

Today this system is striking at the roots of American democracy, for it is the crossroad villages and small communities dotted across the broad countryside of these United States that have sustained the democratic heritage. It is in the atmosphere of these country neighborhoods that traditional American democracy finds its natural environment. To replace these neighborhoods by the anonymous relationships of the great city is likely to lead to the decline of true community and family life, and to the eventual loss of that intrinsic homespun quality men have held priceless in the American scene.

The techniques of The Montana Study are a means through which education can help orient men and women toward the family and the small community and, without undue interference with a normal shift in population, can help young people to appreciate and feel responsible for their home communities instead of trying to escape from them. And by the extension of these techniques education can become a vital process that will function not only for certain age groups, but for all people all through life. In problems of local health, in problems of economics, in problems of social welfare, it is this community-centered education that can help lead America to a finer quality of living.

The Montana Study is significant to America's churches, for here is a technique that can make articulate the principles of Christianity. Through church study groups this technique could help millions of Americans to rediscover the basic human values of religion, and help them to extend those values into the stream of everyday life. To the thousands of ministers and religious leaders today serving courageously in the nation's small communities, the study group program is a tool that if utilized could work modern miracles for the high cause of the country church.

The Montana Study is significant to gcvernment and to the nation's political institutions, for here is a practical means whereby Americans in small communities may become alert to the issues that shape their destiny. Through community study groups people can learn to think objectively, to keep their minds free of prejudice, intolerance, and personal bias, and to form intelligent convictions without pressure from those who contrive to make facts fit their own purposes.

But The Montana Study is of greatest significance to America's small communities themselves, no matter where they may be. For here is a technique through which ordinary men and women can coordinate for their own welfare the forces of education, religion, government, economics, culture, and democratic neighborliness, and by this simple means can lift the whole level of living in America. And, as the people of Conrad and Libby have shown, it can be done without the presence of outside experts. Any group of civic-minded men and women in any small community who desire to improve their own town, and are willing to take the trouble, can of their own initiative utilize the techniques of The Montana Study.

They need only to enlist the participation of a true cross section of the citizens in their town, to sit down together once each week around a common table to study and objectively analyze the past, present, and future of their community. And out of this group process they will discover their local problems, the causes and reasons behind them, and the means by which they may be solved. The history, the problems, the causes, and the means of solution will be different in each community, yet the principle of objective study as a community —not as a pressure group or a special clique—will be the same. But the point to start from is study, not action—for intelligent action can come only from long, arduous, and systematic study, which embraces all levels of local society in one unified effort for the common welfare.

If during the process help is needed from outside experts, that help can be obtained from the educational institutions, the extension services, the federal and local agencies in the state concerned. Thus, the people themselves can find a fuller utilization for the public services which they support. And for those who engage in this unified effort to improve their own community there is in store not only an enriching experience, but an activity that can be the most fun they ever had.

Through the generations of history since a group of patriots signed their country's Declaration of Independence a thousand and more powers have been shaping the destiny of American democracy. These powers have been mighty in strength, they have been dynamic and ever changing. In the national capital, in state legislatures, in cities and small communities, no group has remained in power longer than the people would permit. As one power emerged another was doomed. Each great change has been the prelude to a new era, sometimes worse, sometimes better, than the one before. Yet today the people remain supreme, they alone have the final authority to determine what the destiny of their democracy shall be. They may yield if they choose to ignorance, prejudice, and lack of moral courage, and give away their final authority. Or by their own intelligence, understanding, and honest conviction they may retain it for themselves.

The Montana Study was but a modest experiment in education. Yet inherent in this program was that certain quality of initiative and independence that in times of national emergency has driven men and women into action for the common welfare. And if the techniques here demonstrated were now applied throughout all America this program could become a powerful force for the preservation of our democratic heritage.

Appendix

There is perhaps no means by which the people living in America's small communities could make a more worth while contribution to themselves, and to the stability and welfare of our nation, than through a concerted effort to improve and strengthen their own communities. It may be that many who have read this story of The Montana Study will want to start similar programs for their own communities. For these people I have prepared a much-condensed adaptation of the 50,000-word community study guide written by Baker Brownell, Joseph Kinsey Howard, and Paul Meadows for The Montana Study. Space limitations make it impossible to give the entire guide in this book, but the skeleton outline which follows should be suggestive of additional material which may be filled in by the people of any community wishing to organize their own study group.

It is my belief that any community can, by local initiative, organize and conduct its own study group. However, the citizens of any community should not hesitate to call upon the institutions of higher education in their state if they feel the need of outside assistance.

The success that may be derived from using this guide has been demonstrated in Montana. The technique has been tested by actual field operations. Certain changes may be necessary to meet local conditions, but in the spirit of offering a suggestion, The Montana Study's community study guide, in condensed form, is presented in this appendix for whatever use it may be to any small community in America.[1]

Richard Waverly Poston

TEN WEEKS GROUP STUDY GUIDE

As long as people will talk together as neighbors in the communities of America the democratic way of life will endure. The members of this

---

[1] The study guide, *Life in Montana: As Seen in Loncpine, a Small Community*, has been copyrighted by the Montana Study and is condensed here by permission of the Montana State Board of Education.

group will sit around a table together and try to acquaint themselves with their own community and its problems.

The work is planned in a series of ten sections with the thought that one weekly meeting will be devoted to each section. However, if the group desires, more than one meeting may well be given to certain sections, and the rate of progress may be varied according to the wishes of the group. Much of the value of the course will depend upon going through consecutively all the various sections.

Two cardinal principles for a group of this kind are regular attendance and a definite-without-exception closing time.

Members of the study group should choose a chairman and a secretary. The secretary should keep brief minutes of the subjects discussed, the points made, and the names of those who make them. These notes may be read at each meeting but should require not more than five minutes. At each meeting the group should read together the material outlined for that meeting and discuss the questions presented.

Those who organize the study group should make advance preparations for the first meeting by preparing answers to the questions asked in the first section. Thereafter, the group chairman should each week appoint a discussion leader and question committee to make advance preparations for the following week's work. These question committees should be prepared to supply detailed information in connection with each question asked in the section on which they are reporting. Following the reports of the question committees, each question should then be discussed by the entire group.

If necessary the group chairman may act as discussion leader, but it would be desirable to have different members of the group lead various discussions in order to assure active participation by every member of the group.

Four research problems are outlined in the study guide calling for the work of temporary research committees to be appointed by the chairman once every two weeks. These problems are intended to be of specific interest to the community; however, if others seem more interesting to the group they may be substituted.

In addition to the weekly question committees and the temporary research commitees, two or three standing committees should be appointed to conduct organized research into the community's major long-range problems. One of these committees could make a study to determine what and how many new small industries would be practical for development in this community. Another might make a special study of community recreation problems, another might study local school taxation, another town beautification, and another might study community health and sanitation. These are a few examples that could be mentioned, but the standing committees should undertake problems which may call for future action after the study is completed. They should make periodic progress reports to the group for discussion, and eventually submit a written report showing the issues involved in the problem studied, the findings of research, and recommendations of the committee.

Each member of the group should serve on one or more committees.

FIRST SECTION—Why We Are Here:

We are here to discuss some of the problems of our community, our state, and our nation with a view toward finding out how living in communities like ours may become more interesting and more secure. And we expect to have a good time.

We will use three simple methods for accomplishing these goals.

First, the right kind of discussion. This means objective, friendly discussion that does not dodge the facts or real issues, but which is not a debate. It is cooperative thinking rather than competitive thinking. Can we do it? Can we take as well as give in this effort not to win an argument but to find the answer to a problem? In this form of discussion problems are stated, issues declared, values formulated, solutions suggested, policies recommended. This is a method of preparing for action that will not collapse because it was taken without sufficient study.

Second, cooperative research will be our method for digging out pertinent facts concerning the problems we are studying. This will give us a factual and fundamental basis for discussion. Necessary research committees have already been suggested. They should be made up of people from all walks of life in the community.

Our third method will be objective thinking. This is closely related to the first method and in the words of Thomas Huxley means, "sitting down before the facts like a little child." It implies drawing logical conclusions based on research and discussion. The objective person is fact-minded; he seeks all the facts that seem relevant and which are available; he tries to draw clear and honest conclusions from the facts themselves. He is not swayed by politics and pressure tactics for the personal gain of one group over another.

In beginning this study we should analyze the composition of our community as to nationality, occupation, religion, politics, extent of education, income levels, percentage of homes with electricity, telephones, automobiles, etc. In general what kind of people are we, economically, socially, educationally? How do we compare in these respects with other towns in our state?

Why do I live in this community? Is it from choice? Why? Is it for other reasons? How would I like to see this community changed within reason? Write down the answer and compare it with an answer written after finishing ten weeks of this study.

Communities, especially in America, are constantly changing. They may become more closely integrated, or they may disintegrate for want of neighborliness, or they may simply dry up for want of opportunities to earn a living and enjoy life.

Is our community changing in any important ways? How does it differ from what it was twenty years ago? In population? In wealth? In the occupations of its members? In the ages of its people? In ways of living? In its thinking? In other ways? What are the causes of these changes?

Communities differ. Some are metropolitan, some are open-country neighborhoods. Or they may be classified according to their dominant activity, such as agricultural, commercial, industrial, educational, or political. But whatever the type, the community is significant for it is the stage on which all man's activities occur.

How does our community differ from the two nearest neighboring communities? Consider differences in size, wealth, kinds of services—including educational and governmental—occupations of its members, racial origins, religious backgrounds, other ways. How is it related to the two nearest communities, economically, socially, educationally?

Now follows the first of the four research problems.

Research Problem I

Prepare brief histories of different aspects of our community:
  1. History of the churches in our community;
  2. History of the schools in our community;
  3. Business and economic history of our community;
  4. Significant men and women in the history of our community;
  5. Other important historical aspects of our community to be named by the chairman.

Prepare a map of our community, showing zones. Indicate not only the present features, but also some of those of the past as suggested by the above histories.

The group chairman should appoint one researcher to prepare each of these histories and to have them ready for presentation to the group for discussion at the meeting two weeks hence. The chairman should also appoint one or two persons to prepare the community map.

The chairman should now appoint the question committees and discussion leader to prepare the next week's work.

SECOND SECTION—Our Town and Its People:

Our community is made up of the families that live here. Anything that weakens these families weakens our whole community. So let's examine our families. How many families do we have? How many have been here ten years or longer? How many were started here? How do we compare in these respects with other communities in our state?

Within the past fifty years family life in America has undergone profound changes. Children are living away from their families more than ever before. Modern families are smaller. They produce less for themselves. In many respects they do not mean as much as they did in grandfather's day. How have the families in our community changed in the last two generations? How many children are there in the average modern family as compared with those of grandfather's day? How are people more dependent, and how are they less dependent, on the family now than before? What effect do these changes have on community stability?

One of the most important elements affecting the stability of our community is human companionship. That feeling of belonging to a group of people who know each other, understand each other, and are interested in each other, seems to be a necessary part of human happiness and security. Without this our community would be cold and devoid of feeling. Probably the major source of wholesome companionship is the church, and yet it is doubtful if today the church plays as important a role in community life as it used to. The extent of the church's vitality certainly has an effect on the stability of our community. Is the church in our community more or less important now than it used to be? In what ways? Why?

The school is usually thought of as a place for young people only, but it should be a place where education is extended to old and young alike, through adult classes, recreation, discussion groups, and hobby courses. With strong community backing, the school could become a real community center and lift the level of life and education for the whole town. It is doubtful if most towns get as much return on their school investment as they should. To what extent does our community permit the school to enter into its total community life? To what extent do our schools seek to engage in community life and education? Is this also true of the library, of the church? Are there any recommendations in regard to the work of our schools and churches in the cultural and educational life of our community?

Recreation should be an important part of our community life, but in America recreation has often taken the form of commercialized entertainment. Most of us have become mere spectators. This kind of recreation may be relaxing, but does not provide an opportunity for creative self-expression. When a town forgets how to play, and its people fail to participate in creative recreation, it is likely to become dull and uninteresting. In what ways does our community depend on commercialized amusement? In what ways on play or participative recreation? Which of the two is the more important in our community? Can play opportunities, both for young and old, be increased? How?

The chairman should now appoint the discussion leader and question committees for next week's work.

THIRD SECTION—Our Town and Our Work:

Certainly the stability of our community depends largely on the ability of our people to earn a living.

The work that we do is governed by several things.

There is the geographical environment, including climate, soil, and other resources. America has seen many communities that failed to adjust their economy to the natural environment. How is the work in our town affected by our natural environment?

What has been the culture and history in our region as regards earning a living, and what effects has this had on our present economy?

With what occupations and skills are the people in our community acquainted? List those not being practiced as well as those which are being practiced. How do these differ in different communities? What ones are similar in all?

The relations of our town to the rest of the state and to the nation are another great influence on our work. This includes the geographical relation of our town to large markets. Freight rates penalize manufacturers in interior states of the South and West, but favor the shipment of raw materials. What effects do these influences have on our local economy?

Mass production and modern agricultural machinery have changed our work a great deal in recent years. This productive power means that unless we find new occupations, new markets, and new ways of using what we produce, there will not always be enough employment to go around. This is a serious threat to our small communities and our democracy. In solving this problem people in our small communities are faced by two alternatives. They can move to the cities and let our small towns gradually die. Or they can develop new small industries and occupations, and produce more for home use and local markets. (This problem should warrant detailed attention by the study group's standing committee on small industries.)

Has the character of work changed in our community? What occupations have gained? What ones have declined? Why? What occupations are more efficient? What ones are less? What changes in quantity and efficiency have taken place in housework?

Diversified production for local use carried to the full extent of its practical limits would help greatly toward stabilizing the home and small community, lead to greater economic security, and strengthen our democratic way of life. Modern technology with its mechanical devices, its electric motors and gasoline engines, has made small-scale manufacturing and diversified production for local use increasingly practical. There are many examples of successful small-scale industries such as charcoal making, food dehydration, cheese making, pottery, and others, that have been made possible by the development of modern technology and portable power devices.

What relation does this problem of production of goods at home have to community survival, family life, health, birth rates, domestic happiness, etc.?

Have there been any changes in our community in the kind and amount of goods and services produced for use in the home or local community? Give details. What are the main causes of these changes? What is gained by them? What is lost?

There is, of course, a limit as to how far we can go in local production for home use, but there is also a limit as to how much our democracy can stand the strain of centralized industrial power and financial control, with many people employed by a few, and the consequent dying off of our small communities.

What goods or services does our community produce for sale? What is our chief product? What are some of our other products? About what proportion of the people in our community work for wages or salaries? About what proportion are in business for themselves? What proportion produce for local use? Don't forget housewives. What proportion are unemployed?

These problems concerning the work done in our community affect our institutions, such as our churches, our schools, our lodges and clubs, as well as the general cultural quality of our lives. They affect deeply the quality of living in our community. How has the life in our community been affected by these changes? Is our community as closely integrated as it once was? Is it as much a community? Discuss after reviewing the work of the first section.

There should now be a report on Research Problem I, outlined in the first section. The reports on the historical aspects of our community should be followed by criticism and discussion. The community map should be shown in connection with these reports.

A committee should now be appointed for Research Problem II.

Research Problem II

Study five characteristic families of our community and estimate for each family for one year as accurately as possible the following:

1. What proportion of the goods used in the home are produced in the home? What goods are they? How much are there? How about their cost?

2. What proportion of the goods used in the home are purchased from outside? What goods are they? How about their cost?

3. What proportion of the services used in the home are produced by persons in the family? What are they?

4. What proportion of the services used in the home are purchased from persons not in the family? What are they?

5. Can you suggest any practical ways in which these five families could increase home production for use?

The chairman should appoint a committee of five researchers, probably one from each family to be studied, to make these studies and assemble a report, which should be presented for discussion at the meeting two weeks hence.

The chairman should now appoint the question committee and discussion leader for next week's work.

FOURTH SECTION—Our Town and Our State:

The productive life of our people and the quality of our living are closely related to the resources of our region. If we know our region and adapt our way of life to its characteristics our people will live better.

Our community is one of many that make up our state. We ought to know something about these communities. What percentage of them are urban (over 2500) and what percentage are rural? Is our state predominately rural or urban? What are the advantages and disadvantages of rural life? Urban life?

What effect does the distance between communities have on the life of our state? To what extent are the communities in our state related socially, economically, and politically?

To what extent does life in our state vary from time to time in population, prosperity, and stability in general? What about our own community in these respects? Give reasons.

Are there any geographical variations between the various sections of our state and if so, what are they? Characterize each region geographically, economically, socially.

What are some of the critical factors involved in the welfare of towns in the various parts of our state? Rainfall? Markets: Size? Stability? Diversity? Raw materials? Transportation and freight rates? Other critical factors?

What are the important economic and social relationships between the different sections of our state? Are any of these various sections more related to other states than to the rest of our own state? Discuss this question in respect to transportation, markets, education, newspapers, radio, recreation, sports, art, social life, governmental services, etc.

Where does our community fit into the state-wide picture? What is produced in our community for use in the state; out of the state? Where does it go? What do we use in our community that is produced outside the state, inside the state? Where does it come from? Think of amusement and education as well as other products and services.

Regional development in any one of our forty-eight states is likely to be associated with regional patterns of production and consumption. If not carried to extremes home-centered, community-centered, regional-centered production for local consumption is likely to make for a stable and wholesome society. Under such conditions people are likely to be more responsible socially and morally. They will have a richer culture and a quality of living that is their own.

At this meeting there should be a progress report from each of the standing committees.

Discussion leader and question committees should be appointed for the fifth section.

FIFTH SECTION—Our State, A Place to Live:

Most of us are proud of our state. And we should be. It should have a certain personal meaning to us that makes it different from other states. One of the things that makes up the character of life in our state is its social and economic history. The more we know and understand that history, the more we will appreciate our state and enjoy living in it.

Several good books should be obtained on the social and economic history of our state and a report prepared by the question committee. We should discuss this history with a view toward discovering its effect on life today. This study should include the period of exploration and settlement, and the development of culture, farming, business, and industry.

Are there any remainders of Indian life in our community? Can the work of our state's early settlers and former residents be detected in our community? Are there any ways in which their customs have affected life in our community today? Our political outlook? Our business practices? Our moral, religious, and educational standards? How has farm life in our state affected our attitude toward people, our recreational interests? In what ways have the customs and life of our community changed? What brought about these changes?

What is meant by "modernism" as found in our town? What advantages does it have? What disadvantages? What might be done in our community to help cherish the traditions of our state?

There should now be a report on Research Problem II.

A committee should now be appointed for Research Problem III.

Research Problem III

Prepare a community calendar showing the seasonal activities in the field, shop, and home.

1. Appoint a committee of men to prepare a table showing the different work activities in the community at different times of year.
2. Appoint a committee of women to prepare a table showing the different home activities at different times of year.
3. Appoint a mixed committee to prepare a table showing the seasonal activities in recreation, play, and cultural life.

The chairman should now appoint the discussion leader and question committees for next week's work.

SIXTH SECTION—Our State and Our Nation:

A strong regional consciousness is healthy for our communities, but no one region is complete within itself. It is all forty-eight of our states together that make America the land we love. To be really good Americans we should know something about every state in our nation and appreciate the people in them and their ways of living.

For this section's work we should obtain a map of the United States, classify the country into regions, and list all the states in each region. Each region should be characterized in the following ways:

1. Area, climate, outstanding natural features, and natural resources.
2. Population, age of settlement, stability, birth and death rates, percentage of communities that are urban, and percentage that are rural.
3. Relative wealth, standards of living, financial influence.
4. Proportion that is industrial, and proportion that is agricultural. What are the chief products?
5. Culture, recreation, amusement, education, religion, racial groups, and nationality.
6. Dress, customs, traditions, political and economic attitudes. To what extent is regional consciousness developed?

What relations does our region have with each of the others? Financial? Trade? Religious, educational, and other cultural relations? Travel? Migration? In what ways does our region compete with the others? What do we get from each of the other regions of America? What do they get from us?

The chairman should now appoint the discussion leader and question committees for next week's work.

SEVENTH SECTION—The Future of Our State:

The future of our state is partly in our own hands and partly subject to conditions over which we have no control. We have no control over the weather, the price of agricultural products that we grow, and the price of many things that we must buy for use in our production and consumption. If we recognize these limitations and plan for them, adjust our economy and ways of living to them, we can in a measure become free of them.

One important way to make our families and small communities more stable and secure is to build a way of life and production that is not so dependent on distant markets and the services of people whom we never see or know. If families can produce more of what they use and if small communities can become to a greater extent their own market for some of the goods and services they produce, those families and communities will be to that extent less dependent on the fluctuations of outside production and prices over which they have no control.

Stability gained in this way is, however, subject to two conditions that should not be forgotten: First, that modern methods and technology must be used in home and local production. Otherwise the cost will be too high and standards of living will decline. The other condition is that home and village production for use must not be pushed too far. There is an optimum amount of production for use in the family and community. However, most regions of the country have hardly begun to reach this optimum.

What parts of our state are more favorable to this home production type of economy and society? What parts are less favorable to it? Why?

Many experts believe that the future of America's rural areas, particularly in the western and southern states, depends largely on the development of products and services, including entertainment and recreation, that can be produced and utilized within the region. This kind of planning would be less dependent on large-scale capital investments, and would take advantage of raw materials and markets close at home. Such an economy would be less subject to the shocks of national and world crises. People would not have to rely so much on a single industry, nor be limited by the policies of that industry, as they are in many areas, such as Montana. This, in a word, means planning for regional production and regional markets.

If such planning is desirable for our state, how should it be done? What agencies, private and public, are in a position to give helpful advice? What agencies might be indifferent or opposed? Make a list of things that could be produced in our state for use in our state. Make a list of things in our state that people in the surrounding region might want.

The future of our state depends chiefly on the people in it. The first aspect of this problem is biological. Will enough people be born in the state or migrate to it to maintain a proper balance of population? Or is our state becoming overpopulated? What problems are posed by these conditions?

The second aspect of our state's future is economic. It refers to the problems of making a living. Have the industrial possibilities, preferably on a community or regional basis, really been tapped in our state? For example, are the service industries (small repair shops, machine shops, food shops, etc.) as well developed in our community as they might be? What is being planned for the recreational and tourist "industries"? What plans have been made, or could be made, for improved methods in agriculture and forestry leading toward a greater degree of balanced, diversified production and sustained yields? Do we have natural resources that are not being utilized? Do we have any waste products that could be put to use?

The third aspect in the future of our state is appreciative. Is life in our state interesting enough, valuable and full enough, to justify people living here? This includes many things such as education, religion, the arts, recreation, friendships, freedom, health.

Human values and worthwhileness of living in our state are fully as important as the economic or biological factors in planning for the future. History shows that the more prosperous and educated people become the more they tend to leave their small communities. This is due to the fact that people in rural areas have been taught to look elsewhere for values that they should create in their own towns. Since the life and vitality of our state is tied inexorably to our rural regions, the future of our state depends on our power to make life in the small community rewarding and significant to those in it.

Select the outstanding problem for planning in our community. Is it the result of changes in markets, education, transportation, recreational opportunities, or what? Are specialized agencies needed? (Educational institutions, extension service, state welfare service, public health, federal agencies, etc.) Is the cooperation of these agencies necessary?

Group planning is no different from individual planning in many important ways. It means that people having the same problem get together and identify that problem, examine its causes, consider various methods for its solution, work together for its solution, and periodically survey the results with an eye to improvements. No problem is insoluble if it is stated correctly, and many problems are unsolved because even though correctly defined their solutions are blocked by short-sighted and often selfish interests. All too often our planning measures are not big enough for our problems. Yet they must not become too big for them. But the future of our state depends on how fundamental is our planning, and how well it utilizes the natural resources that we have, physical, economic, and human.

There should now be a report on Research Problem III.

The chairman should now appoint the discussion leader and question committees for next week's work.

EIGHTH SECTION—The Future of Our Town in Relation to Its People:

A residential suburb on the outskirts of a great city produces almost nothing in proportion to what it consumes. It blossoms if the city propers. It wilts if the city slumps. A mill or mining town consumes very little in proportion to what it produces. Its fortunes rise and fall with the market of its principal product. Towns of both these types are usually unstable, their life and culture without roots, because there is no balance between their production and consumption. When the people of a community can always produce enough to earn a living, and at the same time find in the community enough to satisfy their desires for consumption, that community will be stable and permanent. It will have a future.

To what extent has our community this balance between the production of goods and services, and the ability to provide things that our people wish to consume and enjoy? What are our needs in this respect?

Diversification of production is one key to community stabilization.

If the community is primarily agricultural, it should be balanced and diversified, if possible, by some manufacturing and service industries. There is almost no end to the examples that could be mentioned, some of which are soy-bean mills, strawboard factories, dehydration and distillation plants.

If the town depends on one large-scale industry, diversification should be sought by introducing some small-scale industries, services, and small-scale agriculture.

We have already discussed the fact that in many ways science has made small-scale industry in the modern home or small town practical and efficient. If this knowledge is utilized, and the new production planned primarily for local or regional markets, it will have important social consequences in helping to enrich and stabilize the life of our families and village communities.

Are there any practical ways in which the agricultural and industrial production of our community can be further diversified? In what ways can the land be put to more diversified use, particularly in reference to family consumption or local consumption? Are there small-scale industries that might be developed on a practical basis in our community? Name and discuss them.

The ability to produce wealth is not the sole requirement for stable family and community life. Production must be coordinated with the desire to consume and enjoy the things that make living a pleasure. If a community can neither produce these things nor buy them, its people almost certainly will move to a place where life is more interesting and worth while. Thus, it is mainly for two reasons that people leave the small communities of America. First, is the inability to make the grade economically, and second, when a person becomes prosperous or educated he looks for a place that offers a higher standard of living and greater cultural opportunity.

What do we produce in our community for enjoyment and worth while living? How could we increase our production of such things? What about our community education service? Is it merely a program of courses, grades, and classes, devoted to people of certain age levels; or are its educational and cultural services directed toward all the people of our community? Do our churches adequately participate in community educational and cultural services?

There should now be a progress report from each of the standing committees.

The chairman should now appoint the committee for Research Problem IV, to be ready for presentation two weeks hence.

Research Problem IV

List the names of all individuals or families who have left our community within the last three years to stay. Tabulate the reasons for their leaving, so far as can be determined. Interpret these reasons whether due to increasing poverty or increasing wealth or education. If none left, give interpretation as to the reason.

Appoint the leader and question committees for next week's discussion.

NINTH SECTION—How to Make Life Better in Our Town:

One modern technique for stabilizing our community is cooperation. This means the voluntary pooling of effort for mutual benefit. A family usually practices cooperation. Lodges, Rotary, and other service clubs are cooperative organizations. Our study group is another example. The idea of cooperation may be extended to the purchase and marketing of goods to consumers, as in consumer cooperatives. Producer cooperatives handle the storage and marketing of goods produced by the group, such as wheat, fruit, or milk. Some of these cooperatives have become so large and centralized they have lost their original cooperative character. This we should guard against, for any time an organization, political or otherwise, becomes dominant or an end in itself, its members lose in freedom, and the organization becomes more harmful than beneficial.

The success of cooperatives depends on whether they can give better services than other organizations, and on the skill of their management. Cooperatives also depend on a fairly stable and informed community in which to operate, and are likely to be more successful in a small town.

Are there any consumer or producer cooperatives in our town? If so, describe them. What are their advantages and disadvantages? Do we have need for such cooperatives? Why? Discuss the whole problem as to need, difficulty, management, probability of success, etc. Should we or should we not have cooperatives here?

A second technique for stabilizing our community is to gain more direct control over the means by which we earn our living. We have discussed this important matter before, but two points should be re-emphasized. First, it means more production for home use and local markets. Second, it means that small-scale production must be done efficiently through the use of modern technical methods. In this way much small-scale production can be even more efficient than mass production.

A good modern educational system is a third technique for stabilizing our community. Such an educational system should not limit its efforts to young people, but should direct its services toward all the people in the community. It should not be designed to drive young people away from their home community by training them to look to the big city for success, but should teach them how to find success in their own community. It should be dedicated to making our community so productive, both in terms of earning a living and the enjoyment of it, that people will find outlet at home for their abilities, and stability for their plans. They will wish to remain in their home town.

Draw up an outline for a community-centered educational system here. Like a church, or a water system, such an educational system should be serving all of the people in the community all of the time.

A fourth method of improving our town is to develop further the advantages of living in a small community. As a place to live and raise children the modern small town has certain resources immeasurably superior to anything the great cities can offer. The best thing for human beings is other human beings, and it is only in the small community that a full and wholesome relationship between human beings is usually possible. Human relationships under big city conditions tend to be fragmentary, scattered, unstable, extensive in range, but shallow and rapidly shifting in content.

In a small community the expressive arts, or the humanities as they are sometimes called, can have a far deeper significance than elsewhere. If the small community becomes a center for participation in music, drama, dancing, poetry, arts and crafts, and other such interesting activities, it can become immeasurably significant to those who live there. It is significant because these activities then emerge, not from specialists working for pay to entertain large audiences of spectators, but from a community of people who know each other from working together, from playing together, and from actually participating together in the creation of their own art, amusement, and entertainment. This is vital community living.

What resources does our community have in the arts? This means not how many professional musicians or literary people may live here, but what opportunities can be created for our own participation in artistic or expressive activity. Is there a place for amateurs? Is there an opportunity here for a community chorus? A community orchestra? Community drama? Hobby groups? A community flower display or gardens? A community fair? A community Thanksgiving dinner? Draw up a rough plan of activities of this sort that might be possible and appropriate to our community—and that we would enjoy doing.

It might be worth while to work out a tentative program for one year's community cultural events adapted to our particular interests. For example: January, New Year's Celebration and Winter Sports Day; February, Washington-Lincoln Dinner and Home Orchestra Concert; March, Community Drama Day; April, Singing Night; May, Garden Day; June, Graduation Day and Chorus; July, Community Picnic; August, Ice Cream Night; September, School and Teachers' Night; October, Hunter's Day and Game Dinner; November, Harvest Festival and Thanksgiving Dinner; December, Christmas Chorus and Community Tree.

The chairman should appoint the leader and question committees for next week's discussion.

TENTH SECTION—What Have We Accomplished:

During the weeks we have spent in this study course there are at least three things that we should have accomplished. First, we should have developed a greater ability to carry on discussion without undue emotion or prejudice, and for the sake of solving a problem, not of winning a debate. We should know how to cooperate better with other people, and should understand better the mental characteristics of our group.

How much have we accomplished in this first direction? Can we discuss problems more objectively and pertinently than we could ten weeks ago? Do we understand the intellectual outlook of our group better than we did when we started?

Second, we should have learned a good many facts about our community and our state. We should understand more clearly some of our basic problems and their causes, and should have a clearer idea of how to deal with them. If we have accomplished this, our stature as citizens and our capacity for constructive action have been increased, and our time has been profitably spent.

Has our factual knowledge about our community and our state been increased? Is our understanding of basic problems any clearer? What problems in particular? Have we arrived at any more definite decisions as to how these problems should be dealt with? What decisions have we made? Is there any greater clarity in our minds as to what action should be taken? Compare these answers with the answer that was written to a similar question in the first section.

Our third accomplishment should be to have had a good time. Really significant activity should combine the useful with the enjoyable far more than it usually does, and that is something our study group should have done.

Have we enjoyed this study group? Has it made this synthesis of the useful and the enjoyable?

The chairman should now call for a report on Research Problem IV.

Standing committees should make their final reports and recommendations, and appropriate discussion should follow.

During this study course we have been concerned with the enrichment and stabilization of our families and our community. Our approach to these goals has been through a consideration of the social and economic problems that have arisen out of modern civilization. Implicit in all of these discussions has been the belief that a good life is a whole life in which all the normal function of living, the biological, the economic, the social, the intellectual, the appreciative and spiritual, are coordinated with each other, and in which all have opportunity for expression.

This concludes our ten-week study course. The Montana Study followed this course with a second series of meetings to discuss and practice "the humanities" as they are found in the arts and appreciative life of Montana. It would be highly desirable if other groups would follow this same procedure. In such a course the members would read and discuss some of their regional novels, speeches, plays, and essays. They would study regional paintings, craft work, music, and the like, and try to find in them those human affirmations and values that were discussed in the first study. Perhaps the group can bring some of its creative people to the meetings or, better still, perhaps the members can do a good deal of creation for themselves for the sheer enjoyment of doing, as the people in several Montana towns did through their community dramas.

In most cases the study groups in Montana took steps after completing their initial ten-week study to initiate action through which the recommendations of their various committees and the solutions to problems studied could be carried out. A permanent organization for this purpose could function either as a direct action group as in Conrad, or for the purpose of mobilizing community-wide support behind action to be taken by already established organizations as in Libby.

Acknowledgments

Research and investigations connected with writing this book have involved more than 5000 miles of travel in Montana, and personal interviews with hundreds of people both inside and outside that state. In the process I have examined large volumes of memoranda, correspondence, reports, and miscellaneous written material including the files of The Montana Study; files concerning varied aspects of the University of Montana and the Montana State Legislature; files of other state organizations, federal agencies, private institutions; and the personal files of numerous private individuals, most of whom cannot for various reasons be named herein. To those who have made these files available and have helped me obtain the information from which this book was written, I express my appreciation.

For the point of view, the selection of material, and the conclusions that have gone into the preparation of this work no one other than myself is responsible, though obviously my opinions have developed from a great variety of sources, most of them individuals in the communities where Montana Study groups were organized.

To the nearly 300 people in these communities who have given me the benefit of their own knowledge and experience no word of gratitude could acknowledge the indebtedness that I feel. These are the people who have truly made The Montana Study function; they are not only familiar with its program—they experienced it. And I believe that in the final analysis they are most competent to judge its achievements. It is for this reason that I have concentrated my research among these people, and in forming the point of view and the conclusions stated in this book I have drawn most heavily from their testimony.

I regret that space limitations have not permitted a detailed account of operations in all the small communities where study groups were organized, or a complete listing of the names of the many civic-minded Americans who participated either directly or indirectly in this group work; it must suffice to say here that it is what these people have done and the splendid cooperation they have given me that have made the writing of this book possible.

As for people living outside the communities where these study groups functioned I am particularly indebted to Baker Brownell, professor of philosophy at Northwestern University, who was chiefly responsible for developing The Montana Study, and who, without any attempt to direct or dictate the handling of this book, has given me the rich benefit of his broad personal knowledge and experience. Without his generous assistance and patient counseling my task would have been infinitely more difficult.

I acknowledge a large debt of gratitude to Joseph Kinsey Howard, author and newspaperman, whose cordial willingness to cooperate and whose large store of knowledge concerning both The Montana Study and the State of Montana have been of invaluable assistance.

For considerable help and information necessary to the writing of this account I am heavily indebted to Ernest O. Melby, dean of education at New York University, whose remarkable vision caused The Montana Study to be founded; to David H. Stevens, director of The Humanities for The Rockefeller Foundation; to George A. Selke, chancellor of the University of Montana; to Dorothy Green, executive secretary of the University of Montana; to Guy M. Brandborg, supervisor of the Bitter Root National Forest, and member of the State Board of Education; to Bert B. Hansen, professor of English at Montana State University, and associate in community work for The Montana Study; and to Ruth W. Robinson, who was acting director of the Study during its third year of operations.

Other people in Montana outside the towns where study groups were organized, and from whom I received courteous assistance and valuable information include: Charles Baldwin, attorney and member, State Board of Education; Harry Billings, managing editor, *The People's Voice*; R. V. Bottomly, justice, State Supreme Court, former Attorney General, and member, State Board of Education; H. S. Bruce, retired newspaperman; Merrill G. Burlingame, professor of history, Montana State College; Don Chapman, president, Montana Farmers Union; Andrew C. Cogswell, director of public services, Montana State University; Edmund L. Freeman, professor of English, Montana State University; Roy H. Glover, western general counsel, Anaconda Copper Mining Company; P. D. Hanson, regional forester, U. S.

Forest Service; Carl F. Kraenzel, associate professor of rural sociology, Montana State College; Joseph Kramer, associate professor of Botany, Montana State University; Axel G. Lindh, assistant regional forester, Division of Timber Management, U. S. Forest Service; Jerome G. Locke, engineer; James W. Maucker, dean, School of Education, Montana State University; James A. McCain, president, Montana State University; Anne McDonnell, assistant librarian, Historical Society of Montana Library; Harold G. Merriam, chairman, Division of Humanities, Montana State University; Lee Metcalf, justice, State Supreme Court, former state legislator; Melvin S. Morris, associate professor of forestry, Montana State University; Leona J. Peterson, secretary for The Montana Study; Emmet J. Riley, president, Carroll College, and member, State Board of Education; Joseph W. Severy, chairman, Division of Biological Sciences, Montana State University; Branson G. Stevenson, state manager for Socony-Vacuum Oil Company; Tom Stout, managing editor, *The Billings Gazette*, and former state legislator; C. J. Taber, lumberman, and former state legislator; Harold Tascher, associate professor of social administration, founder and head of the social work laboratory, Montana State University; W. Preston "Luke" Wright, capitol reporter and staff writer for the *Great Falls Tribune*. There are many others.

And for valuable assistance in many ways connected with this account I acknowledge appreciation to George Melton Savage, associate professor of English, University of Washington.

R.W.P.

Seattle, Washington
June, 1949

Bibliography

Published Articles, Papers, Reports, and Miscellaneous
Materials Concerning The Montana Study and its Projects

RECORDS OF ACTIVITIES

Day Book of The Montana Study with day-by-day report of all lectures, conferences, travels of staff members, etc.

Minutes, Montana Study Liaison Committee, Montana State University, Missoula, January 9, 1947.

The Montana Committee, report and minutes of organizational meeting of The Montana Study state-wide advisory committee at Bozeman, Montana, February 2, 1945.

Program of lectures and conferences by O. E. Baker, Arthur E. Morgan, and Mrs. Arthur E. Morgan, in Billings, Bozeman, Missoula, Great Falls, Hamilton. A special project of The Montana Study.

Progress Report of The Montana Study from September 1, 1944, to August 31, 1945.

Progress Report of The Montana Study from September 1, 1945, to August 31, 1946.

Progress Report of The Montana Study from September 1, 1946, to July 19, 1947.

ARTICLES AND BOOKS

BROWNELL, BAKER. "The College and the Community," *Journal of Higher Education,* June, 1946.

———. "The College—A Report On a Failure," *Free America,* Autumn, 1945.

———. "The Community Drama in Adult Education," *The Teachers College Journal,* September, 1946.

———. "Community Drama in Montana," *Wisconsin Idea Theater Quarterly,* December, 1948.

————. "The County Newspaper," *The Montana High School Editor*, October, 1944.

————. "Education in the Human Community," *The Saturday Review of Literature*, September 16, 1944.

————. "Four Suggestions for Library Community Work," *Montana State Library Association Bulletin*, November-December, 1944.

————. *Life in Montana—Series II*, an outline for community study groups designed as a follow-up of Series I study guide.

————. "The Montana Project," *Recreation*, June, 1946.

————. "The Montana Study," *School and Society*, December 16, 1944, reprinted in *Montana Education*, February, 1945.

————. "The Montana Study Groups," *State Government*, March, 1946.

————. "A Philosophy of Recreation," *Community Service News*, January-February, 1949.

————. "A Project in Educational Reorientation," *Religious Education*, July-August, 1945.

————. "Social Implications of Forestry in the Inland Empire," *Northwest Science*, February, 1946.

————. "Technology and the Human Limit," *Journal of Higher Education*, March, 1949.

————. "Three Corrupting Principles of College Life," *Mountain Life and Work*, Winter, 1946. Council of Southern Mountain Workers, Berea, Kentucky.

————. "The Value of the Humanities," *Journal of Higher Education*, November, 1945.

————. "War and the Human Community," *Learning and World Peace*, Eighth Symposium, The Conference on Science, Philosophy and Religion, New York, 1948.

BROWNELL, BAKER; HOWARD, JOSEPH KINSEY; and MEADOWS, PAUL. *Life in Montana: as Seen in Lonepine, a Small Community*, for use by community study groups—Series I. Published by The Montana Study, University Press, Missoula, 1945.

HANSEN, BERT. "Community Unification Through Dramaturgy," *Players Magazine*, July-August, 1946.

————. "Darby, Montana, Looks at Itself," *Adult Education Bulletin*, April, 1946, reprinted in *Humanistic Values for a Free Society*, Denver, 1947.

————. "A Project in Community Education," *The Journal of General Education*, January, 1947.

————. "Sociodrama in a Small-Community Therapy Program," *Sociatry*, March, 1947.

———. "Sociodrama in a Speech Communication Program," *Western Speech*, April, 1947.

———. "'A Tale of the Bitter Root': Pageantry as Sociodrama," *The Quarterly Journal of Speech*, April, 1947.

———. "The Use of Sociodrama as a Factor in Community Integration," *Sociology and Social Research*, September-October, 1947.

HOWARD, JOSEPH KINSEY. "Community is Stressed in Indian Education," *The Great Falls Sunday Tribune*, January 28, 1945.

———. "Cultural Handicaps in the Northwest," *The Yale Review*, Spring, 1947.

———. *Montana Margins: A State Anthology*. Yale University Press, New Haven, November, 1946.

MEADOWS, PAUL. "The High School Journalist Reports on the Community," *The Montana High School Editor*, February, 1945.

ROBINSON, RUTH W. "Community-Centered Education for Montana Adults," *Montana Education*, January, 1947.

———. "Community Study—Community Planning," *Montana Educational Journal*, April, 1946.

SMITH, FRANK H. "Folk Dancing in Montana," *The Country Dancer*, Spring, 1947.

———. "Good-Bye to Montana," *The Country Dancer*, Summer, 1947.

MISCELLANEOUS DOCUMENTS

BAKER, O. E. "The Conservation of the Family," an address given at various points in Montana as a special project for The Montana Study; also "The Family, the Church and the State (Government);" also "Population Trends, National, State, Local," July, 1945.

HANSEN, BERT. "An Evaluation of The Montana Study," an undated typewritten report.

"How We Live in Montana," a study plan and Montana bibliography for inclusion in the state high school course of study in the humanities, social sciences, and correlated fields, developed by Ruth W. Robinson, Dean Walter Anderson, Professor Lucia B. Mirrielees, in cooperation with The Montana Study and the Montana State University Summer Workshop of 1945.

KAUFMAN, HAROLD F. and LOIS C. *Toward the Stabilization & Enrichment of a Forest Community*, a joint study by The Montana Study and U. S. Forest Service. Published by U. S. Forest Service, Missoula, 1946.

KRUG, EDWARD A. "The Public School and Community Improvement," a report on an inquiry carried out by the School of Education, Montana State University, as a special project for The Montana Study.

MEADOWS, PAUL. "The People of Montana," a report to The Montana Study, 1945.

———. "Regional Characteristics of Montana," a report to The Montana Study, 1945.

"Montana Handicrafts: Directory of Montana Craftsmen, 1947," prepared by The Montana Study under the direction of Ruth W. Robinson.

Montana Study Groups Association Bulletin, The Montana Study, Missoula, November, 1946.

SELKE, GEORGE A. "Organization and Procedures of Montana Study," a typewritten report and evaluation, Office of the Chancellor, University of Montana, Helena, March 12, 1948.

"Short Courses for Community Leaders," prepared by The Montana Study.

"Suggested Topics for Training in Community Leadership," prepared by The Montana Study, under the direction of Ruth W. Robinson.

LONEPINE MONTANA STUDY GROUP

BRAS, MRS. R. J. "Goods and Services Produced at Home and Purchased by Five Lonepine Families," a research paper.

DONDANVILLE, L. G. "The Economic and Business Development of Lonepine," a research paper.

GANNAWAY, EDNA B. "The Indian As We Have Known Him in the Little Bitter Root Valley," a research paper.

———. "Newspaper History of the Lonepine Region," a research paper published in *The Camas Hot Springs Exchange,* Hot Springs, Montana.

HALVERSON, F. A. "When Our Boys Come Home What Can They Do?" a research paper.

HILLMAN, F. M. "Effects of Irrigation on Agricultural Customs in Lonepine," a research paper.

———. "History of Lonepine Irrigation," a research paper.

HOWSER, C. P. "Persons Who Have Left Lonepine in Recent Years and Why," a research paper.

———. "Significant Men and Women in the History of Our Community," a research paper.

LEE, F. C. "The Families of the Lonepine Community," a research paper.

"Lonepine Historical Drama," by the people of Lonepine, Montana, assisted by Bert Hansen.

Minutes and Committee Reports, Lonepine Montana Study Group, John McCoy, Secretary.

VON SEGEN, MRS. W. W. "Lonepine Church History," a research paper.

DARBY MONTANA STUDY GROUP

"Darby Looks at Itself," a community pageant-drama by the people of Darby, Montana, assisted by Bert Hansen.

Minutes and Committee Reports, Darby Montana Study Group, Pauline Bibler, Secretary.

STEVENSVILLE MONTANA STUDY GROUP

Minutes and Committee Reports, Stevensville Montana Study Group, Esther McFadgen, Secretary.

O'HARE, ED. "Land Utilization," a research paper concerning the Stevensville community.

"A Study Guide on Land Use, 1946," by members of the Stevensville Montana Study Group.

"A Tale of the Bitter Root," a community pageant-drama by the people of Stevensville, Montana, assisted by Bert Hansen.

CONRAD MONTANA STUDY GROUP

Minutes and Committee Reports, Conrad Education and Recreation Association, Jerry Conrad, Secretary.

Minutes and Committee Reports, Conrad Montana Study Group, Veta E. Marsh, Secretary.

LEWISTOWN MONTANA STUDY GROUP

ATTWELL, BETTY. "Significant Men and Women of Our Community," a research paper.

LAY, CONNIE. "History of the Schools of Lewistown," a research paper.

Minutes and Committee Reports, Lewistown Montana Study Group, Almeda Weiser, Secretary.

MOORE, TOM. "Echoes from the Mountains," a play produced at Lewistown, Montana, as "Echoes from the Eighties."

SWAN, ELIZABETH. "A Brief History of the First Catholic Pioneers of Lewistown, Montana," a research paper.

WEISER, ALMEDA. "A Summary of the Churches in Lewistown," a research paper.

WEISER, EARL. "Business and Economic History of Lewistown," a research paper.

ZOOK, ANNABELLE F. "Homestead and Busted," a play.

LIBBY MONTANA STUDY GROUP

AHLSKOG, HOWARD E. "Annual Wild Life Report," a research paper.
FICKE, H. O. "Report on Forest Products, Lincoln County and Troy-Libby Working Circles," a research paper.
GILLESPIE, O. L. "Libby School History," a research paper.
LeDUC, LOUISE. "Business and Economic Development in Libby," a research paper.
Minutes and Committee Reports, Greater Libby Association, Inez Ratekin, Secretary.
Minutes and Committee Reports, Libby Montana Study Group, Mrs. H. W. Redfield, Secretary.
SHELDEN, ARTHUR H. "Agricultural Problems in the Libby Area," a research paper.
STEARNS, WILLIAM C. "Libby Church History," a research paper.

DIXON-AGENCY MONTANA STUDY GROUP

BOURBEAU, LEO. "History of Little Arkansaw," a research paper.
———. "Homestead Days," a research paper.
McTUCKER, ALBINA. "History of Catholic Church of Dixon," a research paper.
Minutes and Committee Reports, Dixon-Agency Montana Study Group, Phyllis W. Morigeau, Secretary.
NYE, ELLEN. "Trails and Landmarks Dixon Area 1946," a research paper.
"A Tale of the Shining Mountains," ("Skol-loomts Ska-kel Whoo-zo-zoot"), a pageant-drama by the members of the Dixon-Agency, and Full-Blood Flathead Indian Montana Study Groups, assisted by Bert Hansen.
TOLIVER, HARRIETT S. "History of the Dixon Methodist Church," a research paper.
TOWNSEND, HARRY. "History of Dixon Schools," a research paper.
WRIGHT, C. C. "General Information About the Flathead Indian Reservation in Western Montana," a research paper.
WRIGHT, GENEVA E. "A Double Decade in Dixon," a research paper.

FULL-BLOOD FLATHEAD INDIAN MONTANA STUDY GROUP

Indian Study Guide, prepared by Bert Hansen and C. C. Wright.
Minutes, Full-Blood Flathead Indian Montana Study Group, Geneva E. Wright, Recorder.
PICHETTE, PIERRE. "Story of Little Mary's Vision."

———. "Story of Mary Sdipp-Shin-Mah."
PICHETTE, PIERRE; COMBS, LOUIE; ADAMS, PIERRE; MOEISE, SOPHIE (Chil-hoom-hoom-shin-nah); KAISER, MARY (Chu-tug); FINLEY, BAPTISTE (Pai-choom). "Discussions and Stories," interpreted by Pierre Pichette, re-corded by Leona J. Peterson, Secretary, The Montana Study.
PIERRE, PETE. "Can Agriculture, Especially Stockraising and Farming, be Enlarged and Improved by and for the Indians," a research paper.

WOODMAN MONTANA STUDY GROUP

FORNEY, LOUISE C. "Woodman School History," a research paper.
MAGEE, MARION. "Lumbering," a research paper.
MILLS, ELAINE C. "The Widening Trail," a research paper.
Minutes and Committee Reports, Woodman Montana Study Group, George F. Wilkinson Jr., Secretary.
WILKINSON, FLORA. "Church History," a research paper.
WILSON, JOHN. "Homes on Lolo Creek," a research paper.

HAMILTON MONTANA STUDY GROUP

Minutes and Committee Reports, Hamilton Montana Study Group, Mrs. Clem Rose, Secretary.

VICTOR MONTANA STUDY GROUP

GROFF, Mr. and Mrs.; and HORNUNG, Mrs. ADAM. "Some of the History of Victor from 1886 to 1946," a research paper.

Other Books, Documents, and Miscellaneous Publications

MONTANA HISTORY

BIRNEY, HOFFMAN. Vigilantes, Penn Publishing Company, Philadelphia, 1929.
BURLINGAME, MERRILL G. The Montana Frontier, State Publishing Com-pany, Helena, Montana, 1942.
CONNOLLY, CHRISTOPHER R. The Devil Learns to Vote: The Story of Mon-tana, Crown Publishers, New York, 1938.
Copper Camp: Stories of the World's Greatest Mining Town, Butte, Mon-tana, W. P. A. Writers' Program, Montana State Department of Agri-culture and Industry, Books, Inc., 1943.

DIMSDALE, THOMAS J. *The Vigilantes of Montana*, State Publishing Company, Helena—first edition Virginia City, 1866.

GLASSCOCK, C. B. *The War of the Copper Kings*, Bobbs-Merrill Company, New York, 1935.

HEINZE, F. A. *The Political Situation in Montana, 1900–1902*, Butte, Montana, 1902.

HOWARD, JOSEPH KINSEY. *Montana: High, Wide, and Handsome*, Yale University Press, New Haven, 1943.

KENNEDY, JOHN E. "The Story of St. Mary's Mission," Western News Print, Hamilton, Montana, 1941.

LAWSON, THOMAS W. *Frenzied Finance*, Ridgeway-Thayer Company, New York, 1905.

MILLS, EDWARD LAIRD. *Plains, Peaks and Pioneers*, Metropolitan Press, Portland, Oregon, 1947.

The Western News; A Magazine Supplement, Hamilton, Montana, 1910.

ARTICLES

GARNSEY, MORRIS E. "The Rise of Regionalism in the Western States," *The Nation*, special western supplement, September 21, 1946.

HOWARD, JOSEPH KINSEY. "Golden River," *Harper's Magazine*, May, 1945.

———. "The Montana Twins in Trouble?" *Harper's Magazine*, September, 1944.

———. "New Trends in American Journalism," *The Montana High School Editor*, November, 1944.

———. "On Montana Education," *Montana Education Journal*, January, 1946.

———. "Towns are Tolerable," *Mademoiselle*, February, 1949.

———. "What Happened in Butte," *Harper's Magazine*, August, 1948.

MEADOWS, PAUL. "The Changing Character of the Culture of Montana," *The People's Voice*, Helena, Montana, October 17, 1947.

———. "The Cliché Experts Come to Town," *The People's Voice*, Helena, Montana, December 14, 1945.

———. "It is Time for Tax Reform in Montana!" *The People's Voice*, Helena, Montana, December 21, 1945.

———. "A Plea for Regionalism in Education," *Montana Education*, April, 1945.

———. "The Primer of The Montana Negatives," *The People's Voice*, Helena, Montana, November 30, 1945.

———. "Some Democratic Aspects of the TVA," *The People's Voice*, Helena, Montana, February 9, 1945.

———. "Some Sociological Aspects of Land Use Policy," *Social Forces,* December, 1945.

THOMPSON, JIMMY. "Blind Indian Uses Braille," *The Spokesman-Review Magazine,* Spokane, Washington, July 6, 1947.

DOCUMENTS REGARDING THE UNIVERSITY OF MONTANA

BRANDBORG, GUY M. An unnamed address.

Higher Education in Montana, Governmental Research Publication No. 1, issued by The Montana Taxpayers' Association, Helena, December, 1938.

MELBY, ERNEST O. "The Role of a State University," Montana State University, December, 1941, an address.

Minutes and Proceedings of the Montana Commission on Higher Education.

President's Report to the State Board of Education, Montana State University, July 31, 1945.

Reports of the Chancellor of the University of Montana to the Commission on Higher Education, also to the State Board of Education.

Report of the Montana Commission on Higher Education with Recommendations of the Montana State Board of Education, September 26, 1944.

Report of Special Curriculum Committee to the President of Montana State University, December 21, 1945.

Report of University Sub-Committee, Appropriations Committee, House of Representatives, Montana State Legislature, February 14, 1947.

"Statement of Policy" by the State Board of Education to the Twenty-Ninth Session of Montana State Legislature.

STATE AND LOCAL GOVERNMENT RECORDS AND PUBLICATIONS

Assessors records and school reports, Ravalli County Courthouse, Hamilton, Montana.

Biennial Reports, the Montana State Board of Equalization.

Constitution of the State of Montana.

House Journal for Twenty-Ninth Session, Montana State Legislature; also for Thirtieth Session, 1945 and 1947.

Report of the Montana Committee on Public Elementary and Secondary School Organization and Finance, November 12, 1946.

Report on questionnaire released by State of Montana Juvenile Commission, 1948.

School reports, Darby High School, Darby, Montana.

Senate Journal for Twenty-Ninth Session, Montana State Legislature; also for Thirtieth Session, 1945 and 1947.

U. S. GOVERNMENT PUBLICATIONS

Bowman, A. B. "Summary and Brief Discussion of the Forest Management Plan for the Kootenai Sustained Yield Unit," U. S. Forest Service, Missoula, Montana, April 15, 1947.

Claims of the Salish and Kootenai Tribes of Indians of the Flathead Reservation, Mont., Report No. 2050, 79th Congress 2nd Session, House of Representatives, Washington, D. C., May 14, 1946.

The Economic Base for Power Markets in Ravalli County, Montana, Bonneville Power Administration, January, 1947.

Farmers in a Changing World, Yearbook of Agriculture 1940, U. S. Department of Agriculture, Washington, D. C.

Haas, Theodore H. "Trends and Portends in the Indian Bureau," U. S. Bureau of Indian Affairs, Washington, D. C.

Hearings on Irrigation and Reclamation, U. S. Senate, 79th Congress, S. 555, September, 1945.

Hurt, Leon C. "Penalties of Heavy Range Use," *The American Hereford Journal,* Kansas City, Mo., July 1, 1946.

Hutchison, S. Blair. "Comparative Marketability of Pine and Mixed Species in the Inland Empire," Northern Rocky Mountain Forest & Range Experiment Station, U. S. Forest Service, Missoula, Montana, June, 1948.

———. *The Forest Situation in Lincoln County Montana,* Northern Rocky Mountain Forest & Range Experiment Station, U. S. Forest Service, Missoula, Montana, March, 1942.

Management Plan for Bitter Root Working Circle, U. S. Forest Service, Missoula, Montana, 1941.

Management Plan for the Kootenai Sustained Yield Unit, Kootenai National Forest, Lincoln County, Montana, 1946.

Meyer, Walter H. "Comments on 'Toward the Stabilization and Enrichment of a Forest Community,'" Yale School of Forestry, December 15, 1946.

"Policy and Instructions Governing the Establishment of Sustained Yield Units Under the Provisions of Public Law 273," a directive issued by U. S. Forest Service, Washington, D. C., July 21, 1944.

The Proposed Kootenai Sustained Yield Unit, U. S. Forest Service, Missoula, Montana.

Public Law 273, 78th Congress (Chapter 146—2D Session) (S. 250), Washington, D. C., March 29, 1944.

Public Law 726, 79th Congress (Chapter 959—2D Session) (H. R. 4497), Washington, D. C., August 13, 1946.

Reports of the Bureau of the Census.
Reports of the Bureau of Foreign and Domestic Commerce.
Soils & Men, Yearbook of Agriculture, 1938, U. S. Department of Agriculture, Washington, D. C.
ZACH, LAWRENCE W.; and HUTCHISON, S. BLAIR. *The Forest Situation in Ravalli County, Montana,* Northern Rocky Mountain Forest & Range Experiment Station, U. S. Forest Service, Missoula, Montana, July, 1943.

NEWSPAPERS AND MAGAZINES

Billings Gazette; Bozeman Chronicle; Camas Hot Springs Exchange, Hot Springs; *Choteau Acantha; Democrat-News,* Lewistown; *Great Falls Tribune; Havre Daily News; Independent-Observer,* Conrad; *Independent-Record,* Helena; *Inter-Lake,* Kalispell; *Miles City Daily Star; Missoula County Times; Missoula Sentinel; Missoulian,* Missoula; *Montana Kaimin,* Montana State University; *Montana Standard,* Butte; *Mountaineer,* Montana State University, Missoula; *Northwest Tribune,* Stevensville; *The People's Voice,* Helena; *Public Spirit,* Hatboro, Pennsylvania; *Spokesman-Review,* Spokane, Washington; *St. Ignatius Post; Western News,* Hamilton; *Western News,* Libby.

MISCELLANEOUS

Anaconda Copper Mining Company. Unpublished manuscripts on Montana.
"Group Work Plan for Education," Social Work Laboratory, Montana State University, 1948.
HOWARD, JOSEPH KINSEY. "Butte," a chapter in *Our Fair City,* edited by Robert S. Allen, Vanguard Press, New York, 1947.
———. "New Concepts of Plains History," a paper delivered before the Mississippi Valley Historical Association, annual meeting, Bloomington, Indiana, April 19, 1946.
KRAENZEL, CARL F.; THOMSON, WATSON; and CRAIG, GLENN H., with the collaboration of Corbett, E. A.; Parsons, O. A.; and Rands, Stanley. *The Northern Plains in a World of Change,* Gregory-Cartwright, Ltd., Toronto, October, 1942.
Minutes and final report of proceedings, Northern Plains Conference on the Social and Economic Implications of the Upper Missouri River Development, Billings, Montana, December, 1944.
Montana County Basic Data, Market Research Department, Farm Journal, Inc., Philadelphia.

Montana's Production 1930–1945, Bureau of Business Research, Montana State University, Missoula.

MORRIS, MELVIN S. "Montana's Resources, a Guide for Your Future," an address.

MUELLER, FRANZ H. *Economic Aspects of Industrial Decentralization,* Aquin Papers No. 8, The College of St. Thomas, St. Paul, Minn., 1942.

Proceedings, The Pacific Northwest Conference on the Arts and Sciences, Missoula, Montana, May, 1944, and Pullman, Washington, November, 1944.

Proceedings, Regional Committee on the Humanities in American Institutions, Denver, Colorado, December, 1943.

Records and proceedings, Class in Community Organization, Montana State University, 1948.

RENNE, R. R. "Montana's Agricultural and Industrial Future," an address.

Report and proceedings, Second Annual University Institute for Social Welfare, Missoula, Montana, July, 1948.

"The Report of a Project in Community Reorientation in Denver, Colorado, 1948," under direction of Bert Hansen, School of Speech, University of Denver, August 18, 1948. An outgrowth of Professor Hansen's experimental work in community reorganization in Montana. Includes minutes of the Cosmopolitan Library Study Club sponsored by the School of Speech, University of Denver, organized among Negro residents of Denver as the initial group of a planned program of self-study by several of the Denver minority groups, and the sociodrama which was an outgrowth of these meetings.

TASCHER, HAROLD. *Summary Report,* Group Study Program in Principles of Group Work, Montana State University, Missoula, 1947.

TASCHER, HAROLD. *Summary Report,* Group Study Program in Problems of Child Welfare, Montana State University, Missoula, 1947.

INDEX

Agather, A. J. (Allo), 158, 162
Agricultural Extension Service, 119
Alder Gulch, 2, 35
Amalgamated Copper Company, 7-9
American Association of University Women, 139
American Legion, Conrad, 100; Stevensville, 85
Anaconda Copper Mining Company, 9-10, 29-32, 53, 65, 67
Anderson, Hans, 60
Anderson, Jessie, 95
Anderson, LeRoy H., 95-97, 99, 186
Anderson, Walter A., 121
Antioch College, 139
Arlee, Mont., 170, 180
Art Is Action, by Baker Brownell, 22
Assiniboine Indians, 3
Atkinson, E. A., 67
Attwell, Al, 103, 106-108
Attwell, Betty, 103, 110-113
Auren, Everett, 96

Baird, Mike, 59
Baker, O. E., 139
Baldwin, Charles, 68
Bannack, Mont., 1-3, 187
Baptist Church, 139
Barnes, Guy L., 139
Barringer, Lyle, 59
Baty, Harvey, 37, 39, 43-44
Beaverhead, Pete, 171
Belknap, Charles, 61
Berea College, 107
Beresford, Howard C., 97, 139
Bibler, Pauline, 52
Big Sam, 176, 178
Big Sam, Ellen, 176
Billings, Sam, 52
Bitter Root National Forest, 53, 131, 147
Bitter Root-Selway Wilderness, 60
Bitter Root Valley, 49, 54, 59, 62, 72, 131, 134, 136, 138, 142, 166, 169-170, 175

Blackfeet Indians, 3
"Black Robes," 74, 82
Board of Education, *See* Montana State Board of Education
Border, Ted, 59, 62
Bosley, G. A., 131
Bottomly, Vic, 131
Bozeman unit, *See* Montana State College
Brandborg, Guy M., 131-132, 142, 189
Bras, Lucille, 38
Bras, Roy, 38
Bras, Verla, 39
Brechbill, Luther, 59
Bretzke, M. W., 81
Brinkman, Fred A., 97-99
Brooks, Mont., 111
Brownell, Baker, 28-30, 32-33, 66, 71, 114-116, 118-120, 122, 124-125, 128-130, 133-144, 185, 187, 189; appointed director of Montana Study, 23; Conrad, 87-88, 101; Darby, 52, 54, 63; Indian Study Group, 166; Lonepine, 34, 37-41, 43-44, 46; Lewistown, 102-107, 110, 113; Libby, 149-150, 153; philosophy of, 22-25, 39-40, 54, 110, 113; returns to Northwestern, 140-141, 144; Stevensville, 74-76, 78, 84
Buck, Charles Amos, 76-77, 79-81, 134
Buck Mercantile Co., 76
Buck, Nellie, 81
Buffalo, destruction of, 4
Bunger, Donald, 138
Burlingame, Merrill G., 19-20, 121
Butte, Mont., 6-11

Camas Hot Springs Exchange, The, 43
Campbell, Elsie, 96
Carroll College, 131
Central, Mont., 2-3
Central Montana Folk Festival, 112
Chamber of Commerce, Great Falls, 139; Libby, 159-160
Charlot, Chief, 82-83, 167
Charlot, Paul, 83, 167, 170-173, 175

225